EGMONT KEY

Stories from Eyewitnesses to History

RICHARD A. SANCHEZ

ISBN 979-8-9885587-1-2

Contents

Contents

Untitled Poem (a riddle)

My name is composed of letters five
 Although dead, I am alive
I am in everybody's mouth
I am what the people talk about
The world I have traveled o'er and o'er
Yet, I'm inclined to travel more
The girls all say that I am pretty
With me, they are made witty
So, you can call me what you please
You will find me taking of my ease
By all the world, I am admired
Always on speede [*sic*] but never tired
I never move but always carried
Though dead my name they have not buried
Egmont Fla.

Author's note: the answer to this riddle is "words."

Author George V. Rickards, written in his journal on Egmont Key, December 1860. **From the collection at the Tampa Bay History Center**

Preface

I have been involved with Egmont Key since my first visit in November 2007 at the annual "Discover the Island" event hosted by the Egmont Key Alliance, a Citizen Support Organization for the Florida Park Service on the island. I was immediately smitten with "island fever" and have been researching its history ever since. My interest in the lighthouses took off when I joined the Florida Lighthouse Association, an organization dedicated to preserving the lighthouses of Florida and discovering and preserving their history. I have since learned of the rich histories of the other Florida lighthouses.

Numerous visitors have come to the island over the centuries: Native Americans, Spanish explorers, English explorers and American explorers and map makers, military personnel, lighthouse keepers and their families, pirates, rum runners, and journalists. They all had stories of where they came from, why they went to the island, and then life afterward. Some achieved greatness after leaving Egmont Key, and some disappeared into history. Some did a lot while on the island; for others, it was a mere stopping-off place on their way to something else. Some came to the island for a short time, others for many years, and some never even set foot there. For the named gun batteries of Fort Dade, the soldiers paid the ultimate price, defending American interests. During the years of visiting the island, hundreds of thousands of visitors and I have walked in the footsteps of the many people whose stories are in the following chapters.

I have chosen a few people in each category and used their stories to tell the bigger story of Egmont Key. They appear in this book in chronological order, as they appeared on the island or in Tampa Bay. Where possible, I used original materials, journals, and diaries from the time to give the chapter a first-person account. I have even included the story of the steamship *Grey Cloud,* which obviously is not a person, but its name appears in many accounts in the historical records from the Seminole War period. It has a rather interesting story as well!

The Appendix will be the place to find full versions of some documents referenced in the chapters.

Richard A. Sanchez, 2024

Acknowledgments

This is my second effort at authoring a book on a historical topic. Given the scope of this work, from prehistoric times to modern times, I used a variety of resources. For some chapters, I could find other books that were written on the subject. Online resources like the Library of Congress and the National Archives provided original documents that gave insight into the people in question. The internet is another source for pictures and information. Local libraries like the Manatee County Library had valuable photos and documents. The Manatee County Records Library staff were extremely helpful in providing access to their documents. Visiting a site like Lake Monroe, the location of Fort Mellon, the site of the Dade Battle in Bushnell, or the "waterfall" that Celi encountered at Hillsborough River State Park gave insight into the events just by being able to "walk the ground" of the people of the event.

Many people helped me with this project. Some answered specific questions I had, and others provided documents and newspaper articles or guided me to other sources of information. Without the assistance of these fellow historians, this book would not be as informative as it is. What follows is a list of those people, not in any particular order, but it is most likely not complete. I appreciate every one of them!

Neil Hurley for my lighthouse history questions; Josh Liller, the historian at the Jupiter Inlet Lighthouse; Dr. Brad Massey, formerly of the Tampa Bay History Center; researcher Bruce McCall for his work on Fort Dade; Dave Scheidecker of the Seminole Tribal Historic Office for fact-checking me on Polly Parker and Billy Bowlegs, Dr. Laura Harrison and Dr. Brooke Hansen for the 3D Scanning project, the book *Egmont Key – a History* by Don and Carol Thompson provided additional information. Also, regarding the history of the Alliance, I want to thank the first president, Susan Kessel, for her information about the Egmont '88 cleanup and past board members Cindi Para and Peter Clark of Tampa Bay Watch. Information about Hubbard's Marina is courtesy of Mark Hubbard and Tara Hubbard. Thanks to Frank Haddleton for sharing the information about his ancestors, Henry M. Walker, a harbor pilot, and his son, Fred, and their tragic deaths.

A special acknowledgment goes to Josh Liller, who proofread my manuscript, made content suggestions, and checked grammar and spelling. This was a daunting task for a book of this length. Also, to the late Candace Clifford, who found the documents on the 1849 expedition at the National Archives as well as other related documents.

Last but most important is the work done by Dan Swanson on the cover and Darlene Swanson for her work in formatting the book for printing.

Introduction

The island has had many names over the centuries; Don Francisco Maria Celi named it "Isla de la Cruz (Island of the Cross)," George Gauld named it "Egmont Key (Island)," and a privateer named David Braddock used it as a base of operations and loaned his name that locals referred to it as "Castor Key" (Island). The Seminoles, who were held there while awaiting removal to the reservations in the west, referred to it as the "Place of Darkness." In the 1800s, it was locally called "Pilots Island" because harbor pilots lived and operated from the southern end of the island.

Many people have mistakenly called the island a barrier island. Even though it may be "barrier-like" in many aspects, it lacks one important characteristic of barrier islands: It is too far from a mainland shoreline. Egmont sits in the middle of the entrance to Tampa Bay and so cannot be labeled a barrier island. So what is it?

I consulted with Albert C. Hine, a professor of geological oceanography at the University of South Florida and author of *Geologic History of Florida*, and what follows is his description of the island's formation:

> "The island formed probably 3-4 thousand years ago when the rate of sea level rise slowed coming out of the Last Glacial Maximum (the end of the last Ice Age), which ended about

18 thousand years ago. The sea level back then was about 415 feet lower than today, and the west coast of Florida was about 125 miles farther from the west than it is today.

Egmont Key is most likely situated on a limestone bedrock high, based on geophysical data. The sand came from an ebb-tidal delta associated with the inlet leading into/out of Tampa Bay. The Bay itself was formed primarily by many limestone collapse features, thus allowing small, local streams to flow into it. Egmont actually behaves very much like a barrier island, but its location at the mouth of a large estuarine system is highly unusual, if not flat-out unique. It has undergone significant erosion in the past 150 years and could eventually disappear in the next 150-200 years, given projected rates of sea level rise."

Before the nineteenth century, the island had no long-term inhabitants, but local fishermen or Cubans may have used it as a temporary fishing encampment. The Tocabaga tribe certainly visited the island but established no permanent villages. Evidence of their visits came from a dugout canoe that washed up on the island's west beach in 2020.

The first permanent residents were the lighthouse keepers and their families, who started in 1848 and continued until the last of the keepers left in 1989.

The Seminole War period, ending in 1858, saw soldiers and captive tribe members being brought to the island to be held for eventual relocation. A few years later, in 1861, the Union Navy, during the Civil War, came to the island and, over the course of the war, built a coaling station and a small hospital. The island was used as a base for intercepting rebel blockade runners. At the same time, the island became a haven for runaway enslaved people and Unionists.

It experienced rapid growth during the Fort Dade period, and after the installation was permanently closed, the only residents were US Coast Guardsmen or State Park Rangers. The Tampa Bay Harbor Pilots have cottages on the south end of the island compound, but they no longer live in them as residences.

The only person who could be considered a resident now is the Assistant Park Manager, who lives in the former US Coast Guard barracks near the lighthouse.

The Spanish were the first Europeans to claim Florida as a possession after visits by various explorers sent to find riches and possibly a new route to the Indies. This period was from 1513 to 1763. Control of Florida then went to the British due to a trade for Spanish control of Havana in exchange for Florida. This exchange resulted from the Seven Years' War in Europe and an expansion of British territory. The British government divided Florida into East Florida, which is the peninsula, with its capital at St. Augustine, and West Florida, which included the panhandle region, extending to the Mississippi River with its capital at Pensacola.

During the American Revolution, Spain sided with France, an ally of the thirteen colonies, and besieged Pensacola, capturing it in 1781. Spain again took possession of Florida and held it from 1783 to 1821.

After conflicts with Andrew Jackson in the First Seminole War, the Spanish government decided that protecting Florida was too much of a burden. A treaty handed Florida over to the United States on July 17, 1821, and it was formally declared a United States Territory on March 30, 1822. Statehood followed in 1845. Egmont Key has been affected by all these events over the decades.

A few books have been written on Egmont Key over the years. Some have been presented as timelines, and others have focused on the history of the lighthouses built on the island or its military history. This book differs from other works in that it focuses on the people who influenced the island's history. Some gave only a name to some features on the island, and some profoundly influenced the island's history. Some spent only a short time on the island, and some stayed for years. Some never even saw the island in person. Even so, they all brought something to the island and left part of themselves there. This has made Egmont Key essential to local, Florida, national, and international history. This book is not intended to be the definitive work on Egmont Key but rather a sampler and quick reference on the people's lives in the chapters. For many, the information provided here will satisfy their interest. For others, it will be a starting place for further research about a particular person. You can read the chapters in any order, each being a stand-alone profile of a person connected with the island in some way.

I hope that you find something of interest in the chapters that follow!

Richard A. Sanchez

Chapter 1

Don Francisco Maria Celi, Spanish Explorer and Cartographer

During this time in Florida's history, three European countries vied for land and riches in the New World: Spain, Great Britain, and France. Florida was a Spanish possession then, but France was also interested in it. The French had explored the Gulf of Mexico and investigated the Suwannee River. They established Fort Caroline near present-day Jacksonville in 1565.

Spanish explorers were convinced there was a passage through the Florida peninsula, connecting the Gulf of Mexico with the Atlantic Ocean. If this passage could be found, it would mean safer sailing for merchant ships traveling from the Caribbean to St. Augustine and then on to Spain. The Atlantic could be treacherous, especially during the hurricane season, and passing around the southern tip of the peninsula was also hazardous.

The Spanish government tasked Don Francisco Maria Celi, a captain in the Spanish Royal Navy, with exploring the central part of the Gulf Coast in search of this passage to the Atlantic and also looking for longleaf pine trees suitable for fabricating ship masts. This expedition was nearly two hundred years after Panfilio de Narvez visited the area. The expedition left Havana on Easter Sunday, April 10, 1757, aboard the *San Francisco de Asis.* The journey was delayed for six hours due to bad weather, but after that passed, the ship was on its way. The boat was an xebec type[1] under the command of Naval Lieutenant Don Jose Jimenez. Celi was in command of the surveying expedition. The total number on board was estimated to be around thirty-four. He arrived in the present-day Tampa Bay area three days later on April 13 but anchored near modern-day Anna Maria at 2 AM, concerned that he may miss the entrance to Tampa Bay at night. He entered Tampa Bay at 8:30 AM via the south channel and anchored near Egmont Key, naming it "Isla De San Blas y Barreda." He named Tampa Bay "Bahia de San Fernando."

Celi began his exploration by surveying the island. The method is well-documented and gives an accurate measurement of the circumference. Starting at a point on the island's southeast side, he stretched a measuring line along the shoreline, sighting along a magnetic compass heading. When the heading changed slightly, the distance was measured in Castilian yards.[2] He then stretched the line along the new heading until it changed again, measuring that distance. By repeating this procedure twenty times until returning to the starting point, the size of the island could be determined mathematically. The sketch of that survey is pictured.

The *San Francisco de Asis* remained at this anchorage for five days and then relocated to the east side of present-day Mullet Key Shoal since it was a more protected location. After recording the shape of

---

1 A xebec is a small three-masted vessel used in commerce, typically in the coastal areas of the Mediterranean. Sometimes, they might be outfitted with oars for use in calm winds, but this expedition has no record.
2 A Castilian yard is 33 inches.

the shoreline and shoals, Celi moved to Boca Ciega Bay, called by him "Estero de Romero." A carpenter and two seamen went ashore near modern-day Lake Maggiore in St. Petersburg to "bleed some pines" (to get pitch for ship repair) and, at the same time, found a source of fresh water.

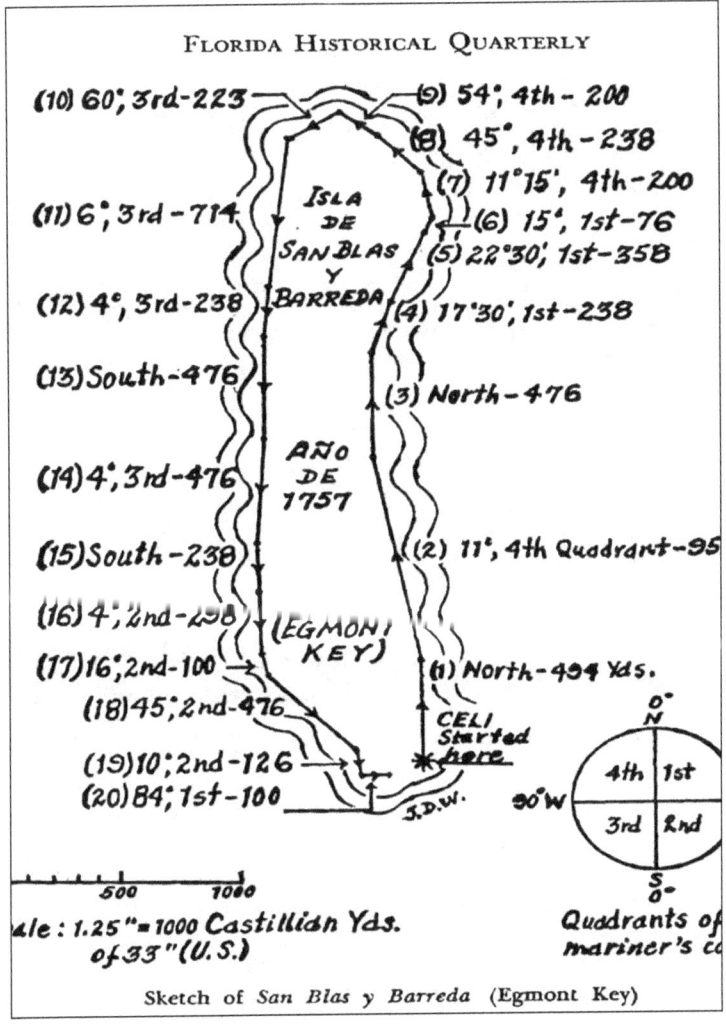

FLORIDA HISTORICAL QUARTERLY

(10) 60; 3rd-223   (9) 54; 4th - 200

(8) 45°, 4th - 238

(7) 11°15', 4th-200

ISLA DE SAN BLAS Y BARREDA

(11) 6; 3rd - 714   (6) 15', 1st-76

(5) 22°30', 1st-358

(12) 4°, 3rd-238   (4) 17°30', 1st-238

(13) South-476   (3) North - 476

AÑO DE 1757

(14) 4; 3rd-476

(15) South -238   (2) 11', 4th Quadrant-95

(16) 4; 2nd-298

(EGMONT KEY)

(17) 16; 2nd-100   (1) North-494 Yds.

(18) 45; 2nd-476

CELI Started here

(19) 10; 2nd -126   4th | 1st

(20) 84; 1st -100   3rd | 2nd

S.D.W.   90°W

500   1000

Scale : 1.25"=1000 Castillian Yds. of 33" (U.S.)

Quadrants of mariner's co

Sketch of San Blas y Barreda (Egmont Key)

Celi Survey Map of the Island

3

Continuing his explorations, the xebec moved into the mouth of "Ensenada de Aguirre" (Aguirre's Cove, now called Hillsborough Bay) and anchored a few miles east of Gadsden Point. During this time, he made contact with the Native Americans who lived in the area. Celi noted that the contact was voluntary on the part of the natives, and they appeared to have no fear of white men.

"El Salto" Rapids photo by Author with permission of the Florida Park Service

The next phase of the expedition was a three-day exploration of the river he named "Saint Julian de Arriaga," the present-day Hillsborough River. At 2:15 PM, the expedition entered the mouth of the river in a longboat and a canoe. The group consisted of about twenty armed men and included the ship's carpenter. It was a difficult trip at times due to the narrow width of the river, the many turns and shoals, and the low overhanging trees. At one point in the journey, the crew offloaded two barrels of water and the mast to shore to lighten the longboat. Sails would be unusable in this terrain. The crew had to push, pull, and struggle to get past the shallow parts of the river. Along the way, Celi made notes about the shoals and made depth soundings.

The expedition continued upriver to a location now within the Hillsborough River State Park boundary. At this point in his exploration, the high banks and slow-flowing dark waters changed to shallower and faster-moving water with limestone boulders in the middle. After passing the first few obstructions, they reached a massive rock formation blocking his path. The party found what Celi called "El Salto" or waterfall.[3] In fact, it was a long stretch of rocky rapids that was too difficult to portage around. At this point, the expedition ended their exploration and traveled back downriver to the place where they left their mast and two barrels of water. They camped there, near modern-day Temple Terrace, in the vicinity of a place now called Riverhills Park. Celi erected a cross at this site and named the pine forest "El Pinal de la Cruz de Santa Teresa" (the Pine Forest of the Cross of Saint Theresa). There is now a historical marker at the site that notes this event. Sampling the river water at the site, Celi described it as "very delicate in taste." While there, Celi sent crewmen out to look for longleaf pine trees suitable for ship masts. He described the trees they found as "pine trees of great magnitude."

After returning downriver to the xebec, he turned his attention to mapping what is now Old Tampa Bay. The survey was not as detailed as the attention Boca Ciega Bay received earlier. He took more care when recording the Interbay Peninsula area, documenting depths and shoals.

---

3 These are the only Class 2 rapids in Florida.

The end of the expedition was nearing, but Celi needed to accomplish a couple of things before leaving. On Friday, May 6, 1757, Celi and the principal officers went ashore on Egmont Key and erected a wooden cross near the southern point where Celi had begun his survey of the island. After a short mass, the event was celebrated with five salvos of gunfire and a dip of the flag from the nearby xebec. Celi made one last attempt to take the depth soundings of Egmont Channel on the island's north tip. Once again, due to adverse winds and currents, he could not accurately make depth soundings, and he considered the north channel suspect for navigational use and noted that on his map. He was incorrect in this assumption since there is a natural ninety-foot hole on the island's north end.

Celi and his crew left Tampa Bay on May 7, bound for Havana. The voyage left via the south channel and was uneventful. They arrived home on May 10 at 5:30 PM.

Celi provides a wealth of detailed information on this voyage of discovery. He kept a journal from when he departed Havana, giving dates, times, names of geographic features, and other interesting information. None of the names Celi gave the places and geographic features remains except for Pinellas Point, which he called "Punta del Pinal de Jimenez." These locations can be visited today to add to the story of the most significant survey and exploration of the Tampa Bay area up to that time.

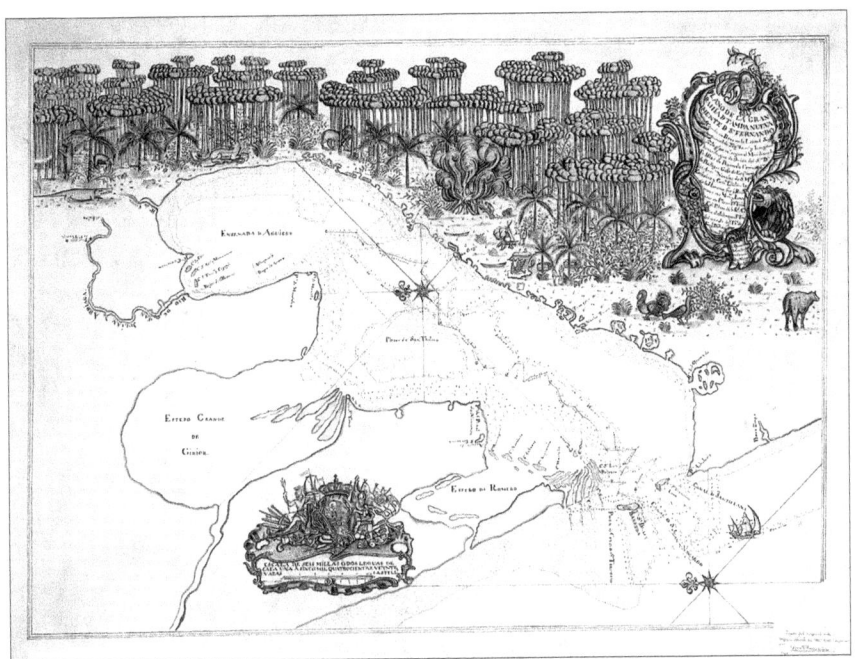

Celi's Chart of the Tampa Bay Area

Chapter 2

Egmont Key's Pirate

The stars called Pollux and Castor are the brightest and second brightest ones in the constellation of Gemini and are well-known by mariners for navigational purposes. The names are also known in Greek and Roman mythology as half-twin brothers who sailed with Jason and the Argonauts. So, what does this have to do with Egmont Key? Read on and learn more about the local "pirate" in Tampa Bay!

In the island's early history, there was a dual naming when Bernard Romans mapped the coastline of East and West Florida. Egmont Key was also called Castor Key, and Burnaby Island (Passage Key) was called Pollux Key. Unraveling the truth about this mysterious marauder has been a journey through a maze of historical records, often leading to more questions than answers. Prepare to be intrigued in this chapter as we delve into the pirate's true identity and connections to Egmont Key and Tampa Bay.

The first clue to his identity emerged from the map crafted by Bernard Romans in 1768, featuring a dual naming of Egmont/Castor Key. My initial assumption was that he named it after himself (pirates are known for their inflated egos, aren't they?), thus the research followed this line of thought. Another tale suggested that the pirate hailed from England and had ties to Savannah, Georgia. I scoured numerous websites using these search terms, even reaching out to the local historical museum in Savannah, but to no avail. They graciously forwarded my inquiry to the State Historical Society in Atlanta. Yet, this pirate named Castor remained tantalizingly elusive.

Undeterred, I turned to a website that purported to list every known pirate from any era and any country, hoping to find a mention of Castor, but my search was in vain.

A random search turned up a website referencing a village called "Castortown," located on Egmont Key's east side about midway down the length. It was supposed to have had about twenty houses, a store, and a dock. No remains of this village can be found today. The website did state that there was a connection to Savannah, Georgia, by this person. The narrative also said he was of English origin. This supported other sources, but the mystery deepened!

Privateers and Privateering

The search persisted, and a new term, 'privateer,' was explored to see where it might lead. The word privateer carries a couple of meanings. It can refer to a person involved in piracy on behalf of a government, commissioned to do so during a time of war, and sharing the seized goods. They are given a Letter of Marque, which specifies the terms of the partnership. It can also denote a type of ship used for such activities. It was not uncommon for a captain to employ his ship for these endeavors, and in the case of Egmont Key's "pirate," it would have been against Spanish or French vessels sailing through the Gulf of Mexico. This new term might hold the key to unraveling more about our elusive pirate.

There is little difference between a privateer[1] and a pirate; privateers allowed a warring country to project naval power beyond what their naval fleets could do. Privateers would attack ships at sea and villages of an enemy nation. Pirates would also attack towns as well as ships, kidnap victims for ransom, and murder at will because they operate outside the law. Usually, pirates would be most active in peacetime when ships were less guarded and when there was a surplus of experienced sailors. A privateer would split his profits with the government that commissioned him to engage in this line of work, but a pirate would not. A privateer was, simply put, a pirate with papers.

Searching for privateer and Castor, I found a website with data about British ships. Two ships were listed: *Castor* and a sister ship, *Pollux*, built in Britain in 1742 and listed as privateers. Their sailing weight was 110 tons each, but their armament was not specified. Then, I had a stroke of luck, which enabled me to piece things together!

When Bernard Romans was mapping Florida, he wrecked his ship in the Manatee River. He trekked across Florida from there to St Augustine, keeping notes on his encounters with Native Americans and wildlife. A few years after completing the journey, he published a book, *A Concise Survey of East and West Florida*. In this book, he described Tampa Bay, the text of which is in the Bernard Romans chapter. He mentions a "Captain Braddock" and his two ships, the *Pollux* and *Castor*.

An online search revealed an academic paper[2] on this captain, David Cutler Braddock. He was born in Southold, Suffolk, New York

---

1 One exception is the privateer Sir Francis Drake, who attacked and burned St. Augustine in 1586. He attacked the Spanish town as a military target but took gold coins, cannons, and other items of value before burning the entire town.

2 Powell, Mark T., "Mariner and Privateer to the Crown: A Modest Analysis of the Life of Captain David Cutler Braddock (1993). Savannah Biographies. 23. https://digitalcommons.georgiasouthern.edu/sav-bios-lane/23

(a British colony) in 1717. He was the only child of John Braddock and Mary (Cutler) Braddock, although he had three half-sisters. He eventually moved to South Carolina.

He began his maritime career around 1730. Early in his career, he faced a harrowing experience when he was captured by the Spanish near St. Augustine while acting as a first mate on a ship named *Acona*, transporting rice. Despite being held prisoner during General James Oglethorpe's siege of Castillo de San Marco, he managed to escape captivity near the end of the unsuccessful siege. This display of resilience and determination led to Oglethorpe employing Braddock to command an armed schooner that was crucial in repelling the attempted Spanish invasion of Georgia. The fighting off the coast of the Georgia Colony and Florida and the ground warfare in the same areas was a minor part of what was referred to as "The War of Jenkins Ear.[3]"

Braddock's life took a new direction when he emigrated to the British colony of Georgia around 1740. Here, he married Mary Lyford of St. Helena Parish, South Carolina, on November 7, 1741. Establishing his roots, he purchased four hundred acres of land in Georgia in 1746 and expanded his holdings by five hundred more. His tract of land was situated on the banks of the Little Ogeechee River, a location that would play a significant role in his future endeavors.

The Savannah, Georgia connection became clear when Braddock was asked to supervise a dredging project on the Savannah River that had become silted to the point that ship navigation was affected. Mr. James Halberstam of Savannah felt the surveyors were not up to the

---

3 The War of Jenkins Ear, also known by the Spanish as The War of the Agreement, was a conflict between Spain and Great Britain that lasted from 1739 to 1748. This war eventually merged into a wider conflict called The War of Austrian Succession.

task of dredging, and Braddock traveled there to assist in the project. Below is an excerpt of a letter sent to Mr. James Halberstam of the Georgia colony.

> "I don't understand the setting of the tides and the method of twining the force of the current into the proper channel to deepen it, and that this must be reported by experienced seaman, which we are at present in want of – Captain David Cutler Braddock, who I mentioned in my Journal of 21ˢᵗ November last to be sailed for New England, is proposed to accompany the surveyors in the *Enquiry* when he arrives here. He's allowed to be an excellent seaman and to be well acquainted with this river, but it is a doubt with me whether it can be remedied with any tolerable expense..."

He then became a privateer to the Crown and eventually set up a base on the island of Egmont Key. He began searching for French and Spanish ships in the Gulf of Mexico. Braddock commanded one of the ships and was active around 1744 or 1745 (other sources place the time as 1749-1750). and was the first Englishman to explore Tampa Bay, with George Gauld being the first to map it in 1767. Braddock acquired a sloop called *Cockspur* that was appropriately equipped with "all stores, ordinance, and ammunition necessary." Bernard Romans account stated that Braddock had also utilized the *Castor* and *Pollux* in his exploits in the Gulf, but how they were acquired is unclear.

He eventually "retired" from his time as a privateer and returned to his land in Georgia. He died peacefully in 1769 at his home in St. Matthews Parrish, Georgia, and is most likely buried there.

The Conclusion

There is still a question of why he named the islands after his ships instead of keeping the names already established. Perhaps he was trying to disguise his town's location and base of operations. The "twin" islands could have possibly reminded him of his twin ships. Or maybe he named them in honor of the two brightest stars in the constellation Gemini. The answer will probably never be known for certain.

Chapter 3

George Gauld, Surveyor

George Gauld was the next in a long line of explorers who came to Florida, particularly Tampa Bay, to map, measure the depth of the channels, and observe the area visually, this time for the British Government.

Gauld was born in Ardbrack, Banffshire, Scotland, in 1731. Little is known about his youth, but he attended Kings College in Aberdeen, Scotland, and earned a Master of Arts degree.

By 1763, after the French and Indian War[1], Great Britain was left with significant land holdings along the eastern seaboard of North America. Not much was known about these areas since no British explorers or surveyors had visited them. The British Admiralty tasked Gauld with charting the coast of West Florida[2] and the west coast of East Florida, the work beginning in 1764 and ending in 1781. His work would not be published until 1790, after his death.

---

1   The French and Indian War was a theater of conflict in the Americas during the Seven Years' War, a global conflict that involved much of Europe. It was between an alliance of Britain and Prussia against France, Spain, Saxony, Sweden, and Russia.
2   The terms "East and West Florida" differed from what we know today. East Florida was the state's peninsula, and West Florida was the panhandle. At that time, East Florida included lands in Alabama and Mississippi, ending at the Mississippi River of today.

Thomas Hutchins, an American military engineer and cartographer, said of Gauld's voyage:

> "It may be proper to observe that I have had the assistance of the remarks and surveys, so far as relates to the mouths of the Mississippi and the coast and foundings of West Florida, of the late ingenious Mr. George Gauld, a Gentleman who the Lords of the Admiralty employed for the express purpose of making an accurate chart of the above-mentioned place."

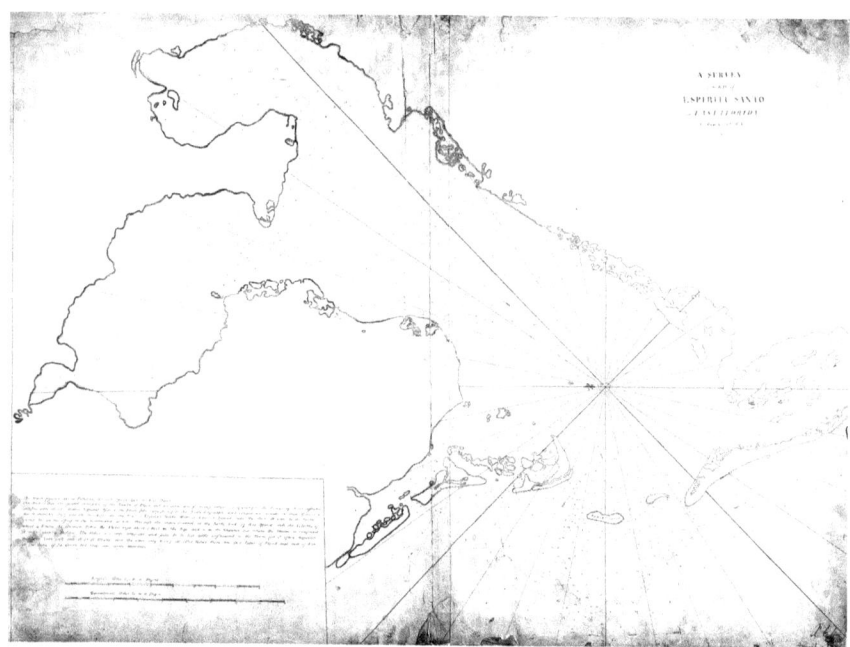

Gauld's map of Tampa Bay in 1767, courtesy of the UK Hydrologic Office Archives

Admiral Sir William Burnaby, while in Pensacola, personally ordered the survey of Espiritu Santo (Tampa Bay) by Gauld in May of 1765. After a series of meetings with Captain Rowland Cotton, commander of the *HMS Alarm*, and Gauld, the trip was planned.

Captain Cotton's ship would be used as the main ship and would be provisioned for a voyage of up to four months. The *Alarm* was a man-of-war of 683 tons and mounted 32 cannons. The crew was one hundred twenty-nine men strong, about fifty less than its usual complement. Gauld's survey crew numbered twenty-two. Because of the size and draft of the *Alarm*, a schooner, *Betsey*, would be sent along to navigate shallower waters as well. James Cook[3] was the *Betsey's* Shipmaster and would prove useful as a surveyor and mapmaker on this trip.

The expedition departed Pensacola on June 13, 1765, and headed eastward along the coastline, carefully avoiding shoals until they could turn south. After three days of sailing, they made landfall near present-day Weeki Wachee/Bayport after crossing the Gulf. After two more days of cautious travel, they reached the bay of Espiritu Santo. On June 21, James Cook set out in the schooner and with a longboat to find a route into the bay for the *Alarm*. The *Alarm* made its way into the bay's protected waters and anchored near the island.

Gauld and his party surveyed the islands nearest to the anchorage and documented his findings. He named the island south of Egmont Key "Burnaby (sometimes seen as Barnaby) Island" after Admiral Sir William Burnaby. It's now called Passage Key but, at one time, was privateer Braddock's Pollux Key. He noted three entrances to the bay: one between Mullet Key and Egmont, one between Egmont and Burnaby, and the third between Burnaby and Long Island (Anna Maria Island). His descriptions and measurements would be familiar to people today. His narrative is below:

---

3 James Cook would later achieve fame with his explorations of the South Pacific. He was killed in 1779 while attempting to kidnap Hawaii's Monarch Kalani-opu u.

"Egmont Island lies North and South, is about 2 miles long, and better than ¼ of a mile broad. The North end is highest, being about 6 or 7 feet above the high water mark; a bank much of the same height and about 40 feet broad runs on the west side next to the sea, almost the length of the whole island, within which there is a valley covered with bushes of different sorts, and various plants that afford an agreeable verdure (green vegetation), though the soil is hardly anything but sand and shells. There are a few freshwater swamps, but the water is not good. A small fort on the North End of this Island could easily command the Entrance of the Harbour."

Gauld is calling it Egmont Island and not by the name given by Celi. He also mentioned the strategic importance of the island and its location in the bay. On his map of the area, there is a legend that notes the tides, water depths, and other details about the island. It is below:

"The black figures denote fathoms, the red signify feet at low water. The arrows show the general direction of the stream of flood, but there are so many inlets or openings, the course of it is affected considerably thereby. Within Egmont Island, the flood gets very strong to the North Eastward and continues nearly in that direction till it divides itself into two bays at the head of Espiritu Santo. Without Egmont Island, near the shore it runs to the Southward, but in the offing to the Northward. It runs through the main channel at the North end of this island with the velocity of about 4 knots. At common tides the flood rises about three foot in the bay and two in the channel, but where the stream is confined, it rises near a fathom (six feet). The tides are very irregular and seen to be but little influenced by the moon, for it often happens that one tide will run 15 or 16 hours and the other only 6 or 7; at other times, there are two tides of flood and two of ebb in the space of 24 hours, but they are quite uncertain."

He then sailed south and charted Johns Pass, Boca Ciega Bay, and Sarasota Pass. In the area now called Pasadena and Jungle Prada, he noted "Oyster Bar." He outlined the Pinellas Peninsula, and in the area now occupied by St. Petersburg, he noted in his journal, "A pretty good place for a Settlement." He showed a circular lake with the inscription "Fresh Water" (this is most likely present-day Mirror Lake, which is spring-fed). He also charted Old Tampa Bay and called it simply "Tampa Bay."

Gauld only conducted a cursory investigation of the eastern shoreline of Old Tampa Bay. He noted but didn't explore the Hillsborough River, Six-Mile Creek, the Alafia River, or the Little Manatee and Manatee Rivers. Gauld wrote little about the vegetation on the islands except to note that most were covered with mangroves and observed that higher elevations had pines and live oaks.

The expedition was not without hazards for the crews. Fourteen crewmen died while in the area of unspecified causes, and three received lashes for drunkenness and theft. Before departing for Pensacola, crewmen went ashore to "sink casks" in the sand to get fresh water. On August 29, the *Alarm* left, this time towing the *Betsy* behind. The expedition returned to Pensacola without incident.

Gauld turned his efforts towards the southern end of East Florida in 1776 by mapping the Keys and Dry Tortugas. His efforts were hampered by the activities of privateers that preyed upon merchant vessels. He returned to the port of Pensacola, but misfortunes followed him there. Pensacola was besieged by the Spanish in 1781. This was the final battle between the two European superpowers for domination of West Florida, ending in the British defeat. Gauld was captured, and he and the other prisoners were taken to Havana, Cuba, and then sent to New York for exchange. Gauld returned to England but died there shortly after arriving. He is buried at Whitfield's Tabernacle Cemetery in London.

Gauld's legacy is naming Egmont Key after Sir John Perceval, the Second Earl of Egmont. Later maps sometimes show it named both "Egmont Key" (Island) and "Castor Key. " Others plagiarized Gauld's work in the years following his death, with copyright laws not being enforced. His work is considered to be of great accuracy even today.

Chapter 4

John Perceval, Second Earl of Egmont

The name "Egmont Key" has been the longest-lasting of the many names for the island. It is named after Sir John Perceval, the Second Earl of Egmont, who never visited the island and, in fact, never even came to North America. He is from a long line of Earls of Egmont. That peerage began in 1733 and was retired in 2011 when the twelfth Earl never married and thus had no heir, which caused the extinction of this line.

Perceval was born on February 25, 1711, to John Perceval (First Earl of Egmont) and Catherine Parker. He was baptized at the Palace of Westminster. Born into a family of nobility, Perceval was destined to serve in a series of appointments befitting of someone with his heritage.

He served in the Irish House of Commons between 1731 and 1749. He married Lady Catherine Cecil in 1737, who bore him five sons. She died relatively young in 1752 at the age of 33. Horace Walpole, a contemporary, said of Perceval, "he was as good-humored [*sic*] as it was possible for a man to be who was never known to laugh; he was once indeed seen to smile, and that was at chess."

Sir John Perceval by Thomas Hudson

In April 1748, he was "created" Lord of the Bedchamber to the Prince of Wales.[1] He was also busy at this time with the design and construction of his home, Enmore Castle, which took from 1751 to

---

1 A Lord of the Bedchamber was a courtier in the Royal Household; the term was first used in 1718. Their duties originally consisted of assisting the monarch with dressing, waiting on him when he ate, guarding access to his bedchamber and closet, and providing companionship.

1757. His second marriage was to Catherine Compton in 1756, and he had three sons and six daughters with her.

Enmore Castle

His next appointment was significant to the story of the Egmont Key. He was made First Lord of the Admiralty, and his tenure was from 1763 to 1766. During this time, English explorer George Gauld was mapping Florida's coastline. Gauld most likely thought it was a good idea to name some of his discoveries after the person who had funded the trip and named Egmont Key after Perceval. It was also called Castor Key (Island). Some later maps show both names.

For the next several years, he sat in the House of Commons for several constituencies. He died on December 4, 1770, at Pall Mall, London, at the age of 59. Upon his death, Walpole commented on Perceval as "a man always ambitious, almost always attached to a court, yet, from a singularity in his turn, scarce ever in place."

Other Egmont Connections

Egmont Key is not the only place that bears Sir John Perceval's name. In Florida, in the seaside city of Fernandina Beach, there is a historical marker that denotes the location of Egmont Plantation. It belonged to the estate of John Perceval, and upon his death in 1770, the executors of his will sent Stephen Egan to manage the property and slaves, which was then in East Florida. It was a very successful indigo[2] plantation. However, in 1776, the plantation was plundered by the Georgia Militia, and Egan, his family, and slaves fled to a plantation on the St. John's River, which was closer to British troops who were at the fort in St. Augustine.

The other location named for him is in New Zealand. It is an active volcano on the North Island's west coast called "Mount Egmont." Perceval favored searching for "Terra Incognita Australis," a continent theorized to be in the South Pacific.[3] Captain James Cook visited the island on behalf of the British government in 1769.

It also has a Māori name, "Taranaki," and both are proper names for the mountain. The English explorer James Cook had given it the name Mount Egmont on January 11, 1770, but in 1986, the New Zealand government deemed "Mount Taranaki" an alternative name.

There is a lighthouse in New Zealand named "Cape Egmont Lighthouse." It is in the Taranaki Region on the North Island at Cape Egmont. The tower was erected in 1877 and was previously located at Mana Island. In 1986, the light was automated, and staff from Maritime New Zealand were removed.

---

2 Indigo is a blue dye derived from *Indigofera tinctoria and Indigofera suffruticosa*. It is used in the textile industry.

3 This idea of an unknown continent in the southern hemisphere balancing out the continents in the northern hemisphere began with Aristotle. It continued through the centuries until the exploration of the southern hemisphere, which is located in present-day Australia and New Zealand.

Chapter 5

Bernard Romans, Surveyor

Bernard Romans was one of several surveyors and explorers who came through Tampa Bay over the years, in Roman's case, East and West Florida. At that time, Florida was considered two distinct regions. East Florida was what is now the peninsula, and West Florida was the panhandle region, extending west to the Mississippi River. The boundary between East and West was the Apalachicola River.

His voyage to survey East and West Florida increased his knowledge of the geography, Native American inhabitants, plants, and wildlife. His observations and recollections would later be published in a book titled *A Concise Natural History of East and West Florida* in 1775 in New York, with the illustration's lithographic plates being made by a metalsmith and engraver, Paul Revere.[1] The book is still in print and provides a detailed look into wildlife and native plants in Florida at that time and the attitudes and perceptions of Native Americans by Romans.

---

1 Map plates were engraved by Paul Revere in 1774. From Revere's account book dated May 4, 1774, Captain Bernard Romans was charged "To engrave a plate for the map of East Florida—ten pounds" and another entry on July 9, 1774, "To engraving on Copper-plate Part of a map of Florida seven pounds."

Barend Romans was born in Delft, Netherlands, a town in the southern part of the country, on June 7, 1741. He eventually Anglicized his name to Bernard. His parents were Pieter Barendsz Romans and Margareta van der Linden. No images of him exist, and little is known about his youth. He emigrated first to England, where he was educated in mathematics, botany, and engineering. He then migrated to the British American colonies in 1756 as a civil service junior surveyor.

On March 3rd, 1761, Romans married Maria Wendel at the Dutch Reformed Church in Albany, New York. The following year, his son, Peter Milo Romans, was born. There is no further record of Maria, who may have died at a young age.

He was appointed Deputy Surveyor of Georgia in 1766. Shortly after that, he was sent to East Florida to survey the property of Lord Egmont (Sir John Perceval) near Fernandina Beach and the St. Johns River, an associate of James Oglethorpe in the founding of the Colony of Georgia.

The Florida Expedition 1766-1767

From 1766-1767, Romans was in command of the sloop *Mary*. On his first voyage, he ran aground in the Dry Tortugas. After this mishap, the ship sank near Cape Florida. Having spent much of his personal wealth, he turned to other ventures.

Romans spent much of this time in the southern colonies, particularly Florida. By 1768, he was appointed by the British government as principal deputy surveyor for the "Southern District of British North America and first commander of the vessels on that service." He also engaged in land speculation and slave trading. His new responsibilities included the new colonies of East and West Florida, which Britain had acquired from Spain after the Seven Years' War.

According to his account, he entered into the King's service as a Commodore: "Sometimes at the head of a large body of men in the woods and at the worst of times …master of a merchantman, fitted out in a warlike manner." After the war, the Romans continued his life at sea as a merchant, traveling as far north as Labrador and south to Central America.

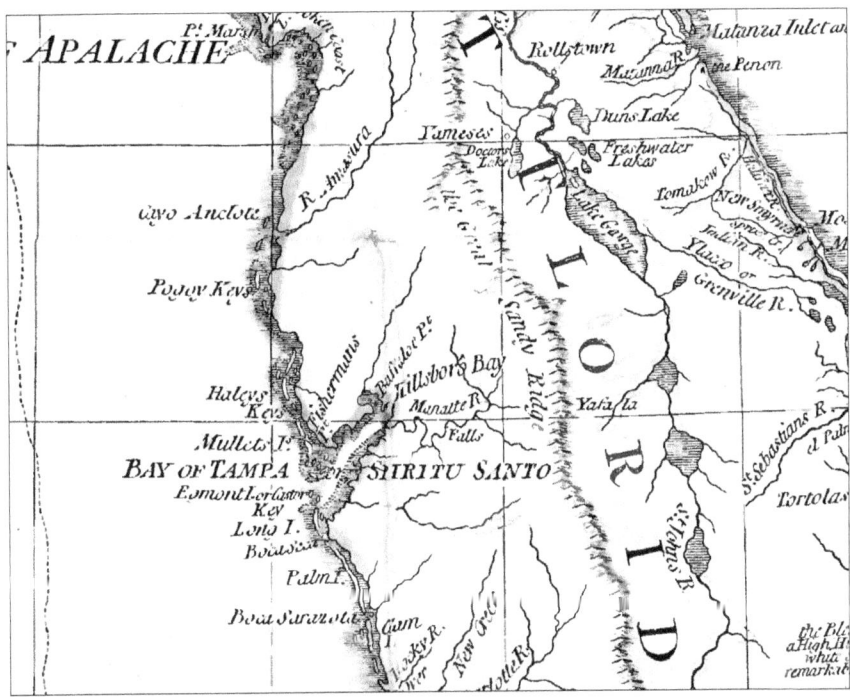

Romans map of East Florida

In 1769, he began his survey of the coastal waters of the Floridas. While on this voyage, his ship sank in the Manatee River south of Tampa Bay. His only option was to walk overland to St. Augustine hundreds of miles to the north. While on this trek, he made notes of what and who he encountered along the way. Realizing this was a historic undertaking, he would publish his findings in a book later.

After reaching St Augustine, he outfitted another boat at his own expense and resumed his coastal survey, reaching Pensacola in 1771. He would record depth soundings, harbors, and freshwater sources along the way. Later, he would draft charts of most of the Florida coastline. The following is an excerpt from his book in which he describes Tampa Bay:

DIRECTIONS FOR THE HARBOUR OF TAMPA BAY OR ESPIRITU SANTO

"This harbour, which is very capacious, will admit large ships and is extremely well calculated for a place to refresh at; here is abundance of wood, water, fish, oysters, clams, venison, turkies [sic], large and small water-fowl, &. The harbour is made by a range of islands lying before it; the southernmost is called Long Island (Anna Maria Island); its northern end called Grant's Point, in honor of Governor Grant[2]; the next lying about a mile North of it, is called Pollux Key(Passage Key); another about 1¼ mile to the NW by N of that is named Castor Key(Egmont Key), in honor of two privateers, one of which was commanded by the late Captain Braddock of Georgia: these two vessels cruized (sic) in those seas about the year 1744 or 1745; and Capt. Braddock was generally acknowledged to be the first Englishman who explored this bay. I have seen his original draught, which (considering the circumstances under which it was taken) was pretty exact. Next is a cluster of keys called Mullet Keys, lying between 2 and 3 miles E to N ¼ N from the north end of Castor

---

2 James Grant was appointed Governor of East Florida from 1764 to 1771.

Key; a shoal runs off from each of these to the westward, to that which runs off from the Mullet Keys the Spaniards give the name of Restingo Largo (Long Sandbar). On the Mullet Keys are huts built by the Spaniards, who resort here for the purpose of fishing. Grants Point lies in lat[itude] 27, 44, and the south end of Mullet Keys 48 N.in Lat. 27."

His narrative continued with instructions on navigating around the bay with depths of channels and landmarks to use while transiting the various channels. The following passage mentions his troubles in the Manatee River:

"Small vessels need not be so scrupulous in regard to these marks, the banks or shoals themselves are pretty deep, as the draughts point out. A.D. 1769 I was employed above 6 weeks in surveying this bay, and after sinking my boat in the Manatee River, where I suppose she lays now, I went across the Peninsula to St. Augustine on foot."

Romans had an argumentative nature and was challenging to work with. In a dispute with his boss, John William Gerrard DeBrahm, and the Governor of East Florida, James Grant, he was fired from government service in 1870 by Wills Hill, titled Lord Hillsborough, President of the Board of Trade and Secretary of State for the American Department (Lord Hillsborough is who the Hillsborough River and Hillsborough County are named after).

After reaching Pensacola, Romans were hired to survey West Florida, including the lands of the Choctaws, Creeks, and Chickasaws. At that time, the Creeks and Choctaws were at war. It was a dangerous undertaking, and rumors reached Mobile, Alabama, that the

Creeks had killed Romans and his party, which later proved to be unfounded. His survey work was completed in 1772.

Publishing *A Concise Natural History of East and West Florida*

In 1773, Romans began planning to publish his exploits and observations in a book. Originally intended as a 300-page work, it gradually grew to 800 pages with two large maps and copper plate engravings. He sought financial backing and also sold subscriptions to meet the cost. The book was conceived as a guide for mariners, but people interested in moving to Florida also wanted it. Romans decided to print it in two volumes, but the second volume's manuscript was lost in a fire and was never printed.

Revolutionary War Service

Bernard Romans sympathies lay with the colonists as war became more likely. He was in Boston during the Tea Party incident and, in his book, described tea "as a despicable weed, and of late attempted to be made a dirty conduit, to lead a stream of oppression into these happy regions."

Romans entered military service when the Connecticut Board of Safety appointed him Captain and tasked him with raising troops. He soon had 200 men and, along with troops led by Nathaniel Greene and Benedict Arnold, were given the assignment to capture Fort Ticonderoga in Canada. This was a defeat for the Americans, and Romans were soon back in Connecticut. He may have witnessed the Battle of Bunker Hill and published an illustration titled *An Exact View of the Late Battle at Charlestown, June 17, 1775*. He dedicated it to John Hancock.

Romans began supervising work on a fortification on Martelaer's Rock across the Hudson River from West Point. He began work, but he was not successful in his endeavors. George Washington wrote of the effort "upon the whole, Mr. Romans has displayed his genius at a very great expense and to very little publick [*sic*] advantage."

Romans's next military assignment was as Captain of the 1st Pennsylvania Artillery. After the unsuccessful battle to capture Quebec, he got into a dispute with another officer. A court of Inquiry was convened on July 24, 1776, under General Horatio Gates. He resigned his commission on June 1, 1778. The following year, on January 28, 1779, Romans married Elizabeth Whiting of Wethersfield, Connecticut, when she was just 19 years old. They had a son, Hubertus Romans, on October 23, 1779.

Bernard Romans reentered military service in 1780 and was sent to join the Southern Campaign in South Carolina. His assignment was unclear. He was on a ship traveling from New London, Connecticut, to Charleston when the Royal Navy captured it. Romans was held captive by the British till the war's end. He died on board the ship on the way home. His widow and an early historian believe he was murdered and his body disposed of at sea. No definitive proof has been published about this. She died on May 12, 1848, in New York at age 87.

RESOLUTION

OF

THE LEGISLATURE OF FLORIDA,

RELATIVE TO

The erection of a light-house on Egmont Key.

FEBRUARY 8, 1847.
Referred to the Committee on Commerce, and ordered to be printed.

PREAMBLE AND RESOLUTION asking Congress to make an appropriation to build a light-house at Egmont Key, on the coast of Florida.

Whereas the port and harbor of Tampa Bay are of the greatest commercial importance not only to the people of Florida, but to the commerce of the whole country; and whereas it is highly important, for the protection and safety of the commercial interest on the gulf coast, that a light-house should be built at the entrance of said harbor; and whereas Egmont Key, situated immediately at the entrance to said harbor, is the most eligible position for the location of said light-house: therefore,

Resolved, That the Congress of the United States be requested to make an appropriation for the purpose of building a light-house on Egmont Key, and that our Senators and Representative in Congress be requested to use their exertions to obtain an appropriation for that purpose.

Adopted December 2, 1846.

D. H. MAYS, *President of Senate.*

H. ARCHER, *Secretary of Senate.*

Adopted December 4, 1846.

ROBT. BROWN,
Speaker of the House of Representatives.

M. D. PAPY,
Clerk of the House of Representatives.

Approved December 14, 1846.

W. D. MOSELEY,
Governor of Florida.

Resolution to build the lighthouse

Chapter 6

Sherrod Edwards, Lighthouse Keeper and Francis Gibbons, Civil Engineer

The first calls for a lighthouse at Egmont Key came as early as 1837. Secretary of the Treasury Levi Woodbury requested that Napoleon L. Coste, captain of the Revenue Cutter *Campbell,* stop at all customs ports of entry between New Orleans and Washington DC and report on the need for additional navigation aids. The Revenue Cutter Service was a forerunner to the US Coast Guard. His report was filed in July of 1837. The following is an excerpt:

"I have the honor to report that the first place which presents itself to me of importance for the erection of a light-house is at the mouth of Tampa Bay, on the north point of Eggmont [*sic*] Key. The western coast of Florida is very low, and similar in appearance, making it necessary for the mariner to have some mark by which he could take his departure, and as Eggmont is the point which all vessels endeavor to make when bound to St. Mark's, Apalachicola, or St. Joseph's, it is my opinion, that by the erection of a light-house on the point above mentioned, the navigation of the coast would be facilitated, and much property saved which is now annually lost by shipwreck. It is also important that I should inform you that a light-house would be a leading mark over the bar into Tampa bay, a bar capable of admitting small class frigates, and navigable to within ten miles of its head for sloops-of-war at all times."

It was not until after Florida's becoming a state in 1845 that the newly formed state legislature petitioned Congress in December of 1846 for funding. Congress granted $10,000 for a lighthouse on Egmont Key the following year. Francis A. Gibbons[1], an architect from Baltimore, signed a contract to build a forty-foot tower with an octagonal lantern room that would house thirteen Winslow Lewis[2] lamps and reflectors at the cost of $6,250. The contract included a dwelling for a keeper, and the Winslow Lewis-supplied illuminating apparatus cost $1,330. Twenty-one-inch reflectors backed each lamp.

Work began on the project in the summer of 1847, with expected completion and lighting of the tower by January 1848. The Customs Collector for St. Marks, Mr. N.H. Walker was tasked with supervising the construction. Walker insisted the tower be built on a foundation of driven pilings (wood) rather than dry shells and sand as suggested by a frugal Stephen Pleasonton, Fifth Auditor of the Treasury. Walker also wanted the keeper's house to "be placed at least one hundred feet

---

1 Francis A. Gibbons constructed the Choptank River Lighthouse in 1870. It was a hexagonal cottage-style, screw-pile structure.

2 Winslow Lewis (1770-1850) was an American lighthouse designer and builder. He also developed a lighting system based on the Argand lamp. He completed the construction of lighthouses quickly and cheaply and became a favorite of Steven Pleasanton for lighthouse construction.

from the tower, so in case of its prostration, the house and lives would not be endangered."

Challenges began to surface immediately with the grounding of the supply ship *Abbe Baker* on Orange Cay in the Bahamas. This unfortunate event led to nearly half the bricks being disposed of overboard to refloat the ship. Despite this setback, by February 1848, the tower had reached a height of twenty feet. However, work was temporarily halted until a new shipment of bricks arrived to complete the project. This was a testament to the builders' resilience and determination. Despite these hurdles, the tower was officially certified in April of 1848, and the first keeper, Sherrod Edwards, had already arrived by October 11, 1847, to activate the light. He recommended that his brother Marvel Edwards be hired as his assistant keeper in July 1848.

Sherrod Edwards was born in 1800 in Thomas County, Georgia. He married Sara (Lovett) Edwards in Thomas County on August 8, 1827. Little is known about his early life or when he moved to Florida.

He had three daughters: Malinda Cathryn (Edwards) Whitehurst, born in 1833; Louisa Jane (Edwards) Whitehurst, born in 1834; and Mary Etta (Edwards) Whitehurst, born in 1840. Each married a man from the Whitehurst family, but they were not brothers.

He served in the 1st Florida Mounted Volunteers from December 10, 1840, to March 1841, when the unit was disbanded. Records indicated he had a Private servant and two horses. At the same time, he was the fourth sheriff of Madison County. Now, he was the first keeper, and his resilience was about to be tested by Mother Nature.

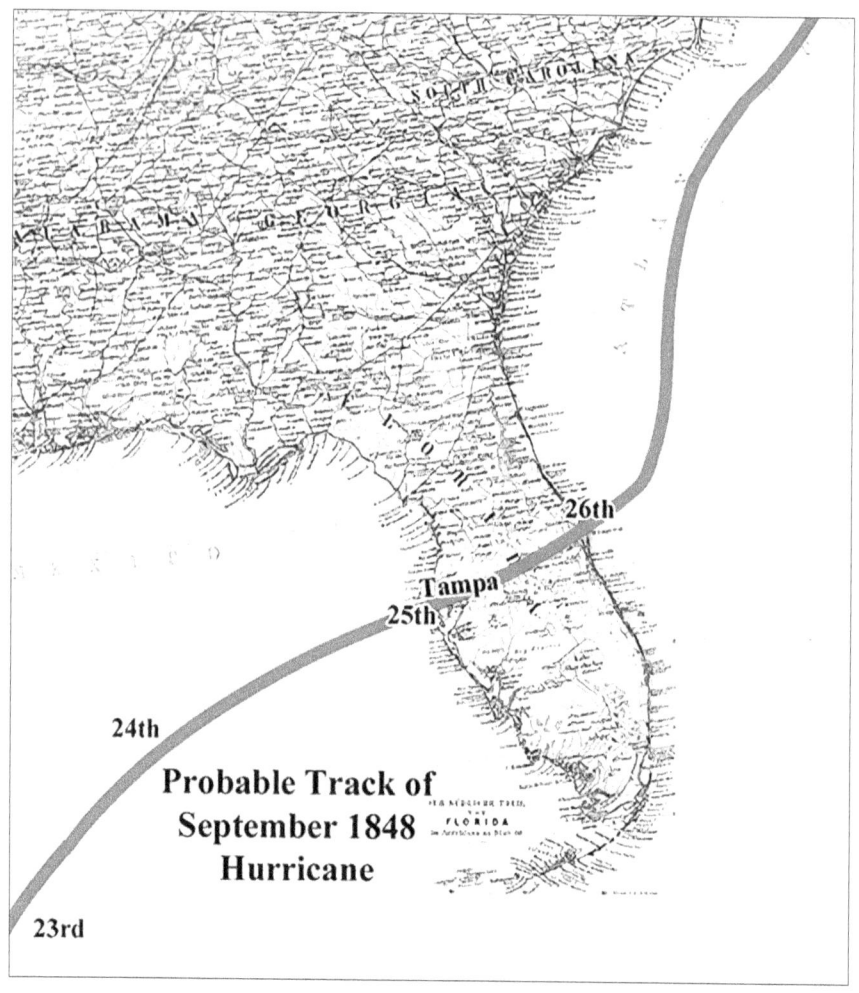

Lighthouse Similar to the 1848 Tower on Egmont Key

Misfortune continued to plague the new lighthouse when, on September 25, 1848, a hurricane estimated to be a Category 3-4, also called "The Great Gale of '48," came ashore at Tampa Bay, near present-day Clearwater. The storm surge was estimated to be fifteen feet, and winds of 100-135 miles per hour. It is the most powerful storm ever coming ashore in the Tampa Bay area in recorded history. In present-day downtown Tampa, Fort Brooke received heavy damage with the loss of all the piers and most of the buildings. The surgeon for the post reported a rapid rise of water between 10 AM and 2 PM. Damage to the fort was so extensive the Army considered abandoning that site and building a fort further south of Tampa. The civilian residences also received heavy damage, and there were reports of vessels in the harbor being driven upriver and destroyed. At that time, Tampa had only about two hundred residents. Only five buildings survived the storm, but all were damaged. Miraculously, there were no reports of any lives lost!

Remnants of the 1848 tower can be found east of the current tower.
Photo by author

The only warning of impending danger was a faint glow of light in the Gulf of Mexico in the hours before daylight on the day the storm made landfall. The storm washed over the Egmont Key with nearly fifteen feet of water, severely damaging the tower. The tides rose so fast that the water was two feet deep surrounding the keeper's house when Sherrod Edwards took action. According to Tampa pioneer John A. Bethell, "He placed his family in his boat and waded with it to the middle of the island and secured it to the palmettos until the gale was over." Sherrod Edwards and his family survived the storm but were exhausted after a night in the storm. When they returned, the lighthouse was heavily damaged, and his house and possessions were gone. According to a local legend that has been passed down for many years, the keeper and his family rowed ashore and promptly, after the storm passed, quit his job! In fact, Sherrod Edwards remained a keeper until 1850, more than two years after the storm,

Mother Nature was not quite finished with the island and Tampa that year. On October 11-12, 1848, barely three weeks after the last, another storm passed through the area. It was not as powerful as the previous one, with a storm surge of ten feet. These storms were referenced by Brevet Colonel Robert E. Lee when a party of engineers from the Board of Engineers stopped at Egmont in 1849 as a part of their coastal survey of Florida, which had become a state in 1845. Lee noted the damage to the lighthouse in his report. Walker's insistence that the foundation be wooden pilings probably saved the tower from toppling after the storms in 1848. Shortly after these storms, the tower was struck by lightning, causing cracks in the brickwork.

After surviving the two worst storms in recent times and working to repair the lighthouse and keep it in service, Sherrod Edwards and his family left Egmont in 1850. Sherrod quit due to the low pay of $400 ($15,000 today) per year, which he felt was insufficient for all the job hazards.

Sherrod Edward's grave. Note the misspelling of his name as "Sherod,"
Photo by Author"

Sherrod Edwards died in Hillsborough County (now part of
Pinellas County), Florida, on June 29, 1880. He is buried in the
Curlew Pioneer Cemetery in Palm Harbor next to his wife, Sarah

Lovett Edwards, who died in 1902. Their three daughters are also buried there.

Francis Gibbons performed engineering work on several lighthouses on the east coast of the United States in the following years. The lighthouse continued in service, although attempts were made to repair it. In 1854, a concrete base was poured around it, attempting to stabilize it. The Lighthouse Board realized a new lighthouse was needed and requested Congress to fund a new one.

History Repeats Itself

During the writing and editing of this history of Egmont Key, weather events occurred that so closely parallel the so-called "Great Gale of '48" that this work would not be complete without a discussion of them. What had transpired was a once-in-a-century hurricane that severely altered the course of life on the island, possibly for decades.

Fast-forward 176 years to September 25, 2024, when Hurricane Helene began to form in the western Caribbean Sea just a few days earlier. Heading northward through the warm waters of the Gulf of Mexico, it was predicted to make landfall in the Big Bend region of Florida.

Unlike conditions in 1848, there was plenty of information about the storm's progress in 2024. Modern satellite imagery, hurricane hunter aircraft from the Air Force and the National Oceanographic and Atmospheric Administration (NOAA), and weather radars along the Florida peninsula could gather data and report to the public and authorities on the storm's characteristics. News media coverage would be around the clock, with new information available every few hours. These advancements in storm tracking allowed local, state, and federal agencies to plan evacuations, provide emergency services, and help with the needs of the local population after the storm has passed, reassuring the public about the safety measures in place.

Even though the storm landed well away from the Tampa Bay Area, the surge of water caused by its passage was forecast to be 7-10 feet with winds of 140 miles per hour. Even with all the warnings and preparation, 214 people died in the United States along the storm's entire path.

Mother Nature was not through with Florida yet! Like 1848, on October 9, 2024, fourteen das after Helene, Hurricane Milton made landfall at Siesta Key, a little south of Tampa Bay. This powerful storm formed in the western Caribbean Sea and began moving north and east, with projected landfall in Tampa Bay. The storm quickly grew to Category 5 (wind 157 MPH or higher) and a storm surge of 7-14 feet. This time, the track would be fifty miles south of the October 1848 hurricane. Due to atmospheric conditions, Milton began slowing down to Category 4 and then arriving as a Category 3. The wind speed at Egmont Key was 105 MPH. Wind damage was severe, with 75 percent of the residents and businesses in Hillsborough County losing power, which would take weeks to restore fully. The wind field of the storm spawned at least forty tornadoes in the state's heartland, destroying many homes and taking lives.

Helene had caused significant damage to Egmont Key with the wind and surge of water. The harbor pilots' compound saw every building damaged or knocked off its foundations. One building disappeared altogether. Substantial damage to their dock and maintenance shed rendered them unusable. The USCG support buildings on the island's north end were flooded, and the ranger house was also flooded. The lighthouse tower remained in service since the beacon didn't require shore power.

The wildlife was also affected, with the gopher tortoise population significantly killed off. Some of the tortoises from Egmont Key were carried by the surge of water nearly two miles to Fort DeSoto

Park. The nesting shore birds had mostly fledged and left the island, so they were less affected. The loggerhead sea turtle nesting was also impacted, but the actual numbers have not yet been reported.

Passage Key, which had disappeared in 1848, was washed away again. It was only about five acres and had only recently returned after disappearing after a storm several years ago. It will eventually reform, but it will take Mother Nature a few more years to accomplish this.

Hurricane Milton further destroyed the island's infrastructure. The final results have yet to be assessed. If another suitable location can be found, the harbor pilots may have to move operations elsewhere. The condition of the ranger house, USCG support buildings, and the US Fish and Wildlife building have yet to be reported.

As of this writing, the total damage to Egmont Key has yet to be assessed. The island will likely recover as it has over the centuries in response to events like these. The loggerhead sea turtles will return next year along with the nesting shorebirds. Gopher tortoises will recover as well. Passage Key has been washed away in the past and will undoubtedly return within a few years.

Chapter 7

The 1849 Expedition to Survey the Coast of Florida

Coastal Forts in Florida in 1849

At the time of the 1849 coast survey, Florida was still primitive and untamed. The state had been admitted to the Union barely four years earlier, in March 1845. The Second Seminole War had concluded indecisively only three years before Florida became a state, and there were still tensions between the military, white settlers, and the Seminoles. The final outbreak of conflict that decided the Seminole's fate would start just a few years later, in 1855.

Various nations had occupied the Florida Territory since the 1600's. The British and Spanish each had possession of it and fought over it. The French attempted to colonize Florida by Huguenots at Fort Caroline but were swiftly driven out by the Spanish. The French may have made explorations of the Suwannee River as well. The Spanish built several forts in the northern part of the peninsula when Florida was their possession. The Castillo de San Marcos in St. Augustine is the most well-known, along with a smaller fort at Matanzas. Spain began construction of these in 1705. At the beginning of the Civil War, the fort at St. Augustine had a single soldier as a caretaker, having been abandoned after the end of the Third Seminole War. The Confederates occupied the fort at the outbreak of hostilities and held it until 1862 when Federal troops reoccupied it. Holding a fort like Fort Marion was difficult for the Confederates since their soldiers were needed elsewhere.

Another Spanish fort from that era is Fort San Marcos de Apalachee near present-day St. Marks, where the Wakulla and St. Marks Rivers meet. During the coastal survey in 1849, this fort was in ruins. The Confederates would put it in service again during the Civil War, but it was rebuilt only as an earthwork fort. It was the last coastal fort to lower its flag in defeat in the Civil War.

The Spanish built a fort at Pensacola in 1787 called Fort San Carlos de Barrancas (Bluff) or the Old Water Fort. It was built on the site of an earlier Spanish fort known as San Carlos de Austria. After the United States purchased Florida from Spain in 1821, the government made Pensacola into a major navy yard, adding additional fortifications. Barrancas was rebuilt, and an additional battery was added to the bluff, connecting it with the older Spanish fort with a tunnel. In addition, construction had begun in 1845 on the Advanced Redoubt on the land side of Pensacola to protect the city from attack. Finally, Fort Pickens was constructed on Santa Rosa Island in 1834, and Fort McRee on land opposite Pickens in 1839, making Pensacola the most well-defended harbor in Florida. All these forts would play a part in the Civil War for both sides, with Fort Pickens being one of the few forts occupied by the Union Army in the Confederate States for the duration of the war.

Further down the Gulf Coast was Fort Brooke, first established as Cantonment Brooke in 1824 and later renamed Fort Brooke after a wooden palisade wall was constructed. Tampa was a small village at the time, with little economic activity. This fort played a part in the Civil War as well. Union troops stationed on Egmont Key for the duration of the war attacked Ballast Point and later Fort Brooke to stop blockade runners operating in the area. The Union forces held the fort for only a few days. In May 1864, the Union Army attacked Fort Brooke again, capturing it and Tampa, occupying it for the rest of the war. Fort Brooke was decommissioned by the Army in 1883.

Construction of Fort Taylor in Key West began in 1845 as a means to protect the United States coast after the War of 1812. After his sudden death in office, the fort was named after President Zachary Taylor. Work was completed in the 1850s and included two Martello Towers, which are more minor fortifications built nearby to support a more significant fortification. The importance of Fort Taylor became clear when Florida seceded from the Union in 1861. The Union occupied Fort Taylor and Key West for the duration of the Civil War.

During the coast survey, the last major fortification in Florida was Fort Jefferson in the Dry Tortugas. Construction began on the fort in 1846; its purpose was to provide a naval station to combat pirates in the Caribbean that preyed on shipping in the area. The site was also considered a good location for a lighthouse, and one was constructed. It became known as the Garden Key Light. The fort was eventually built around the lighthouse tower, and a lantern room was later built on one of the bastions on the fort wall, and the tower was demolished. It was determined that the Garden Key Lighthouse was inadequate to protect shipping in the area from hazardous reefs, so another lighthouse was built three miles west on Loggerhead Key, completed in 1858. Garden Key Lighthouse became a harbor light to guide ships to the fort.

Fort Jefferson is the largest masonry structure in the Americas, even though it was never completed after thirty years of work. Construction began in 1846, and sixteen million bricks were shipped to the location from Georgia and New York. The fort was to be two tiers high, but it began to sink before the second tier was complete. It was decided not to complete the second tier by closing in the firing ports for the cannons. Guns would be mounted on top of the second tier. It never had its full complement of artillery due to weight considerations. Fort Jefferson also played a part in the Civil War and was occupied by the U.S. Navy as a coaling station. At the same time, Navy ships in the area looked for blockade runners transiting between Havana and Florida. It was also a prison for Union soldiers convicted of crimes, as well as the prison that held Dr. Samuel Mudd and co-conspirators of John Wilkes Booth in the Lincoln assassination.

The Need for the Survey of 1849

Since Florida was a new state in the union (along with Texas in 1845), the Army Corps of Engineers saw the necessity to assess potential ports for future growth in economic activity as well as existing ports and reserve land that would be appropriate for building coastal forts. Coastal forts were how the United States defended itself from hostile nations at the time. The greatest fear was to see enemy ships outside a significant port, so coastal forts were located in the harbors of major cities along the eastern seaboard and, later, on the west coast and Hawaii.

The Corps of Engineers, headed by Chief Engineer Joseph Totten, dispatched a group of four engineers to travel by schooner around the coast of Florida and stop at any location that was an active port or that could potentially become a port and make an assessment of the channels, tides, wave action, winds and land in the vicinity of the harbor. They were interested in determining water depths and estimating the size of ships that could access the harbor. Also, they wanted to determine how the land masses and tree cover might contribute to making a harbor a safe anchorage in bad weather. The report doesn't specify what measurements were made, but the contents can provide an educated guess of the report.

Once the assessment was made, a decision on what lands might need to be reserved was made and recommended in the report back to the Corps of Engineers. The expedition stopped at and "examined" seventeen locations around the state and, in their report, prepared a table that expressed the relative importance of several of the sites. Many years later, in 1870, the lands were formally reserved by the Department of the Interior, General Land Office. Most were never used for the intended purpose of coastal defense, and later, they were relinquished and made available for other uses.

What follows is part of the letter from General Joseph G. Totten authorizing the expedition and the table that prioritizes the sites. The only site included here is Tampa Bay. An asterisk indicates the handwriting was not legible enough to determine the word. Spelling and grammar are unchanged. The full document is in Appendix A.

Sir,

"The Board of Engineers will make an examination during the coming winter of the coast of East and West Florida from Amelia island around to Pensacola bay; not including the latter, which has been comprised in previous examinations.

It is hoped that the engagements of the Officers of the Board permit the duty to be taken up in time for the proceedings results to reach the Department before the close of the next Session of Congress. When informed of the time & place appointed by the board for the commencement of the examination, the Dept. will ask the Sec. of War to solicit the Sec. of the Treas. the aid (hitherto granted with great promptness) of a Revenue Cutter, to transfer the Board along parts of the Coast otherwise inaccessible to them.

The main object of the Board, in the contemplated exploration of the Coast of Florida, will be the selection & designation of the Bays, Harbors and Inlets, that should enter into the New System of Coast defence [sic]. To this end, it is expected that they will examine all such, so as to satisfy themselves of the true points of defence in each, & also to be enabled to append to their report, memoranda comprising instructions for the necessary surveys & levellings [sic]. In a general description of the localities of interest as connected with defence, the Board will discriminate to the relative value & importance of each; will mark out the order of time in which they *** should receive the attention of Government in surveys, in the erection of defenses [sic].

In the account of harbors *, should be comprised a description, with a sketch (at least) of all existing works (except Fort Marion, St. Augustine, & Fort at Matanzas inlet now in this office) and the opinion of the Board on the propriety of maintaining the same in the system.

A special board having already reported on the Florida Reef, including Key West & the Tortugas, the Board of Engineers will use their discretion as to further examination of the same or any points thereof in reference to the Commission [sic] of this reef with the general defensive System of the Gulf.

The Board is aware that every other part of the Coast from Eastport to the Sahire[*sic*] has been heretofore examined by the Board of Engineers – whose valuable reports thereon are in file in this office: the design now is to supply the a***pay [*sic*] knowledge for the deficient portion of the Coast indicated in the beginning of this letter. The above general instructions are all that can be a***pay[*sic*] to the accomplishment of this object in a perfect manner.

I have, however, particularly to instruct the Board that in anticipation of the necessity for occupying certain points, islands on the Coast of Florida as defensive sites, reservations have been made of the public lands to an extent that interfers [*sic*] *** in some places, with the progress of improvements & settlement of the Coast and therefore the Board will as soon as practicable, in a special report, point out all the localities that should be reserves – giving limits to each reservation to sufficiently guide the Land Offices (General Land Office).

Applications have been more than once made from high quarters for all land to be liberated that is now under reservation along that shore and I have had action therein postponed only under a promise that at the earliest day practicable, the Board of Engineers would make a selection of the sites actually *** for our purposes.

It may be advantageous for one member of the Board, before going south, to visit this city for the purpose of selecting such maps and reports useful for duty before the Board, as can be procured here.

I have the honor to be
(Signed) Jos. G. Totten
Chief Engineer

The Board assembled at Mobile (Alabama) on the 26th, and the Schooner *Phenix*, being reported ready for sea on the 30th, sailed that day for the Coast of Florida. The various bays, harbors, inlets around the Coast will now be considered under their respective heads, with a view to their being embraced in the general system of defence [*sic*].

VIII. Tampa Bay. The Coast South of Cedar Cays(Keys) as far as Anclote Cay(Key), or Anchor island is so low & shoal that the land is not visible to the naked eye until you get into less than 2 fathoms of water. From that point, it becomes more prominent & bolder. Anclote Cay, about 4 or 5 miles from the mainland, has an anchorage for Coasters (coastal boats) under its Southern point. Like Clear Water Harbor (present-day Old Clearwater Bay), still farther South, this anchorage is open to the north & can only be entered from the South. It is accessible only to small vessels. South of Anclote island, the shore is bolder and covered by a range of low islands (barrier islands). The principle of those which extend across the mouth of Tampa Bay are called Mullet, Egmont, Barnaby & Long islands (present-day Mullet Key, Egmont Key, Passage Key, and Anna Maria Island). The names have changed many times over the years, and even a coastal survey done in 1855 has different names for Passage Key and Anna Maria.

The lower part of this Bay was called <u>Espiritu Santo</u> (Holy Spirit). The upper part is divided into two branches. The western branch is called Tampa and the Eastern, Hillsborough. The whole bay is generally known under the name of Tampa. It is about 30 miles long & 5 miles wide, as far up as Gadsden's Point, where it separates into East and West branches.

There are now two principal entrances from the sea. One on either side of Egmont island. The channel north of Egmont, called the West entrance, runs nearly east & west between the shoals extending from Egmont & Mullet islands seawards, which bound it on either side. Both shoals stretch several miles to the sea & even at high water, are well-defined & mark the channel way. The bar is at their outer termination, where they spread into one & has 21 feet of water on it at common low tide. Within the bar, the channel is from 7 to 10 fathoms deep & about a mile wide to within the bay. The distance from the north point of Egmont island to the South point of Mullet island is about 2 miles.

The entrance south of Egmont island, called East entrance, lies between Egmont & Barnaby islands. This entrance is also broad & open. The bar has 15 feet of water on it at low water & is not so distant to sea as the bar of the west entrance.

Besides these two main channels, there are other minor ones north & south of them, between islands covering the mouth of the bay, which vary in depth from 4 to 7 feet.

All of these channels except the west entrance, change in their positions and depths after every severe storm. The storm of October 1848 (possibly the one that damaged the first lighthouse), washed away a portion of Barnaby (Burnaby) island & diminished the depth of the channel between that island & Long island. In this latter channel there had been previously 116 feet of water. The channel of the west entrance differs from all the rest in not being subject to the alterations produced by storms. It remains always the same.

The islands covering the mouth of Tampa are low & sandy & bear a stunted growth of Spanish bayonet, palmetto. The shores of the bay, as high as Gadsden's point, are also low & subject to be overflowed by storm tides. Above Gadsden's point the banks are higher. Those on the western branch are above the reach of inundation & 3 fathoms of water can be carried up to the head of the branch. The banks at the head of the Eastern branch, the site of Fort Brooke, are barely above the reach of severe storms. Four fathoms water can be carried from the mouth of the bay to Mangrove point. There, the water begins to shoal & the channel becomes winding. Only 8 feet of water can be carried up to the mouth of the Hillsborough river at the head of the Eastern branch and the Hillsborough is not navigable more than 12 miles from its mouth. The Manitee (Manatee) river enters the bay at near its mouth & the little Manitee about halfway up. There are a few settlements on these rivers, but as yet that around Fort Brooke is the principle.

In a military point of view, this large and spacious bay of greater capacity than any on the Coast of Florida of easy access & having as much water over the bar of its principal entrance as Pensacola is diminished in value in consequence of the many & width of its entrances which renders it difficult to defend. In itself it has but little trade & commerce & it would be difficult to state the period when it would be likely to be of sufficient importance to authorize the expenditure necessary for its complete defence. Yet its position intermediate between Cay west (Key West) and Pensacola, the only points on the Gulf where vessels of a certain draft could look for safety, added to its advantages as a harbor, may hereafter render it advisable, if not to close against our enemy's fleet; at least each a work on the on the north end of Egmont island, which in addition to interrupting the passage of the main entrance , would give some protection under its guns to our own vessels, with the aid of war steamers stationed in the Gulf, secure the advantages of the harbor to vessels & wrest them from an *** . The Survey of this part of the coast will honestly establish the relative position of the islands & channels now imperfectly known & show how the defence of the harbor can be best effected. With this view & preparatory to the completion of the Survey the Board have recommended certain islands at the mouth of the harbor be reserved.

The following table is from a report to General Totten, Chief of Engineers dated March 14, 1849, that rates the relative importance of the different sites for possible future development and fortifications.

Tabular statement of the relative value & importance of the points on the Sea Coast of Florida, marking the order of time in which they generally should receive the attention of Government in surveys & in erection of defences.

Name of Place	Class	Remarks
St Georges Island	1	To receive first Attention of Govt.
Tampa Bay	1	To receive first Attention of Govt.
Biscayne Bay	1	To receive first Attention of Govt.
Cedar Cays	2	Ditto Second ditto
St Johns river	2	Ditto Second ditto

Name of Place	Class	Remarks
St Andrews Sound	3	Ditto third ditto
St Josephs Bay	3	Ditto third ditto
St Marks River	3	Ditto third ditto
Charlotte Harbor	3	Ditto third ditto

All of which is respectfully Submitted by the Board of Engineers

Lt. Col R. E. DeRussy

Board of Engrs.

Pres. Pro Tem

R. E Lee, Capt. & Bt. Col. Engrs.

Recorder to the Board

The four engineers sent on the expedition were Lieutenant Colonel Rene Edward DeRussy, expedition leader, Major Richard Delafield, Brevet[1] Col. Joseph K. F. Mansfield, and Brevet Colonel Robert E. Lee, Recorder to the Board of Engineers for this expedition. All went on to further military careers, and some achieved high rank. What follows are short biographies of the four engineers of the 1849 Expedition. What is interesting to note here is there is no mention of this expedition in their biographies except for Lee's, which might only get a sentence or two but not more than a paragraph in the many dozens of books written about his life and exploits. From this fact, it can be assumed that this expedition was a routine task

---

1 Brevet rank was an honorary promotion for exemplary service. Lee and Mansfield were ranked as Captains and received the pay of that rank.

that could have been assigned to any number of engineers on the Board of Engineers at that time.

Robert Edward Lee

Countless volumes have been written about every aspect of Lee's life and service in the Civil War. Lee became the most successful and well-known of the engineers who served on the Expedition of 1849 but, at the time, held a junior post as Recorder to the Board. He kept a journal and submitted a report to Joseph Totten, Chief of Engineers.

Lieutenant Robert E. Lee in 1838

Lee was born on January 19, 1807, at the Stratford Hall Plantation in Virginia, the son of Major General Henry Lee III (Light Horse Harry) and Anne Hill Carter. His father abandoned the family when he was young and died when Robert was eleven years old. He grew up in very austere circumstances.

He was appointed to attend West Point in the summer of 1825 and remained at the top, or nearly so, for his entire time there. He was known as a skilled mathematician and natural leader. Upon graduation, he began his work as an engineer of fortifications on the east coast of the U.S.

In 1829, he courted and got permission to marry Mary Custis, George Washington's great-granddaughter. They were wed in 1831.

In the Mexican War of 1846-1848, Lee distinguished himself as Winfield Scott's aide. He was promoted to Brevet Major, then Brevet

Lieutenant Colonel, and finally Brevet Colonel. On the Expedition of 1849, less than a year after the Mexican War, he held the rank of Captain. In 1852, he was appointed Superintendent of West Point, a post he reluctantly accepted. His oldest son attended West Point during his tenure there and was first in his class.

In 1857, after the death of his father-in-law, he assumed management of Arlington House, his wife's family plantation on the Potomac River near Washington DC. Managing a plantation was not something he felt suited to do. When the Civil War started, Lee was offered the command of the Union Army. He declined, and Lee eventually assumed command of the Army of Northern Virginia, refusing to bear arms against his home state of Virginia. His plantation was seized by the Federal government and was used as a cemetery to bury many of the thousands of Union soldiers killed during the war. This plantation became Arlington National Cemetery, and his home still stands there.

After the surrender of the Confederacy in April of 1865, Lee returned to civilian life. He was appointed Chancellor of Washington College, later renamed Washington and Lee University. Once again, he excelled at the job. He implemented many new programs and transformed the institution into a leading Southern college. He integrated the Lexington Law School into the university. It became the Washington and Lee University School of Law. He served as Chancellor till his death in 1870.

Lee returned to Florida one more time before his death in 1870 to visit his father's grave, "Light Horse" Harry Lee, buried on Cumberland Island, Georgia. He then visited the home of Colonel Robert G. Cole, one of his staff officers from the war who was living in Palatka, Florida.

Lee died from a stroke the same year, on October 10, in Lexington, Virginia.

Renee Edward DeRussy

Born in the French colony of Saint Domingue (now Haiti) on February 22, 1789, to Thomas Benoit DeRussy and Mary Madeline DeRussy. Two years later, the family moved to Old Point Comfort, Virginia, where his parents became naturalized citizens. At the age of eighteen, he was appointed to the United States Military Academy at West Point on March 20, 1807, graduating at the bottom of his class in June 1812. After graduation, he worked as an Assistant Engineer to construct defenses for the State of New York and helped build Fort Montgomery at Rouses Point on the U.S.-Canada border. In the late 1810s, he became a superintending engineer for the defenses of New York Harbor. After completing this work, he was sent to the Gulf of Mexico to build forts along the coast from 1821 to 1825.

Returning to New York, he continued fort construction, namely Fort Hamilton, located in the borough of Brooklyn. While stationed there, he also constructed a home on present-day Dyker Heights in Brooklyn, N.Y., and because of the home's location, it was referred to as "The Lookout."

In July 1833, he was made Superintendent of West Point Military Academy, a post he served for five years. After this assignment, he was sent south to supervise fort construction in Virginia and Delaware; the latter was Fort Delaware, a prisoner-of-war site during the Civil War and later modernized with disappearing guns as part of the Coast Defense System.

He was sent west to build forts in the new states on the Pacific coast and became a member of the Atlantic Coast Defense Board from 1849 to 1854. He briefly returned to the Atlantic coast and was sent back to San Francisco in 1861. He died on November 23, 1865, the oldest active-duty graduate of West Point at age seventy-five. He is buried in the United States Military Academy Post Cemetery. His brother, Lewis Gustave DeRussy, graduated from West Point in 1814 and served as a colonel in the Confederate Army during the Civil War. He was the oldest graduate to serve the Confederacy.

Richard Delafield

Born in New York City on September 1, 1798, the son of John Delafield and Ann Hallet Delafield. He graduated from West Point and was the first to receive a merit class standing, ranking first in his Class of 1818. He spent much of his early career supervising the construction of defenses in Mississippi and Virginia. He also designed and built Dunlap's Creek Bridge  in Pennsylvania, the first cast iron tubular arch bridge in the U.S. Appointed Superintendent of West Point, he designed a new cadet uniform that displayed the castle insignia for the first time. He was supervising the construction of defenses in New York Harbor when he was sent to Florida for the 1849 coastal survey. He later formed the Delafield Commission, sent to study the European military in 1855. Delafield was appointed Superintendent of West Point again from 1856-1861 and was placed in charge of harbor defenses in New York during the Civil War. He was made Chief of Engineers from 1864 to his retirement in 1866. He died in Washington, DC, and the Secretary of War ordered a thirteen-gun salute in his memory at West Point. He is buried in the family crypt in Brooklyn, New York.

Joseph King Fenno Mansfield

Born on December 22, 1803, in New Haven, Connecticut, to Henry and Mary Fenno Mansfield. He was a cousin of Joseph G. Totten, Chief of Engineers, during the Florida expedition of 1849. He entered West Point at the young age of fourteen and graduated second in a class of forty cadets in 1822. He was commissioned into the Board of Engineers as a Second Lieutenant and settled in Middletown, Connecticut. Mansfield served in the Mexican War and was promoted quickly. He was wounded at the Battle of Monterrey, Mexico, and was promoted to Brevet Lieutenant Colonel for his actions there.

During the Civil War, he was Brigade Commander of the Department of Virginia, and his only combat was firing coastal batteries at the Confederate *CSS Virginia*, an ironclad warship, during the pivotal battle between it and the *USS Monitor*, also an ironclad. Later, he commanded the VII Corps, receiving command just two days before the battle of Antietam. He was mortally wounded on September 17, 1862, shot in the chest while on horseback, and died two days later. He is buried in Indian Hill Cemetery, Middletown, Connecticut. In 1880, the $500 United States Note featured a portrait of him in memory of his service to the country.

Conclusion

All of the participants in the 1849 expedition went on to more remarkable accomplishments during their careers, with Robert E. being the most noteworthy. The expedition was a routine part of the projects they worked on, but their recommendations had a lasting effect on the future of Egmont Key and Mullet Key. What they did for Egmont Key, in particular, has allowed the island to be preserved as a historic site, recreational area, and refuge for sea turtles, gopher tortoises, and many species of shorebirds. Egmont Key/Fort Dade has been on the National Register of Historic Places since 1978, and the lighthouse and support buildings are on the Hillsborough County Historic Register.

Chapter 8

William F Raynolds, Civil Engineer and Explorer

Several people have been given credit for being the engineer for the 1858 lighthouse. Robert E. Lee was one of them. He visited Egmont Key once in 1849 and then went on to other projects. George Gordon Meade was the engineer for the Jupiter Inlet Lighthouse and some of the Reef Lights in the Florida Keys. He is known to have visited Egmont Key once for a repair to the tower and keeper house. It was not until a couple of years ago that it was learned that William F. Raynolds was, in fact, the engineer for the current tower. Like many people who visited the island, Raynolds went on to other endeavors for which he is most remembered. But I am getting ahead of his story!

William Franklin Raynolds was born in Canton, Ohio, on March 17, 1820, the fourth of six children of William and Elizabeth Raynolds. Nothing has been published about his early life and education. He was appointed to attend West Point Military Academy and began on July 1, 1839, graduating four years later, fifth in his class of thirty-nine cadets. One of his classmates was Ulysses S. Grant. As with all the graduates then, his degree was in Civil Engineering.

William F Raynolds

Raynolds was part of the army of occupation of Mexico after the Mexican-American War of 1848. He was one of several U.S. Army personnel confirmed to have summited Pico de Orizaba[1], the tallest mountain in Mexico, an alpine record that stood for fifty years. This was not to be his last experience in mountaineering.

The engineer for the 1858 lighthouse on Egmont Key was uncertain for many years. Correspondence from a letter book received by the Lighthouse Board revealed this information through research of the National Archives documents by the Jupiter Inlet Lighthouse historian Josh Liller. Raynolds also supervised some modifications to George Meade's design of the Jupiter Inlet Lighthouse. At this time, Raynolds was the 7th District Engineer. The transcript is below:

Oct 16, 1857

"William Franklin (LH Board Engineer Secretary) to William F. Raynolds (7th District Engineer) Your design and estimate for the construction of Egmont Key Lighthouse has been re-

---

1 Pico de Orizaba, also called Citlaltépetl, is an active volcano and the highest volcano in North America. At 18,491 feet (5636 meters), it is the third-highest peak in North America.

ceived and approved by the Board, and I have been instructed to authorize you to commence construction as soon as possible."

The new lighthouse tower was put into service in 1858 and has been in continuous service ever since. It has weathered storms, floods, and wars. The lighthouse was automated in 1944 when the lantern room and watch room were removed and a rotating beacon installed. That beacon, a DCB-36, was replaced with a series of aerobeacons and finally with an LED light. The DCB-36 is now on static display on the island. The first Keeper of this new lighthouse was Frederick Tresca, whose story is told in a later chapter.

Expedition to Yellowstone

Raynolds was selected in 1859 to lead the first US government exploration of the Upper Yellowstone region of the West. His goal was to study and map the geography, look for mineral resources, determine if railroad routes were possible, and contact the Native American tribes in the region.

The Yellowstone expedition, a testament to the comprehensive approach of the U.S. government, was composed of members from diverse disciplines. It included a geologist/naturalist, a photographer (a new technology in 1859), an artist, a mapmaker, and a topographer. Recognizing the potential risks of hostile Native Amricans, a detachment of thirty infantrymen was also part of the expedition. Raynolds, the lead topographer, was guided by frontiersman Jim Bridger[2]. The team also included a Sioux interpreter named Zephyr Rencontre, highlighting the importance of cultural understanding in

---

2 James Felix "Jim" Bridger (1804-1881) was an American scout, mountain man, trapper, explorer and guide in the Western United States.

the expedition. Raynolds' second in command was Lieutenant Henry E. Maynadier, adding to the depth of expertise in the team. He was a Topographical Engineer, and his work contributed to the most detailed record of the Shields and Yellowstone River systems.

Leaving St. Louis, Missouri, in May of 1859, they traveled by two steamboats on the Missouri River, disembarking at New Fort Pierre, South Dakota, and beginning the overland trek. The expedition encountered Crow Indians early in the journey. The explorers traveled on the Tongue River, a major tributary of the Yellowstone River in southern Montana. A short trip to locate a rock formation, later known as Devil's Tower, was made by James Hutton and Rencontre. Hutton was the first person of European descent to reach this formation in Wyoming.

The expedition made winter quarters at Deer Creek Station on the Platte River in Wyoming. One of the few photographs that remain of the expedition was made by Hutton in 1860, titled "The Great Falls of the Missouri River."

Resuming the exploration, the group split into two parties. One group under Maynadier went back to the Bighorn River region to examine it more fully and the tributary streams connecting with it. The two groups were to reunite on June 30, 1860, at Three Forks, Montana, and while there, make observations of a solar eclipse that was expected on July 18, 1860. Maynadier was late, arriving at the meeting spot a few days after the event, and the observations were not made. The expedition returned home via steamboats and overland to Omaha, Nebraska, and disbanded in October of 1860.

Though the expedition was not successful in exploring the region that became Yellowstone National Park, they were the first U.S. government expedition to reach Jackson Hole and visit the Teton Mountain Range. Traveling over 2,500 miles, the expedition explored over 250,000 square miles. Raynolds noted in his preliminary report that the once abundant bison were being killed at such an alarming rate that extinction was very likely. This history-making expedition was overshadowed by the Civil War, which started soon after the expedition returned. Most of the photographs taken by Hutton were lost, as well as artwork by Schoenborn.

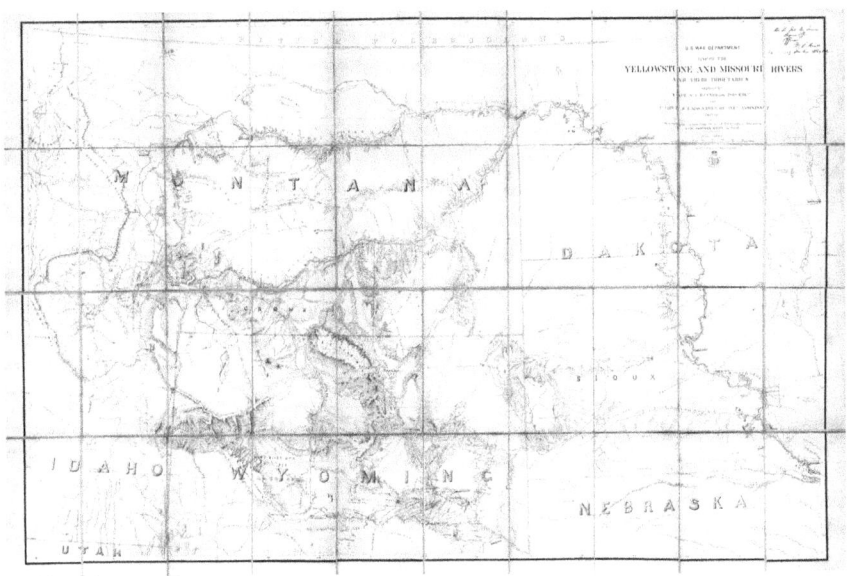

The Civil War

Raynolds served during the Battle of Cross Keys, Virginia, in 1862. It was a relatively small battle, in Civil War terms, and the Confederates defeated a Union Army twice its size. A year after that battle, Raynolds commanded the defensive fortifications at Harpers Ferry, West Virginia. Raynolds was brevetted to Brigadier General on March 13, 1865. He retired from military service on March 17, 1884, with the rank of Colonel, ending a forty-year career. He died on October 18, 1894, and is buried in his hometown of Canton, Ohio.

Holata Micco

Chapter 9

Billy Bowlegs, Seminole Leader (Holata Micco)

Billy Bowlegs, or Holata Micco, was a warrior leader who became prominent in the Second Seminole War. He led the fight to remain in Florida but eventually helped convince the remaining Seminoles of his group to relocate to the reservation in Oklahoma.

Bowlegs was born near Payne's Prairie around 1810 as a member of the Cowkeeper Dynasty. He was a nephew of Micanopy, who also achieved prominence in the tribe and in the struggle to remain on their land. After the Second War, Micanopy was exiled to the reservation in the west in 1838 and relinquished his chieftain's rank. It was assumed by Bowlegs the following year as Holata Micco or Chief Governor.

In 1847, Captain John T. Sprague noted of the Seminoles, "The game of the country, climate, and natural productions places them above sympathy or charity; every necessary want is supplied. Deer skins are the principal articles of clothing and trade, for which powder and lead are obtained. Corn, pumpkins, potatoes, beans, and peas are raised fresh and dried venison, turkeys, sea-fowl, fish, and oysters in abundance, which assures independence year-round..."

Writing of Bowlegs, Sprague noted: "In all respects (he) is qualified for supreme command, which he exercises with skill and judgment. He is about thirty-five years of age, speaks English fluently, and is active, intelligent, and brave."

Bowlegs took refuge in the Big Cypress Swamp Caloosahatchee River area. There were an estimated three hundred Native Americans in Florida. In 1848, an agreement was reached between Sam Jones (Abiaka) of the Miccosukee Tribe and Bowlegs and the Seminoles that the dividing line between the two groups would be the Caloosahatchee River. Bowlegs and his group would occupy the south side.

Tensions between the white settlers and the Seminoles continued in 1849, with attacks on the settlements. War was averted when the Seminoles turned over several members of their tribe to the military. These tribesmen had been implicated in the attacks and were wanted by the authorities. In 1850, General David E. Twiggs met with Bowlegs to arrange for the Seminoles' emigration to the West. In February of that year, seventy-five people left for Oklahoma. Bowlegs, Sam Jones, and Chipco were determined to stay.

One of the methods employed by the US government was to take a delegation of Seminoles, chosen by the tribe, to travel to Washington and New York City to see the White civilization's power to convince the Seminoles that resistance was pointless. In August of 1852, a delegation composed of Bowlegs (a warrior leader), six chiefs, and an interpreter, escorted by General Blake, met President Millard Fillmore, who awarded Bowlegs a medal. Traveling next to New York City, they stayed at the American Hotel on Broadway. The group attended a Broadway ballet performance of *The Barber of Seville*, shopped at Grant and Barton Dry Goods, visited Tiffany's Jewelers, attended a performance of the Christy Minstrels, and toured the P. T. Barnum American Museum. Finally, they met the Mayor of New York, Ambrose Kingsland.

Returning to Tampa Bay via steamer, a reporter for the New Orleans Delta interviewed Bowlegs, who stated, "I saw the Great White Father in the White House. I told him that no one would scare me from Florida; if I wanted to go, I would; if I did not, I would not." Bowlegs returned to Washington and New York again in 1854 but still refused to leave Florida under any conditions.

The year 1855 saw the Army beginning to build a new line of forts and roads into the Everglades and Big Cypress Swamps, leading to the discovery of several villages, including Bowlegs' village. The Seminoles decried these trespassings and warned it could lead to an outbreak of hostilities. This finally happened on December 7, 1855, when a surveying party left Fort Myers to continue reconnaissance of the Big Cypress Swamp. Upon leaving, he discovered one of Bowleg's camps on December 18 destroyed his crops and stole bunches of bananas. This infuriated the Seminoles, and on December 20, they attacked the group of surveyors with about forty warriors, wounding several soldiers and killing three. After the battle, the warriors killed some of the mules and horses, kept the rest, and burned the wagons. This was the beginning of what the military called the Third Seminole War, which lasted till 1858.

The end came in November 1857 when the Army discovered Bowleg's main encampment near Royal Palm Hammock (now part of Everglades National Park), destroying thirty dwellings and a forty-acre plot of vegetables. Negotiations for peace soon followed in March of 1858, and surrender terms were agreed upon. The treaty gave $7500 to Bowlegs, $1000 to each of the four warrior leaders, and $100 to each woman and child. Bowlegs also agreed to be exiled to the reservation in Oklahoma. On May 4, 1858, Bowlegs band of thirty-eight warriors and eighty-five women and children boarded the steamer *Grey Cloud* at Fort Myers with a planned stop at Egmont Key to pick up another forty-one Seminoles there. In the following chapter, there is more detail on the Seminoles' time spent in the Tampa Bay area.

On the way to the reservation, there was a one-week layover in New Orleans. The Seminoles were the focus of curious residents of the city. Many had read accounts of the Seminoles, but not many had seen one. Billy "held court" and met in person with many people. The Seminoles toured the town and shopped at the stores there. A reporter from Harper's Weekly portrayed Billy Bowlegs "as a rather good-looking Indian of about fifty, with a fine forehead, a keen black eye, somewhat above medium height, 160 pounds, with two wives, one son, five daughters, fifty slaves. Bowlegs spoke English well, but when receiving visitors, he "spoke Injun" since that is what people expected. Traveling on the steamship *Quapaw*, they arrived at Fort Smith on May 28, 1858, and continued overland to the Little River in the Seminole Nation, where Bowlegs and his group were received with great enthusiasm.

Bowlegs returned to Florida in December 1858 to persuade the remaining Seminoles to join the ones in Arkansas. About seventy-five agreed and left Florida, arriving at the reservation in March 1859. It is believed that Billy Bowlegs died of smallpox shortly after moving to Arkansas.

At least two other Seminoles, unrelated to the first one, called themselves Billy Bowlegs. They assumed his name to honor his legacy.

Chapter 10

Polly Parker (Emateloye)

The story of Polly Parker (Emateloye) is well known among the Seminole Tribe in the Big Cypress but not as well known outside of the reservation. Her connection to Egmont Key is a part of the Seminole's "Voyage of Tears" and her determined resistance to being relocated to Oklahoma.

Little is known of her early life, but she was born around 1820. Her first records relate to her involvement in the Second Seminole War[1], which started in 1835 with the ambush and defeat of Major Francis Dade and his relief column of one hundred and ten soldiers marching to Fort King. This is referred to as the Dade Battle. This outbreak of hostilities with the Army would last till 1842. There would continue to be skirmishes and attacks between the settlers and the Seminoles. Polly and her husband Chai were forced by the Army to help hunt down other Seminoles so they could be killed or captured. This pair

---

1   The Seminoles maintained that there was one war that lasted forty years, beginning in 1816 and ending in 1858. This part of the Seminole War was referred to as the Florida War. The Army, however, counted three significant outbreaks of hostility with relative peace between them. The Seminole conflict was one of the longest and costliest campaigns against Native Americans in United States history. Their struggles lasted into the modern era, and their fight for their homeland and sovereignty is ongoing.

of guides led the soldiers on long marches through the swamps with little result. They intentionally deceived the army on the whereabouts of Seminole encampments in the hope that the troops would become discouraged. By the end of the war, the tribe was considered the pair outcasts because they had worked with the government.

Polly and her husband eventually settled on the reservation near present-day Bradenton with Holata Micco's group, known as Billy Bowlegs by Americans. Tensions remained between the white settlers and the Seminoles over land ownership. Whites dressed as Seminoles stole cattle and horses and spread rumors among the tribe that the army was going to remove them to the west. The frontier was in turmoil, and it looked like another outbreak of fighting was about to begin.

Billy's group lived in relative harmony with the whites near his encampment, even visiting settlers' homes in an attempt to keep the peace. He also visited the President of the United States to fight for the right to stay in their homeland. However, when surveyors began assessing the tribe's land for sale to settlers, Billy attacked the survey party, thus beginning what was called the Third Seminole War, also known as the Billy Bowlegs War. The Army went to Billy's camp and destroyed the community crops, further aggravating the conflict.

Polly Parker and Chai were once again asked to act as guides for the Army, directing them through the Everglades, but this time, they refused. Chai chose suicide over service, though some accounts suggest Polly murdered him. By the end of the conflict, most Seminoles north of the Everglades had been captured or surrendered and forced to relocate west.

A group of about one hundred and sixty (numbers vary) boarded the steamer *Grey Cloud* at a place now called Billy's Creek for the voyage that would eventually lead to New Orleans and then up the

Mississippi River to Oklahoma. The date was May 4, 1858, which became the official end of the Seminole conflict. The voyage was not without concern on the part of the military. The commanding officers feared the Seminoles might try a last act of desperation to prevent the relocation. An account of this follows from the May 27 edition of the *New York Herald:*

> EMBARKATION OF GENERAL BOWLEGS AND TRIBE AT FORT MYERS "One hundred and twenty-five hostiles being camped near Fort Myers were notified that they must embark on the steamer *Grey Cloud* at 9 o'clock on the morning of the 4th of May. At that hour, the troops of the post, under the command of Captain Brannan, First Artillery, were judiciously posted, without the knowledge of the Indians, at points selected to meet and prevent any treachery that might be contemplated. As the appointed hour drew nigh, the excitement on the part of the whites was intense. But soon, all fears were at an end. The head of the procession was seen to emerge from the hammock and slowly wend its way to the wharf. Silently, they took leave of their much-loved Florida. Warriors that had defended their country to the last shed tears and, with aching hearts, passed on to the steamer's deck. The scene is one to be remembered and calculated to excite the sympathies of the most inveterate Indian hater."

Thus, the voyage began without incident, and the *Grey Cloud* would arrive at Egmont Key the following day. A small group of Seminoles, primarily women and children, had been held on the island for several years awaiting removal. Below is the account from the *New York Herald:*

ARRIVAL OF THE GREY CLOUD AT EGMONT KEY

"On the 6th of May, Colonel Loomis, commanding the Department of Florida, accompanied by Colonel L. Thomas, General Scott's chief of staff, and the department staff-Lieutenant Talbot, Acting Adjutant General; Major McKinstry, chief Quartermaster, and Surgeon McLaren, Medical Director, and a few invited guests (including several ladies), left Tampa in the United States steamer *Ranger* to meet the *Grey Cloud* at Egmont Key and embark the prisoners of war encamped on that island. The party arrived at Egmont at noon, and at 2 o'clock, the smoke of the *Grey Cloud* was visible at sea. Preparations were at once made to meet the redoubtable Chief, Billy. The *Ranger* left the harbor under the press of steam, and all colors flying. As she neared the *Grey Cloud*, spyglasses were in requisition, and it was soon ascertained that the Indians were on board. The two steamers approached each other amid the firing of cannons, the ringing of bells, the steam whistle's shrill voice, and the loud cheers from the respective crews. The Ranger rounded to, under the stern of the *Grey Cloud*. General Billy presented himself, arrayed in his red leggings, silver crown, and feathers, and bowed his acknowledgments. Arrived at Egmont, the steamers were lashed together, and Billy and his principal braves were formally presented to all. He introduced to the ladies his two wives and their children."

Soon, the Seminoles held on Egmont would be brought aboard the *Grey Cloud*:

MEETING OF THE PRISONERS AT EGMONT KEY WITH THEIR RELATIVES – THE EMIGRATING INDIANS

"About 7 P.M., two small boats arrived from the Key with Indian captives. As they neared the steamer the utmost anxiety was depicted on the countenances of the women. The wail of sorrow that burst forth as they threw themselves into the arms of their kindred, from who they have been long separated, would have melted the heart of a stoic. The children, so soon as released from the small boats, ran to their King Billy and clung to his knees. After caressing them for a moment the warrior gave way; and that man shed tears. To the honor of the whites, be it said that their kindly feelings got the better of their curiosity, and they retired to the upper deck. Whilst now and then, a heart-rending shriek would announce that some poor woman had learned the fate of a husband or a father who had perished during her captivity in battle with the whites, then would follow the low, plaintive cry of anguish uttered by relatives of the parties. It was a scene ever to be remembered."

FINAL ADIEU TO FLORIDA

"At 11 o'clock A.M. on the 7th, both steamers got underway. The *Ranger* kept company with the *Grey Cloud* to the outer entrance to the bay, at which point salutes were exchanged, and as we bore up for Tampa, the Indians gave us a war whoop that echoed and re-echoed over the waters, seemingly to startle our steamer into an increase in speed."

Aunt Polly Parker, the Oldest Seminole Indian in the State, Florida.

Emateloye

One stop had to be made by the *Grey Cloud* at St. Marks. At the old Spanish fort, the steamer had to take on wood to fuel the boilers. Polly Parker and a small band of women saw an opportunity to escape. They asked the soldiers if they could go ashore to gather herbs for medicinal purposes. The soldiers agreed and sent the group ashore with one armed guard. The group walked until they were out of sight of the ship before they acted. At a prearranged signal by Polly, the group scattered in all directions. Soldiers fired shots, and some of the women recaptured. But Polly and a few others made their escape.

Their freedom was hardly assured! They were hundreds of miles from home; all they had was what they left the boat with. They had to avoid contact with soldiers and white settlers and navigate their way back to their home on the north side of Lake Okeechobee, a daunting trip, to say the least. In addition, the group had to worry about crossing rivers and avoiding wildlife such as black bears, alligators, panthers, and poisonous snakes. They traveled principally at night, using owl calls to keep in contact, and hid during the daytime. They mainly ate berries and avoided building a fire until the fourth day of travel. They speared garfish and had their first meal since escaping.

They found the remains of their former camp on Lake Okeechobee and a dugout canoe in the sawgrass. Now, with a means to travel over water, they made their way to the protection of the Everglades and rejoined the others who had refused to leave their homeland.

Polly had one daughter, Lucy Tiger, who was born in 1869 and had several children of her own. Today, many people living in the Brighton Reservation can trace their ancestry to Polly.

Polly Parker lived to be more than one hundred years old, passing away in 1921. She is in an unmarked grave between Brighton and the Kissimmee River in a cabbage palm hammock under a live oak tree. The Seminoles revere her, and she is a symbol of their struggle to remain in their homeland. She was known by many early pioneers from Kissimmee to Fort Pierce. In a 1956 letter in the Florida State Archives, Albert DeVane wrote, "She was a very kind and humble Indian and was much loved by her white friends and her band."

Chapter 11

The Steamship *Grey Cloud* (*USS Colonel Kinsman*)

This book's chapters are supposed to be about people, but this is one of the exceptions! The steamship *USS Grey* (sometimes written as *Gray*) *Cloud* features prominently in the previous two chapters, so I thought a little history of the ship mentioned in those chapters is in order. The story of the *Grey Cloud* is well-documented, and its fate is well-known, although the remains have not yet been located. The *Grey Cloud* served as a commercial transport and for the removal of both Sioux and Seminole Indians. "Death Ship" was one of the unofficial names given by the Seminoles who sailed aboard it to exile in Oklahoma. For them, it was a one-way trip to a very different place from their home in Florida. It served in both the Confederate and Union navies during the war. The ship was renamed during the Federal service to the *USS Col. Kinsman*. An old mariner's tradition says that it's unlucky to change the name of a vessel once it is launched, and this ship's history might be an excellent example of the truth behind this superstition.

Construction

The *Grey Cloud* was a typical sidewheel, wood-burning steamship of its time. Constructed in 1854 in Elizabeth, Pennsylvania, on the Monongahela River, this location was an essential center for constructing paddlewheel steamers. There was an abundance of raw materials (primarily iron and hardwood) and skilled labor in the area. The enrollment document stated the dimensions as one hundred and seventy feet long, twenty-eight feet wide, a hull depth of six feet five inches, a "transom" or square stern, and "one deck." The carrying capacity or "burden" was listed as two hundred forty-five tons. The width was determined by the size of the three lock chambers on the Ohio River at Louisville, which were 49.5 feet wide when the *Grey Cloud* was built. The twenty-eight-foot width only referred to the hull as the main deck was probably 14 feet or wider than the hull itself. This would indicate that the main deck could have been 49 feet wide, with each paddle being eleven or twelve feet wide.

The "one deck" term referred to the decks attached directly to the hull and was the location of the boilers, engines, and other machinery and the main storage area for cargo. The machinery was on the main deck as the hull was too shallow to house this bulky equipment. On top of the main deck would be the "boiler deck," which housed a range of cabins, including passenger staterooms and passenger saloons. The top of this deck was the "hurricane deck," on larger steamers, another set of cabins called a "texas" could be added to this deck. It is not mentioned in descriptions that the *Grey Cloud* had a texas, but if so, it would have been for the ship's officers.

The boilers on the western river steamers were located in the forward third of the main deck. These were "flue" type boilers consisting of a long cylindrical tank with tubular flues extending through the center. The size of the boilers of that time ranged from two or three feet in diameter and twenty to as long as forty feet. It is not sure how many of these boilers the *Grey Cloud* housed, but most likely three or four. It most likely had two smokestacks, as this was typical of the steamers of that era, but the *Grey Cloud* may have later been reworked to have only one.

Initially, the *Grey Cloud* had several owners in a partnership and was one of several that operated on the upper Mississippi River. It is not known what the *Grey Cloud's* typical cargoes were, and it was in commercial service for only a short time before it began service as a United States Quartermaster Steamer.

The Sioux Expedition

The *Grey Cloud's* service as a Quartermaster Steamer spanned from 1855 to 1858. During the Sioux Expedition, it served along with the sternwheeler *William Baird* on the Missouri River. This was a military campaign against the Lakota Sioux after numerous conflicts with soldiers and civilians. The expedition was commanded by Colonel William Harney, who had considerable experience in fighting Creek and Seminole Indians and serving in the Mexican War. The expedition's actions covered a large area, and the steamships moved troops and supplies along the upper Missouri River to where they were needed.

Conditions were hazardous on the Missouri River. There were sandbars, underwater snags, varying water levels, and, in the winter, the danger of a ship being trapped by ice. This apparently happened to the *Grey Cloud*, which was stranded for several months and caused $8000 (a large sum at that time) in damage to the hull, requiring repairs to be made at St Louis. The crew was civilian, released from duty, and returned on their own to Sioux City. In fact, the *Grey*

Cloud and the *William Baird* were considered too large and deep a draft to operate effectively on the river in which the water levels varied so much during the year. *The Grey Cloud* was transferred to New Orleans while awaiting new orders.

The Third Seminole War

While the *Grey Cloud* was in drydock for repairs, alterations were made to make the vessel more suitable for service in the open waters of the Gulf of Mexico. The changes were stated in the survey after completion: "said vessel . . . has one deck, no masts, pink stern, has an upper cabin and plain head; that she is in length one hundred & seventy-seven ft, in breadth twenty-seven feet four inches and in-depth, average six feet and that she measures two hundred seventy-five and nineteen ninety-fifths' parts of a ton."

The term "pink stern" refers to a rounded stern rather than the square transom as initially constructed. Also, a single rudder would most likely have been added for open water service. Operations started in November of 1857 when Captain John Parkhill and one hundred and ten men ventured into the Turner River (near Chokoloskee Island) and attacked the last stronghold of Billy Bowlegs. This was the largest battle of the Third Seminole War, and Parkhill was killed during the action. This engagement marked the end of this war. By the end of 1857, the fighting had ended, and Billy Bowlegs had surrendered and was awaiting removal from Florida. In the first few months of 1858, preparations were made for their departure. After agreeing to move to the reservation, Bowlegs was paid $7500 and $2500 for his cattle. Each warrior who surrendered received $1000, and each woman and child received $100.

Historic Marker at Billy's Creek, Photo by Author

They boarded the *Grey Cloud* on a tributary of the Caloosahatchee River near present-day Fort Myers, which now has a historical marker. Departing from there on May 4, 1858, the next stop was at Egmont Key. This date was confirmed in the journal of Elias Rector, Superintendent of Indian Affairs, who was on the ship then. He listed the number of Seminoles and mentioned an Indian guide named Polly (Polly Parker). The numbers of Seminoles were thirty-eight warriors, eighty-five women and children, and an additional forty-one who had refused to surrender and were captured. Upon arriving at Egmont Key, they added an unknown number of Seminoles being held there. The *Grey Cloud* departed on May 7 with the next stop at

St. Marks to take on wood to fuel the boilers. The *Grey Cloud* arrived in New Orleans by May 25, as stated in a letter from Captain A. Montgomery of the Quartermaster Office at New Orleans to Major J. McKinstry, Quartermaster at Fort Brooke in Tampa. The ship had some repairs made to the boilers while in New Orleans and was then sold to a private owner.

Service from 1859-1861

The new owner, Henry Spearing, would use the *Grey Cloud* in the "coasting" trade, transporting goods along the Gulf Coast. The ports served were New Orleans, Pensacola, Mobile, and Galveston. Records show the *Grey Cloud* arriving at the Lake Ponchartrain terminal of the Ponchartrain Railroad. The coasting trade didn't last long, however, and with the coming Civil War, the *Grey Cloud* was soon pressed into service for supporting the Confederate Army.

Civil War Service

The Governor of Louisiana, Thomas Overton Moore, began seizing federal property after the state's secession to prepare for the coming war. This included a U.S. Mint Office, all the lighthouses within the state, military facilities, and several vessels. The *Grey Cloud* was among them and was outfitted for use by the Confederate Navy. It is unknown if it was armed then, but it was used as a troop transport and to deliver munitions and other supplies to forts in the area. The first recorded use by the Confederates is at Ship Island, located at the western end of Mississippi Sound, where they had built a fort to protect the rear approaches of New Orleans. The USS *Massachusetts* attacked the fort, and after withdrawing, the island was further reinforced using the quartermaster ships, including the *Grey Cloud*. The fort was soon abandoned as untenable. The *Grey Cloud* continued to be used by the Confederates as a supply ship in the area. Its final use by the Confederates was evacuating rebel troops from New Orleans after surrendering the city to the Union forces commanded by Admiral David Farragut on April 25, 1862.

USS Kinsman in Foreground at Cornay Bridge

At this time, the *Grey Cloud* became the Union Navy's property and began appearing in official records. It was armed with two 32-pound smooth-bore naval cannons, one at the bow and one at the stern. It was used in various actions in the New Orleans area. Around January of 1863, *Grey Cloud's* name was officially changed to *USS Colonel Kinsman,* likely after Colonel J. Burnham Kinsman, and formally transferred to the Navy.

The *Kinsman* was used in several actions against the Confederates in the following months and was slightly damaged in an engagement with the Confederate gunboat *Cotton* in November 1862. This battle, known as the Battle of Cornay's Bridge, was a ferocious two-hour engagement. The *Kinsman* used its two 32-pound cannons to good effect but received some damage.

At some point, the Union Navy added armor plating around the boilers, which protected them from being damaged by gunfire. The *Kinsman* participated in the second Battle of Cornay Bridge and other actions in the area until the end of 1863.

The end came suddenly and unceremoniously when the *Kinsman* struck an underwater "snag" while operating on the Atchafalaya River on February 23, 1863. What follows is an excerpt from the ship's captain, Lieutenant George Wiggin, to the gunboat fleet commander, Lieutenant Commander A. P. Cooke.

> "I received last night a detachment of the One Hundred and Fourteenth New York Volunteers on board to accompany me on picket duty and started for the fort at about 9:30 p.m. When within 100 yards of the fort, about 60 feet from shore, the engines being stopped, the steamer struck a snag, apparently floating, on her starboard bow, about 15 feet from the stern."

The impact punctured the hull and damaged one of the paddle-wheels. The damage was severe, and the ship began quickly filling with water. Three ships nearby, *Diana*, *Estrella*, and *Calhoun*, were summoned to assist in evacuating the soldiers. The captain tried to run the *Kinsman* aground and attach a line to the shore, but the steamer sank before the line could be connected to a suitable point. Most of the crew was able to escape, but five crewmen drowned. Some of its contents were salvaged, but further recovery was not feasible due to the 18-fathom (108 feet) depth.

Postscript

In September 2000, the US Army Corps of Engineers released a final report on evaluating and analyzing anomalies in the Atchafalaya River bottom that could be the remains of the *USS Kinsman*. The potential remains were discovered during a routine dredging of the shipping channel in the area, which resulted in the location of several "targets" that received further evaluation.

The Corps consulted various reports of the sinking, written shortly after the event, and used maps from a slightly later time period. The presumed wreck area was located in a tidal flats area on the western side of Berwick Bay. What follows is the official conclusion of the study.

"In November and December 1999, diving operations were conducted at the juncture of Bayou Boeuf and Berwick Bay (Atchafalaya River) adjacent to the community of Morgan City in St Mary Parish, Louisiana. The purpose of the diving was to examine seven previously identified magnetic anomalies, some of which were thought to be associated with the United States gunboat *Kinsman*, which sank in Berwick Bay in February 1863. The diving examined an area encompassing 7.2 acres. No vessel remains of any kind were found during the 13 days of diving. Two of the magnetic anomaly sources proved to be modern trash and debris probably derived from recent vessel activity. The sources of the other magnetic anomalies could not be found, and it is believed their sources consist of small and scattered items of modern age or are older objects buried beneath 25 feet or so of sediments that have accumulated at this location in the past 90 years."

That is the story of the *Grey Cloud* as it is currently known. If the remains are conclusively found someday, this chapter may be expanded. More detailed information from the US Army Corps of Engineers records is available online

Chapter 12

Frederick Tresca, Lighthouse Keeper 1856-1859

Frederick Tresca (Tresea) was one of the more interesting of the many keepers who have served on Egmont Key over the years. Tresca spent his life in the maritime industry and played a part in many of the historical events in the area during his time in Florida. Among his many exploits, he was a ship's captain, lighthouse keeper, blockade runner, and horticulturist.

Early Life

Frederick Tresca was born in Dunkerque (Dunklik), France, around 1803, with some sources giving the year as 1802. He was born there while his father, Vincenzo Tresca, served as Ambassador from the Kingdom of Naples to France. Frederick's great-grandparents were Bernardino Tresca, the Mayor of Capistrano, Italy, and Loretta Verdone Tresca, daughter of Baron Francesco Verdone.

HMS Bellerophon

Not much is known about his youth, except that he began his maritime trade as a cabin boy around the age of twelve. He was on the British warship *HMS Bellerophon* when Napoleon Bonaparte came aboard to surrender to the British. Napoleon had been defeated by an alliance of the armies of Great Britain and Prussia at the Battle of Waterloo in modern-day Belgium. The British wanted Napoleon as far away from Europe as possible to prevent his return, so he was exiled for the second time to the island of St. Helena in the South Atlantic Ocean. Historical accounts state that the young Tresca did not make the voyage, only going to Tor Bay, Devon, England, and then returning home. In fact, the *Bellerophon* did not transport Napoleon into exile. The British Admiralty was unsure the aging warship could safely make the voyage, so Napoleon was transferred to the *HMS Northumberland.*

Frederick Tresca later married a French woman and became a French citizen. Tresca grew up working in the maritime trade and was said to be fluent in five languages.

Key West to Tampa

Tresca, like many Europeans before him, emigrated to America to seek their fortunes and for adventure. Tresca came to Key West in 1836 and became a United States citizen on March 15, 1838. The citizenship ceremony was before Superior Court Judge James Webb, who said, "After making proof satisfactory to the said court of his right to be admitted a citizen of the United

States of America by order of the said court took and subscribed the oath of allegiance to the United States according to the form statute in such cases made and provided."

He was a ship's captain and purchased a sloop named *Margaret Ann*. He was involved in trade between Cedar Key and Key West, making stops along the way at Tampa's Fort Brooke and "rancho" trading posts along the Gulf Coast. He learned the Seminole language and bartered with them, trading his goods for animal pelts. He was friendly with several Seminoles, including Billy Bowlegs, whose encampment was in the Fort Myers area along the banks of what is now called Billy's Creek. Eventually, Tresca moved from Key West to the Tampa Bay. In August

1849, he received about 183 acres of land in present-day Pinellas County, north of Phillippe Park in the northwest part of Old Tampa Bay. He sold the land in 1875. Tresca claimed land there under the terms of the Armed Occupation Act of 1842. The Act encouraged white settlers to move into Florida to grow the population. Settlers had to clear five acres and build a house on the land and were expected to serve in the militia if needed.

Tresca and Josiah Gates

Josiah Gates became friends with Tresca while Gates was living in Tampa. Gates ran a small inn at Fort Brooke, and Tresca was a frequent guest there while working as a ship's captain. Gates had also acquired land under the Armed Occupation Act and was the first to look for land to settle south of Tampa. Tresca took him on several scouting trips in the Manatee area, and Gates selected property near the Manatee Mineral Springs. Tresca transported Gates and his family, as well as eight slaves, to his property aboard the *Margaret Ann*. These scouting trips may have convinced Tresca to move to the area as well. Gates was one of the early settlers of the village of Manatee and became its first mayor when it was incorporated in 1888.

Tresca Settles in Manatee County

Tresca moved again around 1850 to land on the Manatee River (Township 34) about one and a half miles south of the village of Manatee (now East Bradenton) in a community now called Samoset. He married Louisa Ellen (Ware)Wyatt, his second marriage, in 1853. They had three children: Walter Francis, born in 1854; William Taylor, born in 1856; and Eugenia, born in 1863. Louisa had been married to Elbridge Wyatt, but he had gone to Mexico to fight with

General Zachary Taylor in the Mexican-American War (1846-1848). Elbridge never returned, and Louisa waited seven years after his departure before marrying Tresca. She had two children with her first husband, Elbridge: Mary Ware, born in 1844, and Henry Ware, born in 1846.

There were established several seasonal fishing camps on the Gulf Coast near Sarasota, which Cubans first operated as ranchos. Tresca opened a rancho, and it was a successful venture over time. Ranchos had originally been fishing encampments operated by Cuban or Spanish fishermen. At the ranchos run by Tresca and other local fishermen like William Bunce, fish were caught and either salted or smoked to be sold or shipped out. It eventually became a trading post where he supplied the Seminoles in the area with trade goods, hunting rifles, and gunpowder. Tresca traded with Seminoles like Billy Bowlegs as well as local inhabitants.

Tresca Accused of Piracy

In 1852, Captain Tresca was accused of robbing dead bodies, victims of a maritime accident, and valuables in New Orleans while on a voyage there. The story, which appeared in the newspaper *Daily Advocate*, described an accident aboard the steamer *St. James* on Lake Ponchartrain, Louisiana, where the boiler exploded, killing several passengers. Tresca went to render aid and found one of the bodies floating in the lake and brought it aboard his vessel, the schooner *George Lincoln*. Because the pockets on the clothing of the body were inside out and valuables were missing, he was accused of stealing the property from the body, was arrested, and charged with theft. An article in the local newspaper, the *Crescent*, called Tresca a "pirate," among other things.

Very quickly, it was determined by the police that Tresca hadn't stolen anything; the charges were dropped, and he was released. The newspaper printed a correction of the story, stating that the charges were dropped. Still unsatisfied, Tresca sued the paper for libel against its owner, Mr. J. H. Maddox. Tresca won the case in District Courts and received $1000. The defendant appealed to the Supreme Court of Louisiana in 1854, and the verdict was upheld. *The Crescent*, according to the Court's ruling, should have merely reported his arrest and charges but not made any statements about Tresca's character.

Around this time, Tresca was involved in the coastal trade between New Orleans and Key West. Several local papers advertised his services. His stops included Tampa Bay, St Marks Apalachicola, and Pensacola, using sail-powered schooners and steamships. At the time, Tresca, Archibald McNeill, and James McKay were the first three commercial ship operators in the Tampa area, handling cargo and passengers.

Tresca also held a mail delivery contract for Route No. 6827 from Tampa to Manatee from 1855 to June 30, 1858. He won the contract in a bid against two other captains. He received $150 per year to transport the mail.

Lighthouse Keeper and the Seminoles

Tresca served as Lighthouse Keeper on Egmont Key from 1856 to 1859. Five different Assistant Keepers served with him during his time there. Daniel Clark (1855 – 1857), John Fagan (1857), J.B. Morrison (1857 – 1860), W.B. Whalton (1860), and Hiram A. McLeod (1860). Tresca was the first keeper at the current lighthouse, which was completed and put into service in 1858.

The story of the Seminole internment in Egmont is one of the bitter chapters in the history of Egmont Key and of the cruel treatment of Indigenous people in Florida. There are records of Seminoles being interned on the island during the Second Seminole War (1835-1842), but the greatest number were interned there at the end of the Third War (1855-1858). In 1856, the *Grey Cloud* stopped at Egmont, having sailed from Fort Myers. The purpose was to examine Egmont Key to assess the suitability for setting up an internment camp for the Seminoles. Tresca must have been happy to have the visitors since he invited everyone on board to a feast of watermelons, most likely grown in his garden. The events about the Seminole interment are discussed in much more detail in other chapters.

What is important here is the relationship between the Seminoles and Frederick Tresca, which was not typical of most people of the time. Being an immigrant to the US, he may have experienced discrimination, but certainly, his trading with the various tribes along the Gulf Coast made him see them as ordinary people trying to survive and prosper. Most white people regarded the Seminoles with disdain and possibly with fear and suspicion. Clashes with white civilians over property were common. Most whites supported the removal of the Seminoles to reservations west of the Mississippi River by whatever means necessary.

Tresca was probably the last citizen of Manatee County who was in contact with Billy Bowlegs before he was transported west to the reservation. Tresca felt great sympathy for how the Seminoles were herded like cattle onto the steamer *Grey Cloud* and removed from their native lands, never to return.

Tresca and Enslaved People

Despite being sympathetic to the plight of the Seminoles, Tresca's attitude towards slavery was quite different. Tresca was a Confederate sympathizer, but most of the people in the South didn't own slaves, and the expectation was that Tresca, being a ship's captain, would not likely own slaves.

SLAVE OWNERS-1860-CENSUS-MANATEE COUNTY			
OWNER	MALE	FEMALE	TOTAL
Addison, Ellen	1	-	1
Boney, D. J. W.	-	2	2
Clark, H. S.	1	1	2
Cofield, J. C.	98	92	190
Crews, Dempsey D.	4	4	8
Cunliff, James	1	-	1
Curry, John	2	-	2
Gates, Josiah	7	4	11
Hooker, William B. -William J. Hooker Agent	6	5	11
Ladd, D. - A. McNeil Agent	2	1	3
Lee, Edmund	1	-	1
Parker, William Estate-John Parker Agent	2	3	5
Smith, William	1	2	3
Tresca, Frederick	-	1	1
Waldron, Oliver	1	-	1
Whidden, W.	-	2	2
Whitaker, William H.	3	2	5
Wyatt, G. H.	2	2	4
TOTALS (18)	132	121	253

1860 Manatee County Slave Census

Typically, slaves were used for big farms or cattle ranching operations where a lot of manual labor was needed.

However, two documents were found that changed the story. First, there was a ship's Manifest of Slaves on one of Tresca's voyages from

New Orleans to Tampa, listing four slaves as cargo. Later, I found a census from 1860 in Manatee County of the names of slaveholders and the numbers of male and female slaves owned by each. Eighteen slave owners held a total of 253 slaves. Tresca is listed as owning one female slave. Since he was away a significant part of the time on voyages, his slave was most likely for domestic work at his home in Manatee County. Two other names were also on the list, and they played a part in Judah Benjamin, the Confederate Secretary of State's escape. One was William Whitaker, with five slaves, and A. McNeil (Archibald) was listed as an agent for the owner of three slaves.

Civil War Adventures

During the Civil War, Tresca worked as a blockade runner, bringing in scarce provisions for struggling Southerners from Nassau, Bahamas, and Havana, Cuba. He made six successful trips through the Union blockade from Havana. Being familiar with the many inlets and hiding places along the Gulf Coast gave him an advantage over the Union blockaders. It was a dangerous business since his ship could have been captured or sunk. He could have been imprisoned as well. Blockade running was a very lucrative business, and several captains in the Tampa Bay area were willing to risk it. Prominent among them was James McKay, who lost several ships to the federal patrols and was held captive for seven months at Fort Jefferson for blockade running.

Judah P. Benjamin's Escape

One of the most exciting stories about Tresca happened soon after the war. After the surrender of the armies of the South, the members of the Confederate government became fugitives and were relentlessly hunted by the Federal forces. The Union feared that the Confederate government would relocate to a sympathetic area and engage in a costly guerilla war that could persist for many years. Confederate President Jefferson Davis, Judah Benjamin, and other officials left Richmond with military escorts on May 3, 1865, heading south to Danville, Virginia. After President Lincoln's assassination on April 15, 1865, the newly sworn President Andrew Johnson believed the Confederate government was involved. In the frenzy following the assassination, there was a roundup of anyone suspected of playing a part.

Jefferson Davis and Judah Benjamin realized their situation was now even more desperate. It was possible they would be killed on sight. Benjamin informed Davis that he would part ways after a final meeting in Abbeville, South Carolina, on May 2, 1865. Benjamin thought his escape chances were better without the military escorts and the other government officials. He convinced Davis he was going on a mission to the Caribbean to meet with Confederate refugees about Davis's plan to reestablish the government in Texas.

After parting with Jefferson Davis in Washington, Georgia, Benjamin continued south with Colonel Henry Leovy in a horse-drawn wagon. Judah Benjamin would rely on Confederate sympathizers and some disguises on his travels south into Florida. While traveling in Georgia, Benjamin became "Monsieur Jules Pierre Bonfals," a Frenchman who spoke little English. Bonfals is Creole for "disguise"- a little wit on the part of Benjamin.

The pair got word of Davis's capture near Irwinville, Georgia, and Benjamin realized his precarious position. He and Colonel Leovy parted ways near Monticello, Florida, with Leovy heading west to his home state of Louisiana. Benjamin continued alone on horseback, now disguised as a North Carolina farmer named Charles Howard, looking to buy farmland.

Benjamin continued south in Florida, first staying at the home of John Moseley before crossing the Suwannee River. He traveled the Gulf Coast, stopping in Ocala at the home of Solomon Benjamin (not his brother), then Brooksville at the home of Major Leroy G. Lesley. Lesley was familiar with the village of Manatee south of Tampa and assured Benjamin he could find passage out of the country there. Leroy enlisted the help of his son, John Lesley, who lived in Tampa, to get Benjamin to the Gamble Plantation.

James McKay also helped Benjamin leave Tampa. He and Benjamin crossed Tampa Bay during a storm to avoid Federal gunboats stationed at Egmont Key, which were patrolling the area, hoping to capture Benjamin or any other rebels on their way south.

Lesley and Benjamin arrived at the Gamble Mansion on the Manatee River about May 28, then occupied by Captain Archibald McNeill and his family. Judah Benjamin wanted McNeill to take him by ship to the Bahamas, but McNeill declined because he was unfamiliar with the routes to avoid detection and capture. McNeill was also concerned for his family in case he was captured or killed. McNeill began looking for someone in the vicinity willing to take Benjamin to safety.

Benjamin holed up at the mansion, seldom leaving his room but watching intently for the Federals from the mansion's balcony. He was nearly discovered when a group of soldiers suddenly stopped at the isolated mansion. He and McNeill ran out the back door and into the brush while McNeill's family stalled the soldiers on the front lawn. After the soldiers left, satisfied that no fugitives were there, McNeill renewed his search with greater urgency for someone willing to make the risky voyage. One person came to mind, whom McNeill referred to as "the Frenchman," Frederick Tresca.

Benjamin made his way with great secrecy and, in the dead of night, across the Manatee River, with the help of McNeill, to the home of Frederick Tresca and his family. Benjamin had barely avoided capture at the Gamble plantation as Federal troops were in hot pursuit. Tresca was undaunted by the fear of capture and was familiar with the many inlets and routes needed to avoid detection. He agreed to help Benjamin escape and hired Hiram McLeod to help on the voyage.

Benjamin stayed with the Tresca family for several weeks. Hiram McLeod had worked at the Egmont Key Lighthouse, where he had been an Assistant Keeper in 1860 (he is mentioned in the chapter on George V. Rickards). During that time, Louise Tresca sewed pockets into Benjamin's clothing so he could hide the gold coins that he was carrying to fund his escape.

Ezekial Glazer and a newly freed slave named Jeffrey Bolden traveled the nine miles by a two-wheeled cart to William Whitaker's house. Benjamin hid under a pile of freshly butchered meat and palmettoes in the back of the wagon in case Federal patrols stopped them. Tresca and McLeod walked the half mile from Whitaker Bayou [1]to William Whitaker's house, and the group returned to the bayou and boarded the boat. Tresca, McLeod, and Benjamin quickly departed on the next part of their hazardous journey on June 23, 1865

On the way to Knights Key, the party was stopped by a gunboat and questioned by the crew. Benjamin had been instructed to say he was the cook and dressed the part, including putting soot and grease on his clothing where a cook might have it. Eventually,

---

1 The Bayou is named after a Florida pioneer in Sarasota, William Whitaker, an early settler with a homestead nearby. Like Tresca, Whitaker was a friend of Billy Bowlegs and shared Tresca's sympathies regarding the treatment of the Seminoles. William Whitaker also traded with the Seminoles and Cuban fishermen who fished in the Gulf of Mexico.

the Federal troops were convinced, and one was heard to sarcastically say "that he had never seen a Jew performing common labor." After arriving at Knights Key, the group transferred to a larger ship, the *Blonde,* to cross to the Bahamas. Upon arriving at Nassau on July 10, 1865, Judah Benjamin paid Tresca $1,500 in American gold, plus paying all expenses. After several harrowing experiences and false starts, Judah Benjamin eventually made it to Southampton, England, on August 30, 1865. To show his appreciation for what the wives of Tresca and McNeill did for him while in their homes, he sent ten-yard bolts of black silk, which would have been unavailable in the South then.

Postscript

Tresca contacted Judah Benjamin a few years later in England via a letter from Mr. G. A. Patten of Bradenton for "some assistance" in a business matter. Now, at the height of his career in Britain, Benjamin had forgotten Tresca's help and never responded.

After the war, Tresca returned to the life of a ship captain operating out of Manatee County. He did try his hand at citrus farming when he planted a variety of grapefruit he had brought from the Bahamas. He had a small grove near his house, where he cultivated the plant. The first year the trees bore fruit was in 1887, after his death. It became a certified variety called the "Tresca Grapefruit." The book *Citrus Culture in Florida* by H. J Wheeler, published in 1923, lists the fruit under Pomelos. Experts at the time classed it as a probable cross of Pomelo and Shaddock varieties. The Foster and Thompson varieties of pink grapefruit later surpassed the Tresca grapefruit in quality, so it hasn't been cultivated in many years.

Frederick Tresca died on May 3, 1886, and the exact location of his gravesite is somewhat of a mystery. At the time of his death, what is now the Manatee Burying Ground was described as an open field near some of the local residents' houses. It was not fenced in or bordered by streets, as it is today. His wife Louise and his daughter are buried there in marked graves. There is an unmarked vault nearby of similar construction that could be his, but the location of his grave may never be known for certain.

His son William Blakely Tresca became a prominent Methodist minister in Key West. His church activities made the society pages of the local newspapers. William wrote of his father about his trip with Benjamin: "A reward of $50,000 could have been gotten by a wave of the hand or a wink of the eye on the part of Captain Tresca, but he did not. The only living son of Captain Tresca, a Methodist preacher, rejoices that his father regarded honor above gold."

The story of Tresca's legacy continued when, in 1944, during World War II, a Liberty Ship, hull number 2471, built in Jacksonville, Florida, by the St. Johns River Shipbuilding Company, was named after him. His great-granddaughter, Lieutenant Virginia P. Tresca, was the ship's sponsor. The vessel served in the Pacific Theater of the war and was sold at the war's end.

Chapter 13

Lieutenant Otway H. Berryman

O tway Henry Berryman was born in Caroline County, Virginia, around 1814. His youth was spent traveling with his successful merchant father. Eventually, his family moved to Washington, DC, where he entered the Navy on February 2, 1829, at the age of 16 as a Midshipman. He married Sara Frances Hipkins on July 9, 1836, in Norfolk City, Virginia. They had a daughter, Columbia Newton Berryman.

Lt. Otway H Berryman

The first mention of his navy service was in 1839 when Berryman was listed as part of a crew departing on a coastal survey voyage on March 30 of that year. He was promoted to Lieutenant at the age of 29 in 1841 and remained at that rank until his untimely death.

At the time of his commission as Lieutenant, he served under the watchful eye of Commander David G. Farragut. His assignment was in the South Atlantic Squadron, patrolling the coasts of Argentina, Brazil, Uruguay, and Paraguay aboard the *USS Delaware,* a 74-gun ship of the line. Their mission was to represent American interests during political unrest in those countries.

Berryman saw his first combat service in the war with Mexico (1846-1848). In a newspaper account from 1846, Lieutenant. Berryman and nine sailors were sent to recover the brig, *USS Truxton,* stuck on a sand bar on the Tuxpan River, 130 miles north of Vera Cruz. The ship's crew had been made prisoners of the Mexicans. When the salvage party, including Lieutenant Berryman, arrived at the *Truxton,* it was being stripped by the Mexicans. The Navy destroyed the *Truxton* with artillery fire.

Due to his heroic service in the Mexican War, Berryman was given command of his own schooner, the *USS Onkahye,* which was recommissioned on April 22, 1847. His mission was to patrol the Caribbean seas in search of marauding pirates and slave trading ships. In 1848, according to a newspaper article, Lieutenant Berryman was commanding the *Onkahye* on a voyage from Rio de Janeiro with diplomatic despatches [*sic*] from the United States Minister in Brazil to Washington, DC.

His efforts were very successful, but disaster struck when his ship rammed into a reef near the Turks and Caicos Islands on June 21, 1848. The collision resulted in the eventual loss of the vessel. After an investigation, he was exonerated from blame.

The Tampa Bay Survey

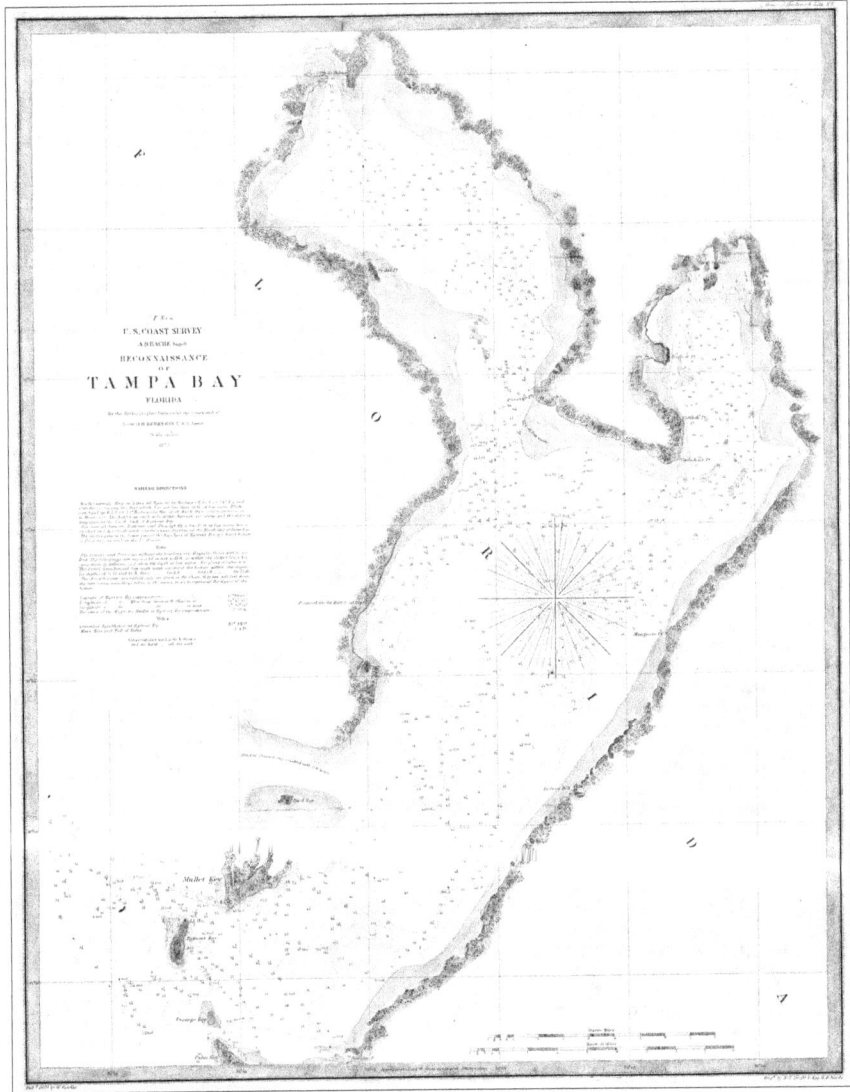

Berryman's Map of Tampa Bay 1855

In 1854, Lt. Berryman and the US Coast Survey were tasked with taking soundings in Tampa Bay for a proposed railroad from Fernandina to a port with access to the Gulf of Mexico. The newly formed Florida

Railroad Company, created by US Senator David Yulee[1] in 1852, was to build a route from the port at Fernandina southward to Ocala. There was to be a line that went to Cedar Key and another line that would go somewhere near Tampa Bay, and the exact location of the terminus was yet to be decided. The purpose of this railroad line was to provide a way to transport goods delivered to Fernandina to places on the Gulf of Mexico without having to navigate the sometimes treacherous route around the southern end of Florida. The company had funding of $1 million from the state, and construction began at Fernandina and headed to Waldo, where it would split into two routes. The survey results appeared in a report dated 1855, which recommended the rail depot location with gulf access as "Piney Point," now downtown St. Petersburg. Construction of the rail line began in 1858. The line to Cedar Key was completed, but the railroad to Tampa was canceled for financial reasons.

Tampa would finally have a rail connection when Henry Plant completed a line from Kissimmee to Port Tampa City, a natural deep-water port, in 1885. This line connected his steamship passenger service from Havana, Cuba. He connected his newly built Tampa Bay Hotel (now the University of Tampa) to this line in 1891.

In 1855, Berryman was sent to the west coast of Florida on the U.S. Coast Survey schooner *Verona* to perform a hydrographical survey of the Aucilla River.

---

1 David Yulee was President and principal investor of the Florida Railroad Company. The Cedar Key section was built first, completed in 1861, and the Tampa connection was never started.

Career as an Ocean Surveyor

Berryman's naval career took a turn for the better when he was selected by noted oceanographer and naval officer Matthew Fontaine Maury, testing new routes and studying the sea currents and winds. This work continued for several years, with travel between North America and Europe, performing deep-sea soundings, and examining shipping routes in the Atlantic Ocean. In 1856, working with the Oceanic Telegraph Company, Berryman surveyed routes between St. Johns, Newfoundland, and Valencia Bay, Ireland. The purpose was to determine the feasibility of laying underwater telegraph cables to connect the continents.

The Civil War

Lieutenant Berryman had been a loyal United States Navy officer throughout his career, but there were political forces in the country that would compel him to make a momentous decision. Threats of secession by the southern slaveholding states were imminent. Berryman was at Pensacola, then an essential naval installation. In the vicinity were three forts to guard Pensacola Bay. Fort Barrancas, near the lighthouse, Fort McRee on the west side of the inlet, and Fort Pickens on Santa Rosa Island.

Florida sent a delegation to Tallahassee in early January 1861 to decide whether to secede from the Union. That crucial decision was reached on January 10th. Florida became the third state to leave the Union after South Carolina and Mississippi, marking a significant turning point in the United States' history.

After his inauguration, President Lincoln was faced with a decision about Fort Sumter, located in Charleston Harbor in South Carolina. The commander, Major Robert Anderson, had abandoned

Fort Moultrie and taken the garrison of ninety soldiers to Fort Sumter to reinforce the troops there. President Lincoln informed the rebels that he intended to resupply the fort with soldiers and supplies. An attempt was made on February 5, 1861, but was repulsed near Charleston Harbor by cadets from the Citadel.

The Confederates saw this as an act of war. A delegation was sent to Fort Sumter to ask for their surrender, and safe passage out of the state was assured. Anderson declined, and the following day, April 12, at 4:30 a.m., the bombardment began. By the next day at 4:30 PM, the battle ended with Anderson surrendering without any loss of life during the battle. The only casualty was during the 100-gun salute when a soldier was killed when a shell prematurely exploded.

At the beginning of the war, the Union still occupied several forts in Florida: Fort Pickens, Fort Jefferson in the Keys, and Fort Zachary Taylor on Key West. Lt. Berryman had been ordered to Florida on the gunboat *Wyandotte* just a few weeks before Abraham Lincoln's election. The navy hoped that Lt. Berryman's southern heritage and patience would calm the situation at Pensacola. He was ordered to protect U.S. interests and see to the provisioning of Fort Pickens.

Fort Pickens, across Pensacola Bay from the Navy Yard, had been unoccupied since the Mexican War but was seized by a small group of Union soldiers stationed at nearby Fort Barrancas. The soldiers drove off a small band of local civilians who tried to retake the fort.

A sizeable armed group of Confederates had forced the capitulation of the Pensacola Navy Yard. However, Berryman used the *Wyandotte* to bring mail, food, munitions, and soldiers to Fort Pickens from the navy yard under a "gentleman's agreement" with the Confederates.

Lt. Berryman now faced a decision that many men in the military faced at the brink of the Civil War. Though he had served in the US

Navy with distinction and loyalty, he was not willing to fight against his native state of Virginia. Robert E. Lee made the same decision after being offered the command of Union forces. It also divided the class at the military academy at West Point with the question, "Which side are you going to serve?" He felt so strongly about his decision that he penned the following letter to a Pensacola newspaper, reprinted by *The Baltimore Sun* Newspaper:

February 4, 1861

Letter from Lieutenant Berryman

"Lieut. O. H. Berryman, in command of the United States Steamer *Wyandotte*, off Fort Pickens, has written a letter to a Pensacola newspaper in which he writes:

My orders from the proper authorities of a government which I have loved and served as faithfully as I could, I still respect, and when that government shall be dissolved by the decision of my great and noble state, (Virginia), I hope to prove myself worthy of holding a commission even under a Southern Confederacy."

However, Lt. Berryman would not live to see that event. Due to the stresses of serving in a very hostile location, Pensacola Bay, he contracted "brain fever"[2] and, after a few days, died at the young age of 47. His death was on April 2, 1861, and his funeral was held on April 4 at Pensacola. Even though the country was on the brink of war, Berryman was honored by both Union and Confederate soldiers and sailors, the mourners numbering in the hundreds. His obituary

---

2 Brain Fever is an old medical term for serious illness caused by severe emotional distress. It can also be encephalitis, meningitis, cerebral cerebritis, or scarlet fever.

appeared in the *Mobile Tribune* and *Vicksburg Whig* newspapers and reads, in part:

> "Lieutenant Berryman's apparent activity and zeal in the service of the United States, during the present complications, had subjected him to severe animadversions[3], but there is no doubt that he was acting under what he believed to be the dictates of his duty, and it is scarcely just or generous to blame, especially since his nativity and citizenship were both outside the limits of the Confederate States. He was unquestionably a man of honor, an accomplished sailor, and a gallant gentleman."

Lieutenant Otway H. Berryman is buried at the Barrancas National Cemetery in Pensacola, Florida. His widow applied for and received a pension due to his navy service.

---

3 Animadversion is an old word of Latin origin, meaning "act of criticizing."

Chapter 14

George Vernon Rickards, Lighthouse Keeper 1861-1862

George Rickards (sometimes spelled as Richards) was the lighthouse keeper on Egmont Key at the start of the Civil War and played a role in protecting the tower and its valuable lens from destruction during the conflict. Like many of these subjects, he has an interesting life story.

Rickards was born in Yorkshire, England on August

George V Rickards

18, 1836. He came to the United States via Key West in 1853 and settled in Hillsborough County (now in Pinellas County) around May of 1855. He had a wife, Jane, and a son, George Jr.

He began serving as the Principal Keeper in May 1860. During his tenure at the lighthouse, he had two assistant keepers: W. B.

Whalton from March to August 1860 and Hiram A. McLeod from August 1860 until Rickards joined the Confederate Army in 1861 (the same Hiram McLeod who was Tresca's assistant).

The Hazards of Lighthouse Duty

On April 20, 1861, the *Atlantic Democrat* of Egg Harbor, NY, reported the following: EGMONT KEY LIGHTHOUSE STRUCK BY LIGHTNING "Last Thursday at 8 PM, the Keepers house was struck and considerably damaged by lightning. Mrs. Ricards [*sic*] who was in the dwelling house, seventy-five yards distant from the lighthouse, was struck down, apparently dead for half an hour. The light house proper received no damage." Central Florida is known today as the lightning capital of the western hemisphere, and it was so in 1861.

The Rickards Journal

The Tampa Bay History Center has acquired a journal written by Rickards between 1852 and 1861, including his time in Tampa as a lighthouse keeper. Unfortunately, the journal did not reveal much historical information but did give insight into Rickards himself. It was primarily original poems, and one story was about a turkey hunting trip where the Hillsborough River was mentioned. He was hunting with a companion he called "Friday," but not much was said about him. The poem at the beginning of this book and the one below are good examples of his creativity.

Midnight Hour

Tis midnight hour the moon shines bright
The dewdrops blaze beneath their rays
The twinkling stars, that trembling light
Like beauty's eyes displays

Sleep no more tho bound by thy heart
Some tender dreams may idly play
For midnight song with magic art
Shall chase that dream away

Tis midnight hour from flower to flower
The wayward gopher floats along
On singers(fingers?) in some shady bower
To hear the night bird song

Egmont Key Light Station, January 6, 1861

The Egmont Key Lighthouse from the Florida Memory Project

The Civil War Comes to Egmont Key

Soon after the start of the Civil War, Tampa became a hotbed of both blockade runners and US Navy ships determined to prevent blockade running. Soldiers and sailors of the East Gulf Blockading Squadron occupied Egmont Key in August 1861. They established a gun battery and a small hospital, while Fort Brooke in Tampa became a Confederate stronghold. Rickards was a Confederate sympathizer along with the Customs Collector[1] at the St. Marks lighthouse. The Customs Collector at Key West, which the Union had occupied, was loyal to the United States.

Like many at the time, especially in Florida, Rickards professed allegiance to whichever side was present at a given moment. He feigned allegiance to the Union while the Union Navy was on Egmont. However, the Union Navy did not continuously keep troops on the island at the beginning of the war. When they were gone, Rickards took the opportunity to remove the Fresnel lens and any other supplies he could transport from the tower, and he brought them to Tampa for safekeeping. He left Egmont Key along with his family and never returned.

There are a few stories about what happened to the Fresnel lens and other lighthouse equipment when Rickards deactivated the light, but what follows is the most accurate. The recently formed Confederate States Lighthouse Bureau instructed its Collectors of

---

1   Superintendent of Lighthouses worked directly for the Fifth Auditor of the Treasury. They mostly nominated new keepers to fill vacancies. As local appointees, it is unsurprising that many of the Superintendents sided with local political views and supported Secession. Before the advent of the Lighthouse Board in 1852, lighthouses were administered by the local Collector of Customs (the primary tax collector on imports, the major source of revenue before income taxes). Many, but not all, Collectors of Customs were also designated Superintendents of Lighthouses.

Customs personnel to safeguard the lighthouse equipment from being confiscated by the Union Navy. Rickards was ordered to remain in charge of the Egmont Key light and "to keep up such relations with the fleet as would induce them to allow him to remain in charge until such time as the property could be safely removed." Rickards would have to bide his time and feign loyalty with the Union until they were away from the island, and he could act.

On August 23, 1861, Rickards seized his opportunity. He removed the lens and ninety-six pieces of equipment with utmost secrecy, transporting them to Tampa. The items were stored at the Florida Railroad Depot, their presence unknown to the Union. Only six days later, an inventory of the removed items was completed. Rickards, now a Florida State Coast Guard member, continued his covert activities. On March 13, he moved the equipment and lens from "M. Walls Warehouse to the Post Office Rooms." Five days later, on March 18, he boxed up the lens and buried it in an undisclosed location in Tampa. On April 4, he was compensated for moving the equipment to Brooksville, Florida, for safekeeping. The lighthouse lens and other equipment would remain hidden from the Union until the war's end.

Soon after the lens had been removed, the Union Navy occupied the island for the duration of the war. They built a small hospital and other buildings, and the East Gulf Blockading Squadron used it as a base of operations against blockade runners and as a coaling station. Three artillery pieces were placed on the island facing towards Tampa to the east. Egmont was also a haven for Unionists who had lived in the area, as well as a path to freedom for slaves in the area who had escaped from their enslavers.

The story of George Rickards continued when he joined Confederate Henry Mulrenan's Florida Volunteer Coast Guards, mustering for duty on December 14, 1861, as a seaman. He is listed as "George Richards" on the Company Roster. Shortly after, on January 9, 1862, he was assigned to the sloop *Mary Jane*. His Coast Guard service was short-lived, however. The Confederacy needed infantry, and the Union Navy had a strong presence on the Florida coast. As a result, in April 1862, Rickards and many others transferred to Captain Robert B. Smith's Company of the 7th Florida Infantry Regiment. They were nicknamed the "Key West Avengers." His enlistment was for a term of three years. At that time, they were stationed in Tampa.

George Rickards was not interested in becoming a foot soldier due to the high casualty rates of the land battles. He and twenty-four other sailors wrote a letter to Stephen R. Mallory, Secretary of the Navy, requesting duty in the Navy. Below is the letter:

Fort Brooks [*sic*], Tampa, Fla., May 1, 1862

To the Hon. Stephen R. Mallory, Director of the Navy, Confederate States of America,

Sir

"The undersigned marines, Citizens of Key West, Fla., would respectfully represent that they have been in the service of the State of Florida Coast Guard since the month of December last, that lately they have been reorganized and are now members of Captain Robert Smith's Company, 7th Regt. Florida Volunteers regularly mustered into the service of the Confederate States for three years of the war and are stationed at Tampa, Fla. That they are sincerely anxious to render good and efficient service to their country and are satisfied that the Army is not the proper place for them, that they been informed that Seamen in the Army can be transferred to the Navy, and therefore make this application, and pray to be transferred to a Gun Boat or other vessel of war where they may have a chance to meet the enemy and strike for their Country's cause. Very Respectfully, "Your obedient servants."

All the seamen signed the letter, including George Rickards, who was listed as Ships Carpenter.

The request was of no avail. The 7th Florida Volunteers became a part of the Army of Tennessee under the command of General Braxton Bragg. However, Rickards was not destined to fight with the infantry for long. On November 1, 1862, he was present on the muster roll and was dispatched to serve as a hospital orderly, guard, and cook at the University Hospital in Knoxville, Tennessee. A year later, in November 1863, he was reported as sick in the Newsome Hospital in Cassville, Georgia. Later, muster rolls at that hospital listed him as present and employed as a nurse.

He was promoted to First Sergeant between January and July of 1864. His fortunes took a turn for the worse when he was captured near Atlanta, Georgia, on July 22, 1864, the day after the Battle of Atlanta. The circumstances surrounding his capture were not explained. One account stated he was slightly wounded in the right leg. By this time of the war, President Lincoln had ended prisoner exchanges at the urging of General Ulysses Grant, so he was sent to Camp Chase in Ohio, arriving on July 31, 1864.

Camp conditions were typically harsh, and food was scarce and of poor quality. Sanitation was inadequate, and deadly diseases such as smallpox were rampant, caused by overcrowding. By 1865, the camp had 9,400 Confederate soldiers. George Rickard contracted erysipelas[2] and died on April 17, 1865, only eight days after the surrender by General Lee at Appomattox. He is interred in a marked grave in the Confederate Cemetery, Grave Number 1884. The cemetery holds 2,200 Confederate soldiers. The war lasted only a few more weeks and officially ended on May 9, 1865.

The Egmont Key Lighthouse was returned to service on June 2, 1866, and has guided ships into Tampa Bay since then. Company K, a group of Civil War reenactors in the Tampa Bay area, keeps the history of the 7th Florida Volunteers alive.

---

2 Erysipelas (Latin for "red skin") is an infection, typically a skin rash caused by the Streptococcus pyogenes bacteria entering the skin via minor trauma. It is usually on the face but can also be on the legs. Also called St. Anthony's Fire, affected individuals typically develop symptoms including high fevers, shaking, chills, fatigue, headaches, vomiting, and general illness 48 hours after initial infection. The infection can spread to the joints, causing septic arthritis and even death.

Chapter 15

Captain William McKean

Early Life and Naval Career

William Wister McKean was born in Huntington County, Pennsylvania, on September 19, 1800. He was the grandson of Thomas McKean, the state Governor and one of the signers of the Declaration of Independence. He married Rosa Davis Clarke in Philadelphia on August 25, 1824, and had one child, Mary. He entered naval service and

William W McKean

was appointed a Midshipman in November 1814. This was shortly before the end of the War of 1812. He served on shore assignments, one being at the Naval Asylum (Hospital) in Philadelphia. The rest of his service was commanding naval vessels. His final combat tour was as Flag Officer (a Senior Captain in the Navy) of the East Gulf

Blockading Squadron based in Key West, from January 20, 1862, to June 3, 1862. His final rank as Commodore was awarded on July 18, 1862. He died on April 22, 1865, at the age of 64, in Binghamton, New York, and is buried there in the Spring Forest Cemetery.

Union Blockade of the South, "Anaconda Plan"

Only a week after the start of the hostilities at Fort Sumter, the strategy of a blockade of the south was proposed by General-in-Chief Winfield Scott. It was a controversial idea since some felt that declaring a blockade would be tantamount to recognizing the Confederacy as a nation rather than a rebellion. President Abraham Lincoln, nonetheless, declared a blockade in April of 1861 called Proclamation of Blockade Against Southern Ports. The press dubbed it as the Anaconda Plan after the snake that strangles its victims. It included the Atlantic coast from Virginia to Florida and the Gulf Coast, including Texas. The Union also wanted to control the Mississippi River since it was a significant transportation route for Texas cattle going to the Confederate Army. It was a bold strategy since the coast was 3500 miles long with twelve major ports, including Mobile, Alabama, and New Orleans.

The Union Navy consisted of seventy-six vessels of all types in the fleet. Ships that could operate in shallow coastal waters and rivers were most needed for blockade duty. Only twelve were available for this type of service; of these, only four were ready for immediate use. The Union Navy began a program to acquire suitable ships and construct new ones as rapidly as practicable. This was accomplished by building new ships, purchasing ships from European countries like Great Britain, and retrofitting existing ships for blockade duty. Captured Confederate blockade runners that were seized were also put into service as blockaders. Crews had to be enlisted and trained as well. It would take until 1863 to have enough ships to stem the flow of goods into the Confederacy.

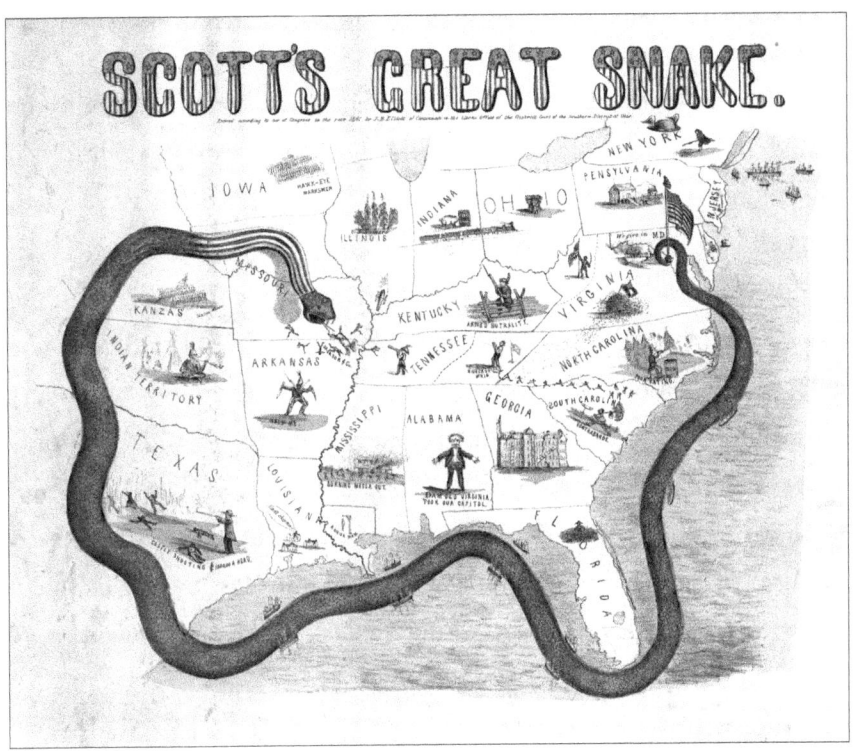

General Winfield Scott's Anaconda Plan

Florida was very active with blockade runners due to its long coastline, many rivers, and barrier islands that could provide hiding places for them. The South was eager to get its cotton harvest to England to supply the textile industry there. Cotton sales provided hard cash for the Confederate government, and Britain bought all the South could provide. Britain would supply the South with arms, ammunition, and other goods necessary for the war effort.

James Dunwoody Bulloch, an uncle of Theodore Roosevelt, became a purchasing agent for the Confederate government in Liverpool, England. He arranged the purchase of arms, ammunition, medicines, and uniforms and warehoused them until they could be brought through the blockade.

The Confederate government demanded ships that could be armed and put into service for their navy. There was also a flurry of shipbuilding to provide suitable shallow draft vessels for British captains willing to run the blockade.

Florida's coastline provided another needed commodity for the rebel army in the form of salt. Salt was used for several purposes, like meat preservation and leather tanning. There were many salt distillery operations along the coast, from very large operations to sites with only a few kettles. Seawater was boiled to extract the salt, and the distilleries were near the shoreline by necessity, so the Union Navy easily spotted the fires. Landing parties would go ashore and destroy the distillery, but within a few days, the site would be back in operation again.

Gulf Blockading Squadron

At the beginning of the blockade, the Gulf of Mexico was under one command, patrolling from Key West to the Mexican border. Still, the Navy soon realized that the area was too large to be effectively managed by one command. The Gulf Blockading Squadron operated for only nine months, first under Flag Officer William Mervine and then under McKean.

East Gulf Blockading Squadron

Flag Officer McKean was appointed to command the newly formed East Gulf Blockading Squadron on January 20, 1862, and his headquarters were set up in Key West. The squadron was assigned to patrol from Cape Canaveral on the east coast of Florida to the east of Pensacola and was considered a minor command. This was due to Florida having few ports on the peninsula.

Sailors in this squadron endured endless hours of boredom and the fear of tropical diseases such as yellow fever, broken up with occasional combat or the seizing of a blockade runner. It was considered much safer than other posts in the navy that would experience major naval engagements, mostly against shore fortifications.

Naval Operations in Tampa Bay

The Union Navy and Army conducted several operations in the Tampa Bay area besides routine patrolling in search of blockade runners. The *USS Tahoma* captured the blockade runners *Crazy Jane* and *Statesman*, as well as the British schooners *Harriet* and *Mary Jane*.

On October 13, 1863, the *Tahoma* and the *Adela* entered Tampa Bay with orders to capture the *Scottish Chief* and *Kate Dale*, owned by Captain James McKay, Sr. and supposed to be about five miles up the Hillsborough River. The *Tahoma* and *Adela* opened fire on Confederate shore batteries in Tampa Bay after landing a party of about one hundred infantry near Ballast Point. The Confederates sent a force to engage the Federals. The battle ended in a draw with the withdrawal of Union forces, but they succeeded in burning both the *Scottish Chief* and *Kate Dale*[1]. The *Kate Dale* was rebuilt and resumed blockade running as the *Josephine*. It was captured again with seven bales of cotton bound for Havana.

Another well-known Union attack was in February 1862 on the home of Abel Miranda near present-day Big Bayou in St Petersburg.

---

1 In 2009, the Florida Aquarium located the wrecks of the *Kate Dale* and *Scottish Chief* in the Hillsborough River.

Earl settlers John Bethell and Abel Miranda had built homes and operated fishing camps nearby. They were also known to harass the Union blockaders. In February of 1862, a group of Union soldiers landed near Miranda's farm after bombarding it with artillery on the boat. They burned the house, killed all the livestock, burned orange trees, and took anything of value. Some accounts said it was in retribution for the killings of John and Scott Whitehurst. This is incorrect since the deaths of the Whitehursts happened several months later. Most likely, the attack was because of Bethell and Miranda's militia activities. Miranda escaped to Tampa but returned to the area in 1867. Bethell would later join Company K of the 7th Florida Infantry Regiment. He wrote about his experiences in the book *Pinellas: a Brief History of the Lower Point*.

Raids on local saltworks continued throughout the war. In November of 1864, there was an unsuccessful raid at Gadsden's Point by the *USS Nita*. There was a successful raid on a small saltworks owned by a "Mr. Hooker" after sailors noticed a plume of smoke coming from shore.

On May 5, 1864, the Union Navy landed at Fort Brooke, a small fort built during the Seminole War period, and captured about forty Confederates. They threw the fort's armaments[2] into the Hillsborough River nearby. Even this victory did little to stop the blockade runners in the Tampa Bay area.[2]

---

2   Charlie Spicola of the Tampa Rough Riders related a story about how that organization recovered two of the cannons from Fort Brooke, which are now at the University of Tampa's Plant Park. After the Union captured the fort, they tried to destroy the cannons by firing one at the barrel of the other. That didn't do enough damage, so the trunnions were broken off, so the guns couldn't be mounted. I went to Plant Park, located the two cannons, and after inspecting them, I found one with a large dent in the barrel, and both had one trunnion broken off. The Rough Riders funded the preservation and mounting on new carriages.

Operations on Egmont Key

Egmont Key was one of several locations around the state that Union forces would occupy for the duration of the war. Fort Pickens at Pensacola, Fort Taylor in Key West, and Fort Jefferson in the Dry Tortugas were occupied at the war's outset. Fort Marion at St. Augustine and Seahorse Key were occupied in 1862.

The first mention of Union troops on Egmont Key appeared in the *New York Herald*, reporting that troops with field artillery came to the island on August 20, 1861. They must have been fearful they would find Confederate militia defending the island. The rebels decided not to contest the possession of the island due to its distance from Fort Brooke and the overwhelming presence of the Union Navy in the area. The Union Navy built a coaling and watering station and a small hospital. They placed a temporary lantern in the lighthouse (the article misstates the height at 40 feet) and used it as an observation tower as well. The newspaper article is below:

New York Herald, August 24, 1861

Egmont Key Occupied by a Federal Force

"The Tampa, FL Peninsular of the 20th ult. says – From a reliable source, we receive information to the effect that the steamer *Cuyler*, blockading this port, has landed thirty or forty men, with three eighteen pounders, on Egmont Key, who have erected a battery on the east side of that island. Egmont Key is at the entrance to Tampa Bay. On it is a lighthouse, showing a fixed light, forty feet high."

Not long after the Union established an encampment on Egmont Key, local community refugees started coming to the island to escape persecution by their neighbors and the rebel militia. A significant number of residents of the surrounding towns were against slavery and secession or were not willing to be drafted into the Confederate Army. This meant that living in their homes and communities was a dangerous proposition and could result in being killed at the worst or, at the least, their businesses being boycotted by others. They chose to abandon their homes and livelihoods and opted for the relative safety of Egmont Key. The Union military was not always present on the island at the beginning of the war, but its distance kept them out of harm's way. The refugees or "Unionists" occasionally had to venture ashore in search of food or other goods but did so at their risk. The tragic story of one of these refugees is told in the following chapter. Another factor that made their lives hazardous was the military using them as a source of intelligence on what the rebels were doing and where they were located. The rebel militia knew this fact, so they were on the lookout for them. The number of refugees on the island numbered thirty-eight whites. Runaway slaves, called "contrabands," who sought protection from Federal forces, were initially sent to Key West. As the war progressed, additional camps were established on Egmont Key, Fort Myers, and Seahorse Key. The Union encouraged them to leave their owners and work for them as a militia force or as paid laborers. They also were a valuable source of information on rebel activities. It's not known accurately how many slaves there were, but it could have been as many as two hundred. Captured Confederates were held on Egmont Key as well, but no numbers have been suggested.

Results of Blockade

The blockade of the south was not very effective at first due to a lack of enough patrol vessels to properly enforce it. Only about two of every ten blockade runners were intercepted in the early years around the Florida peninsula. By the war's end, that ratio had reversed, and now only two of ten managed to run the blockade successfully. There is little doubt that it had a significant impact on the Confederacy's ability to wage war. The inability to sell cotton to England and import goods needed for the war effort helped convince the rebel leadership to end the war. Removing the contrabands from the state forced the Confederate military to shift manpower from combat operations to supply operations.

In a larger sense, the blockade had a longer-lasting impact on the Southern economy. Before the outbreak of hostilities between the North and South, England, the biggest importer of Southern cotton, began stockpiling bales of cotton in anticipation of shortages. They also began developing a suitable replacement in India, which was then one of their colonies. By the end of the war in 1865, England had a variety of cotton that would work in their textile machinery. With the devastation of many plantations in the South, they didn't need to wait for the South to recover from the war. In Florida, cotton was grown as far south as Orlando, and with all the farm labor that went to fight in the war, the cotton crop went to seed and never recovered. A replacement cash crop didn't appear until the citrus industry emerged in the mid-1870s, with the first boom continuing until the first devastating freezes in 1894 and 1895. By 1909, the citrus industry began a recovery.

Chapter 16

John Alexander Whitehurst, Unionist

The story of John Whitehurst and his family on Egmont Key is a local example of how divisive the Civil War was for the whole country, especially in Florida. The Whitehursts were from Telfair County in southern Georgia. John was born on January 12, 1816, to parents Daniel Scott Whitehurst and Jincy Fletcher Whitehurst. The US Census of 1850 shows John Whitehurst living on property adjoining his father's in present-day Hernando County, in the Annuttaliga Settlement. That land was purchased by Daniel Whitehurst in 1820. The Census of 1860 shows John Whitehurst living in Hillsborough County (now in Pinellas County) on one hundred-sixty acres near the modern town of Safety Harbor, his occupation listed as a farmer. The property was bounded on the south by present-day Drew Street and on the west by US 19 in Clearwater. The land was granted to him in 1852 under the Bounty Lands Warrant Act of 1850 for service in the Florida Mounted Volunteers during the Seminole Wars.

Unionists and Contrabands on Egmont Key

In Florida, the conflict was often described as a civil war within a civil war. Florida sent 15,000 soldiers to the armies of the Confederacy, but 2,000 volunteered to serve in the forces of the Union. There were few regular soldiers in Florida during the war, most being sent to the Army of Northern Virginia or the Army of Tennessee. Still, a substantial militia force remained for duty within the state. The battle at Olustee, the largest battle in Florida, had only about 5000 participants on either side. Several forts changed hands without much combat, and Union forces occupied several places throughout the war. Fort Pickens near Pensacola, Fort Marion in St. Augustine, Fort Zachary Taylor, and Fort Jefferson in the Keys were held by Union forces for most of the war, with Fort Myers occupied in 1863. Egmont Key and Cedar Key became islands of refuge for Unionists and contrabands (runaway slaves). Most of the military action in the state was an attempt by the Union to disrupt commerce and stop the blockade runners, who provided much-needed supplies to sustain the South. Salt distilleries[1] dotted the coastline and, by boiling seawater to extract salt, provided this vital commodity for meat preservation and tanning leather. The distilleries were operated chiefly by enslaved people.

Egmont Key was quickly recognized as a strategic location for the Union Navy to establish a base from which to operate to prevent blockade running. Fort Brooke remained in Confederate hands (until 1864), and so did Mullet Key. The Union Navy occupied Egmont Key in 1861, eventually building a coaling station and a small hospital. They had artillery aimed at Mullet Key as well. The lighthouse

---

1 One salt distillery was located at Cypress Point in Tampa, now a city park. The Confederates operated a small still there during the war. A historical marker tells the story of salt making in the area.

keeper (George Rickards) had abandoned the lighthouse, and the lens and other equipment were relocated to Tampa for safekeeping. The tower was used as an observation point, and a temporary light provided by the Union Navy replaced the missing lantern.

With the presence of Union troops, local people with sympathies for the Union saw Egmont as a haven. Tampa and the surrounding communities were sparsely populated, and everyone knew who the Unionists were.

About thirty-eight Unionists abandoned their homes and businesses and fled to the island. An additional danger was that the Union forces relied on these refugees for information on Confederate activities and movements. The local militia forces were very aware of the Unionists' efforts to gather intelligence for the Union.

It was also a safe place for escaped slaves. As the distilleries were discovered and destroyed, the Navy would take the enslaved people to Egmont Key for protection. From there, they might work with the Navy or join militias to fight the rebels. At the outset of these efforts to remove the enslaved people, there was an understandable reluctance to go with the Union Navy. They were unsure of their intentions, but eventually, they saw Egmont as a path to freedom.

The story of Egmont Key as a haven for Unionists began on February 17, 1862, when the bark *USS Ethan Allen* and *Mary Nevis*, a sloop, went to Clear Water Bay (present-day Old Clearwater Bay) and retrieved John Whitehurst and his wife Elizabeth and six children, his first cousin Daniel Scott Whitehurst and a few others and at 4 PM, put them ashore on Egmont Key along with their baggage. John Whitehurst owned about 160 acres of land near present-day Safety Harbor. They were now under the protection of the US Navy and relative safety.

The local militia had threatened the Whitehurst's to join the Confederacy, but John Whitehurst steadfastly refused. He said he "had only served under the American flag and wasn't going to serve under any other."

Even though they were protected on Egmont Key, these refugees faced hardships and dangers. The Navy did not have adequate provisions for them, so from time to time, they had to risk going ashore and returning to their abandoned property, looking for food or anything that would be useful on the island. The account that follows is the report of Lieutenant J. C. Howell, commander of the *USS Tahoma*, on the fate of John Whitehurst:

> "I have the honor to report that on the 26th August, ultimo, while three of the refugees who have been for some months at the light-house on Egmont Key under the protection of the United States were on the main land [*sic*] endeavoring to procure potatoes, beef, etc., from their farms near Old Tampa for the support of themselves and families, two of them, John and Scott Whitehurst, while shoving from the shore in their boat were barbarously set upon by guerrillas, and Scott Whitehurst was immediately killed, and John Whitehurst mortally wounded. The latter had strength enough to pull the boat out of fire, then fell and laid two days in the boat exposed to the rays of an August sun and was at last discovered by another refugee named Clay and brought to this place. The third man, named Arnold, is supposed to have been murdered during the day. All these men were Union men, and only a short time ago, John Whitehurst offered to raise a company of loyal Floridians if he could be assured it would be accepted. I sent a boat

and recovered the body of Scott Whitehurst and buried it. John Whitehurst died last night and was decently interred by us this morning. His dying request was that his three little sons should be received into the United States naval service. I have no vacancies for them but will take them on board and ration them (which I shall be obliged to do under any circumstances) until I receive permission to ship them, which I am confident will be granted. The boys are quite young - the eldest, I should think, about twelve years of age, the youngest about seven or eight.

These guerrillas are scouring the woods, looking after deserters and conscripts; they rob, murder, and steal indiscriminately, if the reports of the refugees are to be credited; Union men they threaten to hang, and do shoot, as we have lamentable proof. It is said that every man capable of bearing arms has been forced to join the rebels in this part of Florida."

Although accounts vary, the group's landing location was probably near present-day Johns Pass. John Whitehurst's property was quite a distance away.

As mentioned in the previous chapter, the Union attack on Abel Miranda's farm on Pinellas Point was rumored to be retaliation for the Whitehurst killings. Since his death was after the destruction of Miranda's property, this isn't possible. However, could it be the other way around? Maybe the Whitehurst murders were in retaliation for the destruction of Miranda's farm, who was known to be a militia member. Or maybe there's no connection at all, just a series of unrelated events.

Scott Whitehurst was most likely buried on Mullet Key, and John was buried on Egmont Key. John Whitehurst's dying[2] wish was mainly fulfilled. His sons, Christopher Columbus and Winfield Woodbury, enlisted in the US Navy[3] on October 4, 1862, and served on the *USS Tahoma.* The third son, Harney, was not old enough to serve. Whitehurst had three daughters as well: Georgina, Susana, and Frances.

The two sons were later trans-

Whitehurst headstone, photo by author

ferred to the schooner *Wanderer,* next to the sloop of war *San Jacinto,* and finally to the *Ariel.* Christopher was probably killed in action before the end of the war or deserted. Winfield survived and was later shown in a census of Hillsborough County with mother Elizabeth and brother Harney. Elizabeth later remarried to a man named Stevens and lived in the Hyde Park section of Tampa.

Postscript

In 2012, I was contacted by one of the descendants of the Whitehurst family. She told me that in their family history, they had heard that John Whitehurst had died on the Egmont Key and was buried "some-

---

2 Sources differ on the exact date of his death. Some list September 2, 1862, and others list August 26, 1862.

3 Children served in the navies of both sides as cabin boys or "powder monkeys" on warships. They had the dangerous job of bringing kegs of gunpowder to the cannons during a battle.

where near the lighthouse" and that the grave had apparently been lost. The family was planning a reunion, and their tradition was to have it in different places that had significance to their family history. The family wanted to have the reunion on the island, and she asked when would be a good time of the year to visit. I suggested that our annual fundraiser, "Discover the Island," which is held in early November, would be best since there were a lot of things to do while they were there.

To my pleasant surprise, a group of about ten or twelve came to the island during the event, and I got to meet them and share their stories and information about John's fate. I was then asked a question that caught me off guard! I was asked, "How would we know if he had ever really been on Egmont Key?" I hadn't spent much time thinking about that, but I quickly remembered the historical plaques in the cemetery that listed all the known burials there. The information had been compiled by Egmont Key Alliance members many years prior and placed at the cemetery. I suggested they go over and look at the names and see if he was listed.

Of course, it was, but it was uncertain if he might still be buried somewhere there with the grave lost or if he might have moved when the cemetery was closed. Many of the military men had been relocated to the National Cemetery in St. Augustine and some to private cemeteries. The family later discovered via research on the internet that he was, in fact, buried there.

When I visited the cemetery a few years later, I searched for the headstone and found it among the others from Fort Dade. It was gratifying to know that the Whitehurst family finally got answers to the whereabouts of John Whitehurst and that he was located in a place that the military would properly maintain.

Chapter 17

The USS Narcissus

The tugboat *USS Narcissus* met a tragic fate just off Egmont Key in 1866, and its story is integral to the island's history. Unfortunately, the ship's appearance isn't captured in any known photographs or drawings, but it was a typical tugboat of its time.

Constructed in 1863 during the height of the Civil War, it was intended to be added to the fleet of Union Navy ships that were blockading the South. This blockade, called the "Anaconda Plan," started in 1861, even though the Union Navy didn't have nearly enough ships to enforce it adequately. It was an enormous undertaking, trying to stop Confederate supply vessels from entering or leaving the South. The blockade extended from Virginia to Texas. Thus, the Navy began a shipbuilding and purchasing program to equip the blockading fleets.

The *Narcissus* was built at East Albany, New York, and launched in July 1863 as a screw (propeller) steamer called the *Mary Cook*. It was purchased by the Union Navy on September 23, 1863, and was commissioned as the *USS Narcissus* at the Brooklyn Navy Yard, New York, on February 2, 1864. It was armed with a 12-pounder smooth-bore cannon and a 20-pound Parrott rifle.[1] With a length of 81 feet 6 inches and a beam of 18 feet 9 inches, it had a draft of six feet. Classed as a fourth-rate vessel[2], its maximum speed was twelve knots but typically ran at five knots.

After commissioning, the *Narcissus* sailed towards the Gulf of Mexico, stopping for fuel in North Carolina. Joining the West Gulf Blockading Squadron, she began patrolling in the Mississippi Sound. She quickly captured a Confederate sloop, the *Oregon,* and took her prize to headquarters in New Orleans. In the summer of 1864, the *Narcissus* participated in the Union operations at Mobile Bay, although it was not directly involved in the famous naval battle.

Her luck finally ran out when she struck a Confederate torpedo (underwater mine) and quickly sank. This time, all hands managed to escape to safety. The *Narcissus* was raised and sent to Pensacola for repairs to the hull, but she was not returned to service until the war's end.

With the war finally over, the US Navy began disposing of the many ships acquired for blockade duties, including the *Narcissus* and its sister ship, the *Althea.* On New Year's Day in 1866, they set sail from Pensacola, heading for New York to be sold for commercial duties.

The vessels began traveling along the Gulf Coast. On January 4, the captains encountered storms and decided to anchor near Egmont Key and await better conditions. The *Narcissus*, moving at full speed, ran aground on Egmont Shoal, a sandbar near the island. The *Althea* fared better and was able to power her way off the shoal and anchor safely nearby.

---

1 The Parrott Rifle was a muzzle-loading, rifled artillery designed by Robert Parrott in 1860 and used extensively by both sides as land-based and shipborne weapons. It was made with cast iron for the barrel and a wrought iron reinforcing band at the breech end.

2 Fourth Rate refers to the size of the ship, the number of crewmen, and the number of guns it carries.

At 6:15 PM, the *Althea* saw signal flares from the *Narcissus* and, fifteen minutes later, returned the signal. The crew of the *Althea* could see more signals from the *Narcissus* but could not understand them. Before 7 PM, the crew of the *Althea* tried one more time to signal the grounded ship, but there was no response. The deck logs of the *Althea* noted that at 7 PM, the boiler on the *Narcissus* exploded. The *Althea* crew stood by in shock as the *Narcissus* broke apart, realizing the entire crew had certainly perished!

The following morning, the *Althea* anchored off Egmont Key, and two crewmen went ashore and found wreckage strewn down the shoreline. The badly burned body of one of the crewmen had washed ashore as well. Finding no survivors, they reboarded the ship and continued their journey to New York. This spot off Egmont Key would be the final resting place for the *Narcissus* and would remain known to only a few people until the 1980s, when the site was rediscovered by local divers and some artifacts looted.

In 2008, the Florida Aquarium in Tampa began a program to map and survey underwater wrecks in Tampa Bay. State grants funded the program, and the idea of adding this wreck site to the state underwater preserve program soon arose. In December 2011, The Bureau of Archaeological Research, Division of Historical Resources, Florida Department of State, proposed to dedicate the wreck site of the *Narcissus* as a Florida Underwater Archaeological Preserve. Archaeological work continued through 2015, and the site was formally nominated and then declared Florida's 12th Underwater Archaeology Preserve. But, for this location, the local dive community wanted to do more to commemorate the sailors who lost their lives there.

The idea developed to do something more than just put a plaque on a piece of concrete and place it near the wreck site. With much input from many interested people and organizations, it was decided to construct a reef ball to attach the plaques. The memorial would also be a place for marine life to inhabit. The final monument was a large reef ball, with a plaque on one side listing the names of the crewmen who were lost there and a plaque on the other side with a likeness of the *Narcissus*. Eternal Reef Company of Sarasota, Florida, constructed this reef ball. The US Coast Guard placed the reef ball at the site on January 15, 2015.

Given the significance of this site and what happened there in 1866, just placing a reef ball would not have been appropriate. The Florida Aquarium went all out to make this an event to be remembered! First, Danny Redmond, whose great-granduncle, William Wilkerson, one of the crewmen, came to Tampa Bay. A boat with him and several divers from the Florida Aquarium aquarium staff and underwater video equipment went to the location. The video signal was transmitted back to the Florida Aquarium building, where a large group of people were seated in the Jeff Vinik Room.

There, a ceremony ensued, and everyone saw the reef ball and a wreath of flowers placed in the water. At the Aquarium, the Coast Guard dignitaries rang a bell once for each lost crew member as their names were read. Fortunately, I got to witness this as a guest of the Aquarium. All these events took place on January 20, 2015. It was a fitting way to wrap up this project and recognize everyone who participated in this event.

Many years after all this work, I had an opportunity to scuba dive at the site along with other divers from the Gulfport Dive Club. It is a challenging dive because of the depth and the currents that can sweep over the shoal. It had to be dived at slack tide when the tide was not moving in or out. Finding the wreck was difficult because the reef ball had been covered to the top with sand, giving no visual clue to the exact location. The tides will continue to move the sand, so the reef ball will eventually be visible again.

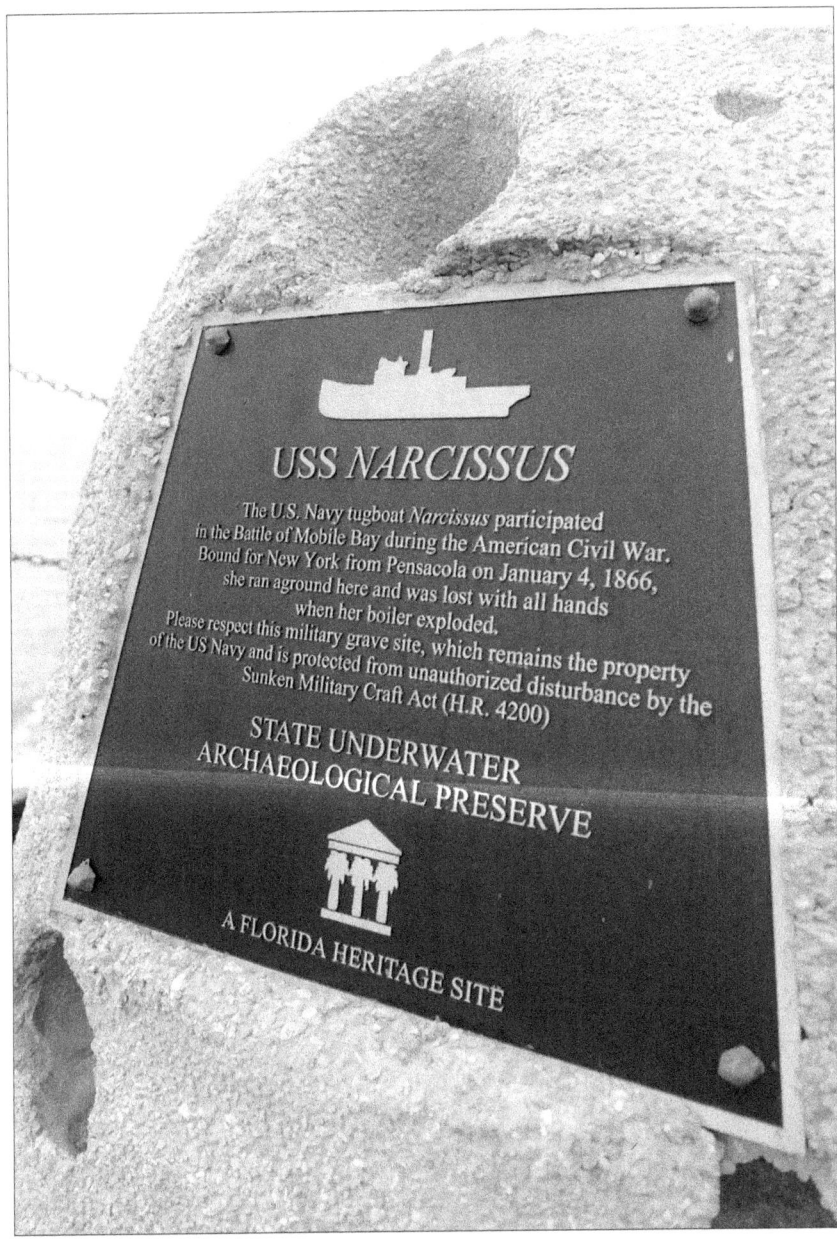

The U.S. Navy tugboat *Narcissus* participated in the Battle of Mobile Bay during the American Civil War. Bound for New York from Pensacola on January 4, 1866, she ran aground here and was lost with all hands when her boiler exploded.

Please respect this military grave site, which remains the property of the US Navy and is protected from unauthorized disturbance by the Sunken Military Craft Act (H.R. 4200)

Reef ball and plaque

If you visit the site, you will see the remains of the steam engine, boiler, and propeller. The *USS Narcissus* is now the twelfth underwater preserve in the state accessible to divers. Nicole Morris of the Florida Aquarium and Southeastern Archaeological Services completed her Masters Thesis on the history of the *Narcissus*. Her work helped get the site designated as an underwater preserve. The *Narcissus* was added in 2018 to the National Register of Historic Places.

Chapter 18

Charles Moore, Lighthouse Keeper

Charles Moore was the longest-serving keeper on Egmont Key, his service spanning more than thirty years. He was witness to the most significant changes to the island when the quarantine camp was established after the Spanish-American War and then the construction of Fort Dade, which saw the clear-cutting of the vegetation on most of the island, construction of five concrete gun batteries, approximately seventy support buildings, a narrow gauge railway, brick paved streets and all the infrastructure associated with a small town. He went from living in relative isolation for twenty years with his family, the assistant keeper, and his family to an island now a part of the US Coast Defense system with hundreds of soldiers, civilian workers, and their families.

In geopolitical terms, his time as a keeper started about ten years after the post-Civil War Reconstruction era of the South after the Civil War, to the emergence of Tampa as a major port city and the United States as a world power during the Spanish-American War. He was a keeper when Henry Plant brought his railroad to Port Tampa City in 1884 and built the Tampa Bay Hotel in 1891. The increased shipping activity in the Port of Tampa used this lighthouse to navigate into Tampa Bay safely.

Guests from the hotel would occasionally take a steamer to Egmont Key and spend the day picnicking and touring the island. Over the years, he had several distinguished visitors, some of whom will be discussed in this chapter. His little corner of paradise became a place of modern civilization with all its good and bad aspects.

Early Life

He was born on September 22, 1838, in Connecticut. Little information has been found about his boyhood. He attended college and spent some time in Alabama, where he met and married Emily Rayfield, who was thirty years younger than him. His first child, Charles Mortimer Moore, was born in Tampa near the present-day Cass Street Bridge when Charles began as Assistant Keeper in 1876. Charles and Emily had two more children who died very young: Henry, born in 1878 and living until 1881, and a daughter, Nettie, who was born in 1881 and passed away the following year. He held several jobs before becoming a lighthouse keeper. He had been a caretaker at Fort Brooke in Tampa, then later operated a saltworks and transported mail under contract to Cedar Key.

Lighthouse Service

His long career as lighthouse keeper at Egmont Key began on October 23, 1876, as Assistant Keeper under Walter Burgess. Upon Burgess's departure (removed for neglect of duty and letting the light go out) in 1878, Charles Moore was promoted to Head Keeper, a position he held until his retirement in 1910. His duties included maintaining the tower and keeping the lamp lit, which required daily climbs to the top of the tower to replenish the fuel. The six-foot-tall windows of the lantern room had to be kept clean, and the lens had to be kept in good working order. He also had a small boat, provided by the government, which occasionally needed maintenance and repairs. It was noted in a local newspaper that he went to the Fogarty Shipyard in Manatee County to have repairs made.

In addition to his keepers' duties, Charles had to provide for his family. He kept a garden for vegetables, certainly had some chickens, and did a lot of fishing. He periodically had to go to Tampa for other supplies. He was somewhat of a local celebrity known by many as "Cap'n Charlie." His comings and goings were frequently noted in the society pages of Tampa newspapers as visiting friends or conducting some business. Visitors to the island were noted in the local newspapers as well.

In 1872, a buoy depot and coal shed were constructed on the island. This allowed buoys on the Florida west coast to be kept in good repair, and the shed stored coal to fuel lighthouse tenders (ships).

George O. Shields' Visit 1883

George Shields was a noted author of the time and wrote many articles on the outdoors. His topics included hunting, fishing, camping, and sporting dogs. He was an avid outdoorsman and traveled around the United States looking for adventures he could write about. He was published in *American Field Magazine* and *Harpers*. He authored several books on the outdoors and stories on cavalry battles with the Nez Perce Indians.

His visit to Egmont Key was one stop on a trip down the Gulf Coast to Sarasota on the steamer *Valley City*, where he planned to fish, hunt, and see some tropical fruit trees (citrus was a novelty in those days). He was Theodore Roosevelt's contemporary and an avid outdoorsman, and both advocated for wildlife conservation and sportsmanship while hunting.

The *Valley City* docked at Egmont at 1 AM, and Shields went ashore at sunrise after having a cup of coffee in his stateroom. The ship's captain gave him one hour to "take a walk on the beach." He met Charles Moore and described him as an "intelligent, kindhearted, and hospitable gentleman." Shields described Egmont as a "picturesque isle that is a half mile wide and one and a half miles long." Moore told him about a heron rookery on the island about a half mile from the keeper's house that he considered "pets" and wouldn't allow them to be shot or disturbed in any way[1]. Moore estimated the heron population to be about 2500 birds.

Moore talked about a large herd of deer on Mullet Key that he used as a food source whenever he wanted fresh venison. Moore estimated he had killed one hundred ninety-two deer over two years. The brief walk around the island allowed Shields to see some local fish species due to a cold front that had recently passed over the island, stunning the fish and washing them ashore. He wrote of seeing "cow-fish, sea-horse, dog-fish, lamper-eel (lamprey-eel), and varieties of toad-fish." Shields collected specimens of coral, sponges, shells, and sea moss.

His time on the island is at an end, and Shields bid farewell to Moore, who urged him to return for a longer visit. Shields described Egmont as a most fascinating place and was hoping he could accept

---

1 In those days, the demand for colorful feathers for women's hats drove what was referred to as the plume trade. There were no regulations governing the killing of wildlife for commercial purposes, which decimated many seabird rookeries in the Tampa Bay Area.

the offer of a more extended stay. Shields boarded *Valley City* and continued his voyage, stopping in Tampa, a city of 1800 inhabitants and shipping hub for the Tampa Steamship Company.[2]

Moore on the Steps of the Keepers House Courtesy of the Manatee County Public Library Digital Collections.

Later Life

Charles Moore lived an idyllic life on the island, tending to the lighthouse and raising his family. A 1900 island census showed his son, Charles Mortimer Moore, as a ship's carpenter. Charles had seven Assistant Keepers during his time there.

---

2 George Shields never returned to Egmont Key but continued his adventures elsewhere. He died in Manhattan, NY, in 1925. American Field Magazine is the oldest publication of its type in the U.S. and is now called American Field and Sporting Dog Magazine.

During the Spanish-American War in 1898, the Army came to Egmont Key to construct temporary earthworks on the north and south ends of the island. The earthworks served to protect cannons guarding the shipping channels from the threat of attack by the Spanish Navy. It was a serious concern since Tampa was a central embarkation point for troops and supplies heading to Cuba. However, in their haste to build the earthwork (near present-day Battery Mellon), the Army located it on Lighthouse Service property. There was a flurry of letters back and forth between the two agencies, and in the end, the Army claimed it was a national emergency. The earthwork was not manned for long since the Spanish Navy wanted nothing to do with attacking Tampa, and the artillery was needed in Cuba. The earthwork remained until after the construction of Battery Number One, later rebuilt and named Battery Mellon.

In 1899, a separate, wood-frame, two-story house was built for the Assistant Keepers. Before this, they lived in the same house with the Head Keeper and family. It was located just north of the present-day Park Ranger's residence. When the Coast Guard took over maintaining lighthouses, the house became the first barracks for the Coast Guardsmen.

In 1908, Charles Moore contracted throat cancer, which he battled for two years. In the 1910 Census, he was listed as a "boarder," his son Charles M. was now acting as a Civil Engineer, and Edward Woodward was the Head Keeper. Charles retired from the Lighthouse Service on May 3, 1910, and went to Tampa to live out his retirement. According to newspaper accounts, he returned to Egmont Key to live out his final days with his son, who was now managing the Tampa Harbor Pilots. Speaking to a newspaper reporter, he said he felt the loneliest when the Army came to the island and built

Fort Dade since they clear-cut much of the island and built so many buildings. He died on November 10, 1910, and is buried at Major Adams Cemetery in Bradenton. His wife Emily died the following year and is buried at the Woodlawn Cemetery in Tampa along with her children, Charles Mortimer, Henry, and Nettie.

Charles Moore's grave in Bradenton. Photo by author

Postscript

There would be many more keepers after Chares Moore retired, but none would serve nearly as long as he did. The life of a lighthouse keeper on Egmont Key, as Moore had known it, was about to end.

In 1922, Fort Dade, whose construction had ended Moore's paradise, was declared obsolete and closed down, with only a small caretaker group on the island. Eventually, all the artillery was removed and scrapped or repurposed elsewhere. World War II saw the fort looted for scrap metal and the destruction of the many wooden buildings there. The only building to survive other than the gun batteries was the Guardhouse, made of solid concrete.

In 1939, the US Coast Guard took over the duties of the Lighthouse Service. Lighthouse Keepers were offered the choice of duty in the Coast Guard or continuing as civilians. Coast Guard personnel now staffed the lighthouse on Egmont Key, and in 1944, during World War II, the lantern room and watch room were removed, a concrete deck was poured, and an automated DCB-36 beacon was installed. Later, the USCG built a modern, one-story concrete barracks, a foghorn, and a low-frequency radio navigation beacon. The Keeper house, built in 1858, at the same time as the tower, and the Assistant Keeper house, built in 1912, which had seen so many keepers and their families come and go over the years, were considered safety hazards and nuisances and had were demolished. Eventually, the radio beacon and foghorn were declared obsolete and removed.

In 1974, the island became a part of a National Wildlife refuge under the management of the US Fish and Wildlife Service. This refuge extends from Cedar Key in the north to Passage Key, south of Egmont Key. It includes a bird sanctuary on the south end of the island.

In November 1989, the USCG removed the personnel from the island, and the Florida State Park Service began operating a park there. They manage the park in cooperation with US Fish and Wildlife.

The DCB-36 beacon, now on display at the island, was eventually replaced with a single aerobeacon. In 2017, after Hurricane Irma had damaged the tower's electrical wiring, the USCG replaced the aerobeacon with a battery-powered, solar-charged LED strobe that was visible for eight miles. The lighthouse is now considered unnecessary for navigation, and the lighthouse property's future is uncertain.

Chapter 19

Charles Mortimer Moore

Charles Mortimer Moore[1] was born on October 15, 1876, at a home in Tampa near the present-day Cass Street Bridge. He was taken to the island as an infant because his father, Charles "Cap'n Charlie" Moore, had just been appointed Assistant Keeper at the lighthouse. His time on Egmont Key would span most of his adult life.

His early schooling was at Williamsburg Academy, a two-room school in Manatee County. He also attended a school in Fogartyville (now part of Bradenton). Later, he attended Rollins College in Winter Park, Florida, from 1891 to 1894

At Rollins College in the 1890's, the courses of study were quite different from modern college curricula. He began in what was called the "Sub-Preparatory Department." Courses readied students for the more advanced courses. He entered the "Academic Program," which was not a degree program but consisted of advanced studies in English, history, natural science, and modern languages. In the list-

---

1 According to his daughter Roberta, Charles abhorred his middle name. He was called "Charles", "Young Charlie," or "Charlie."

ings of students in the Annual Catalog, Charles listed his residence as both "Egmont Keys" and "Braidentown."

Charles M. Moore at Rollins College. Courtesy of the Manatee County Public Library Digital Collections.

He married Roberta Lightfoot and soon got a job at the Fogarty Boat Works under Bartholomew "Bat" Fogarty. The boatyard had been established in 1865 by Bartholomew "Tole" Fogarty. His son was Bat. They built hundreds of boats of all types for local captains over the sixty years of operations. The land owned by the Fogarty family totaled 135 acres[2].

Charles Mortimer Moore and his wife Roberta Lightfoot. Courtesy of the Manatee County Public Library Digital Collections.

---

2 One of the buildings and many of the tools from the Fogarty Boat Works are preserved and on display at the Manatee Village Historical Park in Bradenton.

The business fell on hard times, so Charles began working at the newly established Detention Camp on Egmont Key. The year was 1898, and the Spanish-American War had ended after only three months of combat. However, due to the real threat of yellow fever, a tropical disease common in the southern United States, South America, and the Caribbean, the 20,000 troops returning from Cuba had to quarantine for about ten days. The Marine Medical Service had a large quarantine site on nearby Mullet Key, but the number of troops and the amount of baggage that had to be fumigated justified opening a new site.

The site on Egmont Key was hastily chosen, but a worse location could not possibly have been selected. It was in a marshy area just south of the lighthouse. The tents used as housing had been left over from the Civil War more than thirty years prior. The food was terrible, mosquitoes plentiful, and the soldiers operating it were not the best the Army could offer. There were numerous complaints from people forced to live there, and medical care was poor at best. Charles became a property clerk for the Marine Medical Service, but he soon quit due to the camp's poor conditions. He referred to the Egmont Detention Camp as a "sick camp."

The camp was soon closed because the Army decided to add Egmont Key and Mullet Key to the Coast Defense System under the command of the Coast Artillery Corps. At this time, these coastal forts were how the United States protected its major ports from attack by a foreign navy. Henry B. Plant, who built the Tampa Bay Hotel and the railroad that brought guests to it, had friends in Congress who ensured the Army had used his hotel as a headquarters for the commanders planning the war in Cuba. Henry Plant convinced these same congressmen to add Tampa to the Coast Defense.

The detention camp was shut down since the Army was concerned about the possible transmission of yellow fever to the construction workers. This transition presented another opportunity for Charles to gain employment.

Even though he was not a civil engineer, many of the tasks he performed were sometimes handled by engineers. He oversaw the construction of gun batteries, caissons, five sixty-inch searchlights, docks, and storerooms and installed a telephone cable to Bradenton. At its peak, Fort Dade had over seventy buildings, five gun batteries, an airfield, and two mine casemates. This work would last twenty-four years until the Army declared the forts obsolete and decommissioned around 1922.

Charles's career would take another turn after the closure of Fort Dade. The Tampa Bay Pilots Association's harbor pilots, who had been guiding ships into Tampa Bay since before the Spanish-American War, now opened an office on Egmont Key. Charles became the first manager, bookkeeper, dispatcher, and agent, a job he would hold until his retirement in February 1948.

Charles had one daughter, Roberta, who lived an idyllic life. She grew up on an island where her father worked and her grandfather was the Lighthouse Keeper. In an interview shortly before her death, she described what it was like to visit. She often said, "Egmont was my teacher." She later married E. Ward "Bud" Cole II from Temple Terrace, Florida.

Charles had purchased a home at 316 West Columbus Drive in Tampa, constructed in 1921. Charles and his wife Roberta lived there at his death on January 3, 1967, at the age of 90. His life spanned from the post-Reconstruction era after the Civil War to modern times, including the Spanish-American War and both World Wars. At his funeral, there were many harbor pilots and others from the local maritime community. He and his wife are buried at the Woodlawn Cemetery in Tampa. In 1970, E. Ward Cole and Roberta sold the home on Columbus Drive. It is still standing and has been converted into duplex apartments.

Chapter 20

The Tampa Harbor Pilots

The story of the Tampa Harbor Pilots goes back to the pre-Civil War period. Tampa was a sparsely populated town with only about one hundred residents, and Fort Brooke was a prominent military installation in the area.

Soon after Florida became a Territory, after being ceded to the United States from Spain in 1821, the legislative framework for managing port traffic was created. On September 16, 1822, the Legislative Council for the territory approved an act for appointing pilots. It wasn't until 1839 that Act Number 17 provided for the appointment of three "discreet and proper persons" to perform the duties of what was then called Port Wardens for the harbor at Tampa Bay.

The first pilots appointed under this legislation were Louis G. Covacevich and Juan Gomez. Covacevich was born in Trieste, Austria, emigrated to Tampa in 1837, and became a citizen in 1842. Juan Gomez was listed on census records from 1850 as living in the Covacevich household, and his occupation was listed as Pilot

An interesting revelation from Gomez was that during the early 1850s, Egmont Key was an internment site for the Seminoles, who were soon relocated west to Oklahoma. He would take "excursionists" to the island for picnics. His ship was named *Red Jack*. This would mean recreational visitation to the island by paying passengers started much earlier than previously known.

He was a pilot for the East Gulf Blockading Squadron during the Civil War. In his later years, he moved to Panther Key near Charlotte Harbor and became locally known as "Panther Key John.'

In those days, the strategic importance of natural channels and deep water sites in determining port locations was evident. There was little need for extensive dredging to create ship channels or docking facilities. The naturally occurring channels and deep water sites, such as those around Fort Brooke, played a crucial role in determining the location of ports. While Fort Brooke and the surrounding waters could support shallow-draft boats, larger ships required deeper water.

When Henry B. Plant built his rail line into the Tampa Bay area in 1887, he wanted the terminal at the deepest water he could find to handle his steamships that would dock there. His steamship line traveled to Havana, Cuba, and other ports in the Caribbean. The deepest water was at what became "Port Tampa." The town that grew up around this port became Port Tampa City[1].

A dredging project was authorized in 1880 under the Rivers and Harbors Act. It called for a nineteen-foot channel to be dredged to Port Tampa and the mouth of the Hillsborough River. The project took a decade to complete.

Henry Plant would build a hotel to accommodate guests, as with all his rail lines. In this case, he built two, the St. Elmo and the Port Tampa Inn. The hotels were built on a long dock extending out over the water. The rail line went to the end of this dock. Passengers arriving by ship could go to one of the hotels or get on the train and travel into Tampa, a nine-mile journey through Florida scrubland.

---

1   Port Tampa City was also called Passage Point or Black Point.

The first person to give navigational information to ships entering the bay was Charles Moore, the lighthouse keeper on Egmont Key. Captains would stop at the lighthouse dock, and Cap'n Charlie would loan them a nautical chart of the bay and surrounding waters. Charles would tell the captain to return the chart when he left Tampa. The captain was on his own, determining the best route to either Port Tampa or the City of Tampa.

An interview with Charles M. Moore, son of the keeper, in 1966 best tells the story. Charles M. would eventually become the first paid employee of the Tampa Bay Pilots after working as an engineer on the construction of Fort Dade. This narrative is courtesy of the Manatee County Library collection.

"Charles Moore, who was appointed Senior Lightkeeper for Egmont Key Lighthouse in June 1877, told his son Charles M. that a lighthouse about 60 feet in height was built on the island about 75 feet northeast of the present (1966)[2] lighthouse. According to the report, it became unsafe and was replaced by the present lighthouse in 1848. This latter structure was severely damaged that same year by perhaps the worst hurricane ever experienced in Tampa Bay."

"Before there was an organized pilot group, the small foreign tramp steamers would stop inside of Egmont Key and borrow a chart of Tampa Bay from Mr. Moore, the lightkeeper, to find their way to Port Tampa, returning the chart on the outbound passage."

---

2 This date is apparently the year the interview was done. His account is somewhat confusing about the different towers. A storm damaged the 1848 tower, and the 1858 tower stands today. Charles M. died in 1967 at the age of 90.

"About 1883, shortly before the Henry B. Plant System extended their narrow gauge railroad from Kissimmee to Tampa, a drifter appeared on the Tampa Bay scene. "Dutch Bill," as he was known, offered his services as a pilot to those schooners, barkentines, and brigs that brought the locomotives and rails into Tampa for this extension. It has never been clearly established whether Dutch Bill was brought here and hired by the railroad or if he came on his initiative."

Charles M. Moore continues in the interview, speaking about the beginning of the Tampa Bay Pilots:

"The birth of the Tampa Bay Pilots as an organization might well be said to be in the early 1890s when Captain Harry G. Warner started bringing ships out of Port Tampa. Captain Warner owned a ship chandlery business in that city and piloted out the ships that Captain Switzer brought in. Warner had a naphtha-powered motor launch, which he would tow astern of the outbound vessel to provide his own return transportation to Port Tampa. Captain Switzer did not maintain a station on Egmont Key for some time but came over from Tierra Ceia, staying at the lightkeeper's home as he awaited an incoming ship. The elder Mr. Moore would say in jest that Captain Switzer must surely have glue on the seat of his pants, that he would rather be cold than get up and replenish the old woodstove with fuel."

"John Fogarty, who later became a Tampa Bay Pilot, worked in his father's boatyard at Fogartyville, later running his father's schooner, the *Ino*. He later ran a side-wheel steamer, the *Manatee*, between Tampa and the Manatee River. The

Independent Line, a H. B. Plant Line competitor, owned this vessel."

"From about 1888 until some years later, there was a channel of only 9 to 10 feet from Gadsden Point to Tampa on the Hillsborough River. Vessels exceeding this draft were required to anchor at Gadsden Point, from which passengers and cargo were transported to and from Tampa. In early 1888, a channel was completed to Port Tampa, and in June of that same year, the Steamers *Mascotte* and *Olivette* of the Plant Steamship Company began docking there."

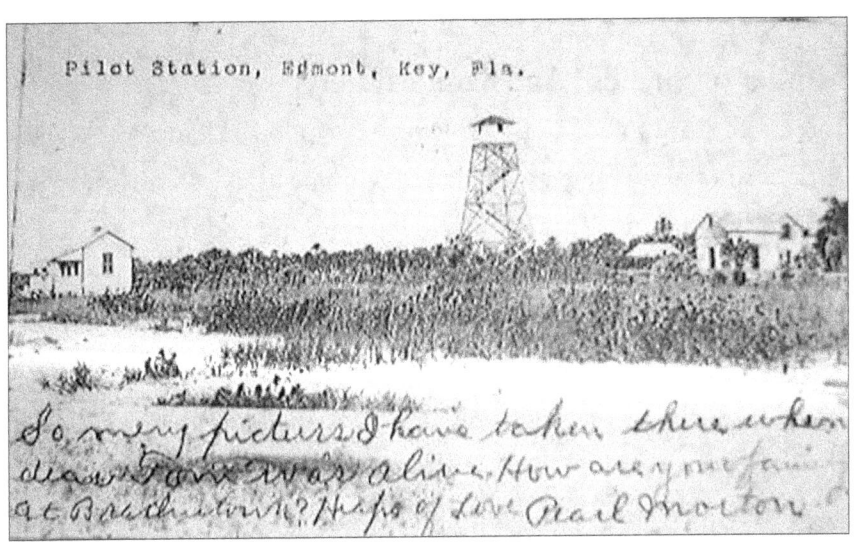

A postcard with the pilots' observation tower.

Another primary source of early pilot history comes from Captain C. W. Bahrt[3]. His narrative reveals the beginnings of the pilots on

---

3 Captain Carl William Bahrt (1880-1937) was a Tampa pilot for 27 years, sometimes known as "Captain Billy."

Egmont Key. Captains Harry G. Warner and W.A. Switzer purchased a sloop, *Gunars,* and used this vessel for transportation. They constructed a fifty-foot lookout tower to be able to observe ship traffic. It was on the south end of the island. Captain Switzer built a home on the island, and Captain Warner lived in Port Tampa City (his house still stands there). Switzer would meet the ships as they entered the port, and Warner was on the ships as they left. Carl Bahrt was only ten years old then, and one of his duties was to man the tower and look for ships that would need the services of a pilot. He was also a "handy boy" for everyone on the island. Carl Bahrt was joined by his younger brother Arthur C. Bahrt as a pilot in 1936 and served until his death in 1939.

Murder or Suicide? An Island Mystery

The tragic stories about one of the harbor pilots, Henry M. Walker, and his son, Fred Walker, were shared with me by a descendant, Frank B. Haddleton. One death occurred on the island and the other across Tampa Bay at a place called Indian Hill, which is a little south of the Little Manatee River.

Henry Marshall Walker was born into a maritime family in Harwich Port, Massachusetts, in 1843 to parents Marshall and Rebecca Walker. By age seventeen, Henry had settled himself in a maritime career, apparently undeterred by the number of his family lost at sea over the years. He married Louisa Eldridge, also from a maritime family, on November 16, 1862. They had two children, Frederick Barzillai Walker and Henry Marshall Walker, Jr. They also entered maritime careers, following in the footsteps of many of their families.

By 1878, Henry Walker had established himself as a successful captain. The same year, Walker, two partners, and a steamship company purchased a steamship called *Valley City* and moved to Tampa to begin commercial operations. The company would eventually become the Tampa Steamship Company. The decision to relocate to Florida was most likely driven by the decline in shipping activity due to the increasing use of railroads in the Northeast. This move coincided with a period of rapid growth in Tampa, the population increasing from eight hundred in 1880 to 15,000 by 1900. Also, the growth in the citrus and cattle industries increased the demand for shipping. The construction of Henry Plant's railroad line and hotel in Tampa brought tourists to the area in the winter months. Plant had constructed a port facility in Port Tampa City (now Port Tampa, annexed by Tampa) that connected Florida with cities like Havana, Cuba.

Walker operated along the Gulf Coast from Pensacola to Key West and Havana. The *Valley City* was eventually lost near Cape San Blas, Florida, and replaced with the *Wateska*. By 1890, Walker was now operating a schooner, the *Albert Woodbury*, while his son, Henry Jr., took over the command of the *Wateska*. In January 1891, the *Wateska* became grounded on Passage Key bar, just south of Egmont Key. Efforts to remove the vessel from the bar were unsuccessful, and it was abandoned there.

By 1893, Henry Walker's maritime career changed from being a captain to becoming a harbor pilot. He joined the pilot operation on Egmont Key along with Harry G. Warner and W. A. Switzer. He lived in a house on the island along with his wife Louisa and two boarders.

Walker captained a steamship on a very part-time basis for the Plant System, Henry Plant's system of hotels, railroads, and steamship lines. He became a friend of Plant and took guests on fishing excursions in the Gulf of Mexico aboard the steamer *Florida*, a 230-foot steel, screw-driven vessel built in Glasgow, Scotland.

While at Egmont Key, Henry Walker's life was good. He was a successful and well-paid pilot, private captain, and ship owner. He had purchased eighty acres of land, half of which is now Lake Vista Recreation Center in St. Petersburg. The other half is now the campus of Lakewood High School. There was no reason to believe he was anything but happy with his life.

In June 1900, Walker's wife, Louisa, returned to Massachusetts as she had done every summer. His son Fred's wife and children had also left the area for Massachusetts, which they hadn't done in the past. On June 5, 1900, Henry Walker's friends noticed he had not left his room all day. Upon entering the locked door, they found him on the floor in a pool of blood. A gunshot from a revolver to his chin aimed upward at his brain caused his death. It appeared to be suicide, but was it?

Frank Haddleton, a great-great-grandson, offers up a possibility that it was murder. There was no will, so would he have left his personal affairs in such disarray? There was no suicide note explaining his actions. There was no real investigation of the case, and close friends suspected foul play. The door was locked from the inside, but there was a possibility that an intruder could have left through a window. No suspects have been named in the years since. It is unknown if valuables were missing, but some people on the island may have known of valuables and wanted them. The death of Henry Walker will be one of the mysteries of Egmont Key that will never be solved.

Meanwhile, just a short distance across Tampa Bay, another Walker family tragedy was about to unfold, with some unanswered questions as well. Fred Walker, Henry's son, had been living in a wood frame house at a place called Indian Hill after having moved from Cape Cod. Indian Hill was accessible only by boat, located three miles south of a settlement called Gulf City (now an unincorporated subdivision in Hillsborough County). Indian Hill was fourteen miles as the crow flies from Egmont Key. The site was dotted with burial mounds made by indigenous people. He fished a lot and maintained a beacon in this isolated location.

His job was maintaining a navigation light built by the Coast Guard and used by ships as a marker. It wasn't an actual lighthouse but a light placed on a short tower. Sometimes called a "lens-light," they were less expensive to build and maintain.

Fred's family was still in Massachusetts at the time, not having returned to Florida after Henry Walker's death in June. Locals in Gulf City noticed that Fred's navigation light had been dark for four nights and worried that something had happened to him. On October 25, 1900, concerned locals and a sheriff's deputy went to the house to investigate. They found Fred's decomposing body, and according to an article in the *Morning Tribune* dated October 26, he was "erect on a chair in his cabin, the head thrown back, a ghastly hole in the forehead. The right hand grasped a shotgun, of which one barrel had been exploded (fired). The position of the gun indicated that the deceased had rested the stock of the gun on the floor, pressed his forehead against the muzzle, and pulled the trigger." The house was otherwise undisturbed. His body was in such bad condition that it was buried at Indian Hill but later moved from the island. So, was it suicide as the authorities decided or murder as the locals suspected? It will be another of the tragedies and mysteries of the Walker family and Egmont Key. Today, the area around Indian Hill is an aquatic preserve. (Authors note: Frank Haddleton has published a murder mystery titled *Walkers Key* that is based loosely on the deaths of Walker and his son).

Currently, the Tampa Harbor Pilots are a team of around twenty-two and remain vital to Port Tampa Bay's maritime operations. They no longer live on the island but use the houses there as weekend get-aways. Modern navigational methods such as GPS aid ship captains in transiting Tampa Bay into the port of Tampa. However, the harbor pilots are still on the bridge of ships as they guide them in and out of the bay, ensuring safe navigation into and within the port itself.

Chapter 21

The US Coast Guard on Egmont Key

Egmont Key has a long history of aiding ship captains safely navigating Tampa Bay. Some accounts state that the Spanish built a "blockhouse" at present-day Safety Harbor in 1565 and one on the north tip of Egmont Key. This may have included some light for navigation.

Florida changed hands between the Spanish and English, with ownership being decided by the outcomes of wars in Europe. There is some evidence of exploration by the French around 1640 around the Suwannee River and as far south as Tarpon Springs.

In a significant turn of events, the Spanish Empire, facing a decline and perceiving little value in Florida, decided to sell the land to the United States in 1821. At the time of the sale, Florida was a territory, and due to concerns about hostile Indigenous people, a military installation was built where the Hillsborough River meets the bay. It was first called Cantonment Brooke after the Army officer who established it, Colonel George Mercer Brooke. Colonel James Gadsden was also a part of the founding of the fort, and Gadsden

Point is named after him. Later, the name of the military installation would be changed to Fort Brooke.

The first known navigational aid was erected in 1836 at the island's north end. In a letter to Commodore Alexander J. Dallas at Pensacola, the installation and use are described:

> "I have the honor to inform you that I have planted a beacon on Egmont Island to point out the entrance to Tampa Bay. It is a spar (pole) 80 feet high with a *barrel* on it, painted *white and black,* and may be seen before the land. To enter the bay in safety, bring the beacon to bear E & S by compass, then run for it until you strike 3 fathoms of water, which will take you over the bar, then steer E & N until the beacon bears E by S and then follow the northern bank which can always be seen a cable's length. Run for the beacon to near a cable's length, and you will have 10 fathoms of water, the beacon bearing south, then run E by S to 4 or 5 fathoms, then E N E 6 miles, and N E to 3 fathoms off Mangrove point, then north to 4 fathoms and N E to the anchorage at Gadsden's Point."

This "beacon" was not lighted but simply painted black and white. It could only be used during the daytime under good weather conditions.

The first lighthouse was built on Egmont Key in 1848 and, at the time, was the only beacon between St. Marks to the north and Cape Florida to the south. This first tower was damaged by a hurricane in its first year of operation and was never adequately repaired. A second and much better-designed tower was completed in 1858 and has stood the test of time, still serving as the beacon in Tampa Bay. The second tower was completed at a cost of $16,000, which included a two-story brick keeper's house. Although four alcoves were built inside the lighthouse for storing oil, a separate brick oil house was constructed in the 1890s, with its door facing south. Later, it was enlarged, and the door was now facing west. In 1899, a second house was built for the assistant keepers, and it was a two-story, wood-framed building.

The US Lighthouse Establishment was the agency that managed lighthouses in the United States. Other functions now handled by the Coast Guard were separate services. The US Life-Saving Service evolved from private organizations that did search and rescue and became a government entity in 1848. The function of armed customs enforcement started in 1790 as the Revenue Cutter Service. In 1939, these three separate services were combined into the United States Coast Guard. Lighthouse Keepers were given the option of becoming Coast Guardsmen.

Over the years, when the lighthouse was manned, there were thirty-two Head Keepers and twenty-five Assistant Keepers. The Head Keeper and his family were the island's only inhabitants for many years. Later, the Assistant Keepers and their families lived on the island as well. Initially, both families would live in the same house, but that proved to be problematic. The second house, built in 1915, resolved the problem of families living in close quarters.

When the Coast Guard took over the lighthouse maintenance and navigational aids, they lived in the assistant keepers' house. In 1954, the Coast Guard built a solid concrete single-story dwelling for their staff living on the island and demolished the old frame house. The barracks building is now used by the park ranger who lives on the island full-time. The concrete cistern from the assistant keeper's house remains the only evidence of the original house and is still used for collecting and storing non-potable water.

Aids to Navigation

Fog Bell on Egmont Key

Over the years, many supplemental aids to navigation have been used at Egmont Key Light Station. As technology has improved, they have ranged from primitive to sophisticated. There have been three different audible fog warning devices over the years. The first was a conch shell! In the *Light List* of 1907, a notation stated that a conch shell horn would be sounded during foggy conditions in response to an audible signal from a passing ship. This was replaced in February 1916 with a fog bell on the island's north end. This bell was struck via a clockwork mechanism that would be activated in fog conditions. This building is now underwater due to the erosion of the island's tip. The bell, however, is on display in a small museum near the lighthouse. The bell was cast in 1915. The last fog signal was a horn mounted on a tower next to a building that housed a compressor and large air storage tank. The date it was put in service is uncertain, but it was eventually removed along with the support equipment. The only remnants are the concrete pads on which the tower legs were mounted.

Finally, there was the low-frequency non-directional radio beacon adjacent to the compressor building, installed in 1930. The radio antenna tower was about fifty yards to the east. The radio signal was sent out omnidirectionally, and a ship or even aircraft that the proper receiver could home in on the station. The station identifier was the letter "H" in Morse Code (dot-dot-dot-dot). Two transmitters worked together at the station. One was the online radio, and the other was a standby. They were switched every Wednesday so that each radio got equal use. The procedure was to power up the standby radio and let it come to operating condition by waiting about ten minutes. The radios were equipped with vacuum tube components rather than solid-state devices. After warmup, the radios were switched, and the standby unit powered down until the following Wednesday. This procedure allowed for uninterrupted service.

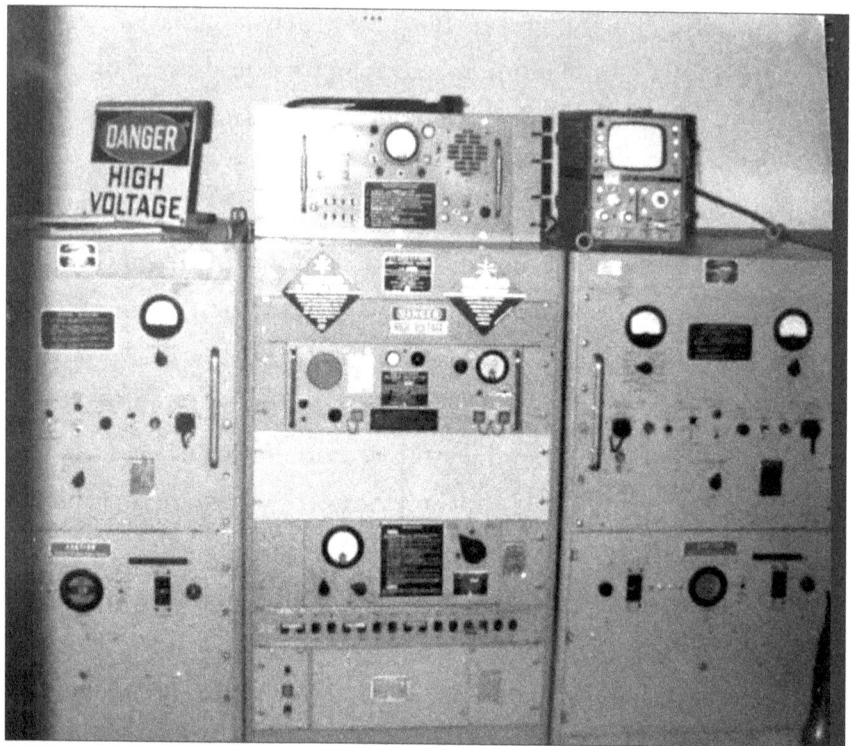

Egmont Key Radio Transmitters. Photo courtesy of David Barker

Lighthouse Beacons

The station's tower lighting has also evolved over the years. In the 1848 tower, there was a Winslow Lewis argand lamp array. Lewis's lamps were a copy of the lamp invented in 1780 by Francois-Pierre Argand of Geneva. However, Lewis used inferior materials and manufacturing methods, but his lamps were less expensive. Lewis also resisted the introduction of Fresnel lenses in the United States until it became clear that they were far better than argand lamp arrays. This tower lasted for only a few years and was replaced with a much sturdier and taller structure.

The tower that is in use today was completed in 1858 and designed to "withstand any storm." It has fulfilled that design requirement. The first light was a fixed (non-rotating) Fresnel lens manufactured in France by Augustin Henri-Lepaute, along with the cast iron lens pedestal.

A double DCB-36 rotating beacon was installed in 1944 when the site was automated. The lantern room was in disrepair, and the new beacon was too large to fit inside, so the lantern room and watch room below it were removed and a concrete pad installed. The electric motor that rotated the beacon was on a mount inside the top of the lighthouse. The rotation speed gave it a flash interval of fifteen seconds, called its night mark. Eventually, this beacon was replaced in 1989 by a series of aerobeacons, which featured self-contained electric motors, making the replacement of the beacons simpler. When a beacon needed replacement, a helicopter would lift the old one off the tower and carry the new one to the top. The DCB-36 beacon was installed near the Coast Guard flagpole as a static display.

After Hurricane Irma in 2017, the electrical wiring that fed power to the beacons was damaged, and repair or replacement was deemed too expensive. The aerobeacon was replaced with a battery-powered, solar-charged VLB-44 LED array visible for thirteen nautical miles. Due to its low intensity, this light is only used at night and is the current lighting system. It still has the same fifteen-second flash interval as the previous beacons. The beacon does not rotate, so the flash interval is via an electronic strobe.

Other Navigation Services

A buoy repair depot and associated pier were constructed in 1874. Within a few years, all buoys between St Marks and Key West were serviced there. After the Spanish-American War in 1898, Egmont Key was the site of a yellow fever quarantine camp for troops returning from service in Cuba. Part of the buoy shed was sealed and converted into a place to fumigate baggage and equipment with formaldehyde vapor. Eventually, this building was demolished, and buoys were serviced at sea by Coast Guard maintenance ships.

David Barker Interview

I met with and interviewed David Barker, past vice-president of the Egmont Key Alliance and former US Coast Guardsman who had been stationed on Egmont Key. His recollections are of the operation of the site and his day-to-day activities.

David Barker's first assignment after joining the service and completing his initial training was at the historic Egmont Key Light Station. He was assigned there from June 1974 to February 1975, working with three other Coast Guardsmen. They lived in a solid concrete barracks building that replaced the wood frame assistant keeper's house built in 1915. This concrete building was designed to be hurricane-proof.

One of the unique aspects of life at Egmont Key Light Station was the transportation method. Workers, including David Barker, were transported to and from the island via helicopter. The helicopter would land on a concrete pad about one hundred yards south and east of the tower, also used for transporting supplies. This method of travel ended when the air station moved from Albert Whitted Airport in St. Petersburg to St. Pete/Clearwater International Airport, where it still operates today. Transportation to the island was then done via boat.

The daily routine consisted of "colors" or raising the flags at 8 AM every morning. There would be some routine housekeeping tasks, but outside crews brought to the island would handle any more involved maintenance. Occasionally, they would patrol the beaches, but these patrols were infrequent. During World War II, beach patrols were done regularly, looking out for German submarines known to operate in the Gulf of Mexico.

The island has no potable water source, but the cistern left over from the old assistant keeper's house provided water for other purposes. Drinking water was brought from Mullet Key at the old Bay Pier in large plastic containers.

Egmont Key Coast Guardsmen provided local news outlets with weather information daily. The staff measured the water temperature and described the sky conditions. Later, this task was also automated.

In 1988, plans were made to have the Coast Guard vacate the fifty-five acres of Coast Guard property on the north end and turn it into a State Park. Congressman Sam Gibbons helped accomplish this management arrangement. By then, the lighthouse was the only aid to navigation, and all other aids had been decommissioned and removed. The park opened in 1989 and remains in operation.

When the State Park Service took over the supervision of Fort Dade, and the buildings were overgrown with foliage. The Guardhouse building was derelict, and one room was filled with steel pallets. They jokingly referred to it as "Howard Johnsons" because the red tile roof resembled the roof on the hotel chain. When the Egmont Key Alliance was established, one of the most successful projects was the restoration of the Guardhouse to create a visitors center. They were able to get new red tiles to replace the originals.

The Coast Guard periodically visits the island today for maintenance and repair of the lighthouse and beacon.

Chapter 22

Clara Barton

Clarissa Horton Barton was born on December 25, 1821, in North Oxford, Massachusetts, the youngest of the family of Captain Stephen Barton, an Army officer, and Sarah Stone Barton. He was considered a leader in progressive thought in Oxford Village, well-off financially, a Freemason, and a lifelong Democrat. Three of her siblings were teachers, and Clara was found to be bright and precocious. Her brother taught her to be a fearless horsewoman while helping her develop physical strength that would be necessary for her future.

Her first experiences as a caretaker and humanitarian came when her brother became seriously ill and was an invalid for two years. Clara became his sole caretaker until he recovered. She became a painfully shy, bashful, and sensitive girl, so much so that it was a cause for concern for her parents. They enlisted the help of Mr. L. W. Fowler, a phrenology[1] practitioner who gave the following assessment: "The sensitive nature will always remain," was his reply, "she will never assert herself for herself, she will suffer wrong first, but for

---

1 Phrenology was a theory of psychology based on the belief that the shape of the skull could determine certain character traits and mental faculties. It was popular in the 19th century. It is a pseudoscience theory.

others, she will be perfectly fearless. Throw responsibility upon her; give her a school to teach." Fowler was incorrect in his assessment

in that she became assertive for causes she believed in, as shown in her later endeavors.

Her early work was teaching, starting in 1838 in Canada and later in West Georgia. Her mother died in 1851 when Clara was just 30. Clara was contracted by the town leaders to open a free school in Bordentown, New Jersey, the

following year, in 1852, teaching 600 pupils. The school was so successful that it was decided to hire a male principal to run the school; the town leadership felt it was unfitting for a woman. Clara was so outraged at this slight since she had started the school that she gave up teaching altogether. She changed her career when she went to work in the United States Patent Office in Washington, DC, as a clerk in 1855. She experienced discrimination because she was a woman working in a government job. She was harassed by coworkers who tried to get her fired. Her boss protected her from this, but his successor demoted her to a copyist when he left, earning ten cents for every 100 words she copied.

The Civil War provided another career change that would dominate her life until the end. She began working with the wounded soldiers, both Confederate and Union. She helped in the aftermath of the battles at Cedar Mountain, Second Bull Run, Fredericksburg, and Antietam. There were thousands of casualties at each of these battles. She was skilled at her work because, in 1864, Union General

Benjamin Butler appointed her "Lady in Charge" of the hospitals for the Army of the James.

After the Civil War ended, Clara was chosen to run the Office of Missing Soldiers. There were tens of thousands of soldiers killed in battles, and it was an overwhelming task. She worked to identify 13,000 POWs at Andersonville, the notorious Confederate-run prison in southern Georgia. In the four years she worked at this job, she identified 20,000 Union soldiers and located 22,000 missing soldiers.

Clara became an activist in the women's suffrage and civil rights movements after the war. She was active in the Black Civil Rights Movement and the Women's Rights Movement. She collaborated closely with Susan B. Anthony and Frederick Douglass on these causes.

In 1869, Clara went to Europe, where she worked to gain recognition from the International Committee of the Red Cross. It was clear that her life's work would be working with wounded soldiers in the coming conflicts around the world. Her next endeavors were preparing military hospitals in Europe at the beginning of the Franco-Prussian War (1870-1871). In that 19-month conflict, more than 900,000 were killed and 232,000 wounded.

In 1881, she became the head of the American branch of the Red Cross. The Red Cross was not just involved with war-wounded soldiers. The organization also aided with natural disasters. The American Red Cross assisted victims in the floods in Ohio, famine in Texas in 1887, a tornado in Illinois in 1888, and the Johnstown Flood in 1889.

Clara Barton went overseas to Turkey to assist with medical services after the Hamidian Massacres. This conflict was a genocide of Armenians by the Ottoman Empire that took place between 1894 and 1896. This resulted in casualties estimated between 80,00 and 300,000, with 50,000 orphaned children.

The Spanish-American War

Barton's subsequent humanitarian work was in Cuba, a population under harsh Spanish colonial rule for many years. The Cubans had been waging guerilla warfare for thirty years to end Spanish atrocities and domination. The civilian population had suffered tremendously from disease, starvation, and imprisonment in concentration camps called reconcentrados. Tens of thousands of civilians died in these camps, which were built as a means of depriving the guerillas of civilian support in the conflict and isolating them from their families.

America's military involvement started when the *USS Maine*, an armored cruiser, went to Havana Harbor as a show of strength and support for the Cuban guerillas. An explosion on the *Maine*, later determined to originate in the coal storage bunker inside the ship, was blamed on a Spanish torpedo (underwater mine). The coal dust fire caused the detonation of five tons of gunpowder stored on the ship, sinking it within minutes with a loss of 252 sailors. The incident created the rallying cry for war: "Remember the *Maine*!"

War fever was high in the United States for several reasons. First, it was to avenge the loss of the *Maine*, then to aid the Cuban population in ridding themselves of Spanish rule. The Hearst newspapers helped to fan the flames of intervention by the United States. America also saw an opportunity to gain new possessions like the Philippines, Puerto Rico, and Guam. Finally, since it had only been thirty years since the end of the Civil War, it was seen by some as an opportunity for the states to fight a war together as one nation against a common enemy and promote reconciliation. The combat only lasted three months, with an American victory over Spain and the liberation of Cuba.

Clara Barton and the US Army

Clara Barton had been on the *USS Maine* at a reception given by Captain Charles Sigsbee the day before the explosion occurred. Clara was at work in her office the following day, and when she heard the blast of the ship, she hurried to the Spanish Hospital, San Ambrosia, to assist with the wounded sailors. Her description of the injured follows:

> "Their wounds are all over them—heads and faces terribly cut, internal wounds, arms, legs, feet and hands burned to the live flesh. The hair and beards singed, showing that the burns were from fire not steam. Further evidence shows that the burns are where the parts were uncovered. If burned by steam, the clothing would have held the steam and burned all the deeper."

Clara and the Red Cross followed Theodore Roosevelt and his Rough Riders to Guantanamo Bay, with the Rough Riders continuing on and landing near Siboney. There was resistance from Army surgeons about a woman being near a battlefront and female nurses taking care of male patients. In fact, she was the only female nurse allowed to work near the front. She was criticized because she wanted to give medical care to Spanish soldiers and have them returned to their regiments under a flag of truce.

Army officers continually told her that the front was no place for a woman and that the Army could care for its own. She faced criticism for spending too much time in the field, not at headquarters, and helping Spanish soldiers. She was criticized because she acted independently and authoritatively; it was even suggested that she was too old for the job (she was 77 at the start of the war).

QUARANTINE CAMP, EGMONT KEY, FLA.

Quarantine Camp on Egmont Key. Note Lighthouse in the Upper Left

Quarantine Camps on Mullet Key and Egmont Key There were several quarantine sites around the southeastern United States in the 1800s to protect against yellow fever, a major concern at that time. During the war, thirteen soldiers would die from yellow fever for every soldier who died in combat. The cause, at the time, was not known for certain; there was no cure available, and there had been deadly outbreaks in several US coastal cities. The cause of this dreaded disease was first theorized to be mosquito-borne by a Florida physician, Dr. John Wall[2], as early as 1857. People entering the coun-

---

2 Dr. Wall became mayor of Tampa from 1878 to 1880 and held other city offices. He contracted yellow fever in 1871 and passed it to his wife and two-year-old daughter, both of whom died. He dedicated his life to determining the cause of the disease. Dr. Walter Reed of the US Army got most of the credit for what Wall had discovered before the Spanish-American War. Wall died in 1895 and is buried in Tampa's Oaklawn Cemetery.

try were sent to a quarantine site and had to stay for up to ten days to ensure they were not infected with yellow fever.

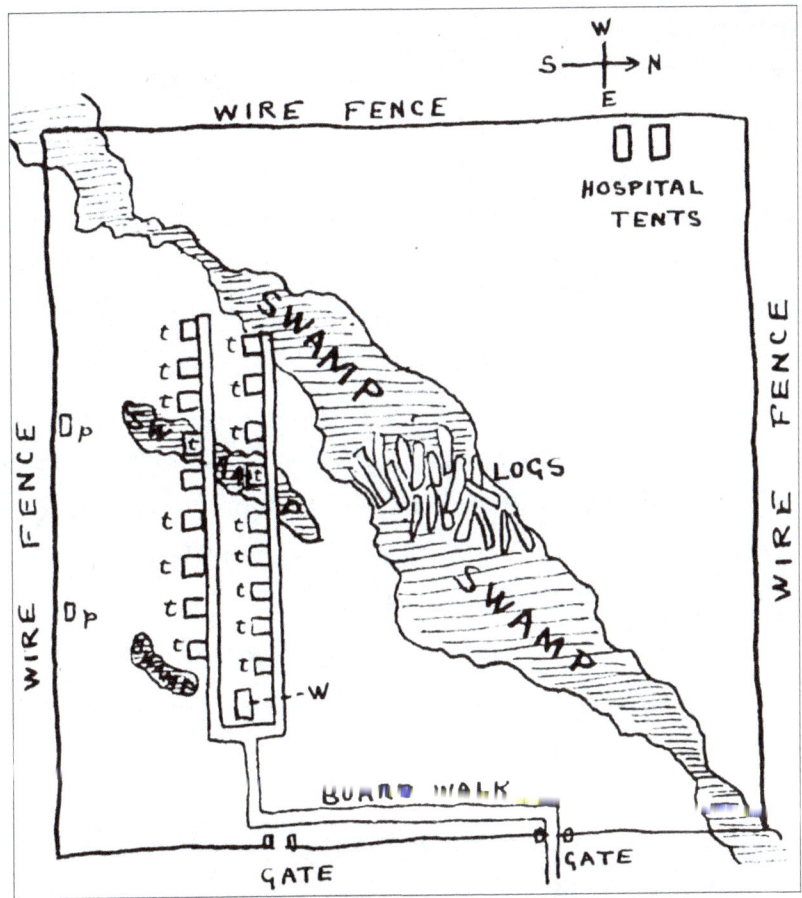

Sketch of camp made by Alfred G. Mayer. The letter "t" is tents, "p" privy and "w" is a water barrel. North is to the right in the drawing.

The quarantine camp on Mullet Key was a more permanent site operated by the Marine Hospital Service. Establishing a site at Egmont Key was in response to the urgent need for more locations because of the large number of troops and other personnel returning from Cuba. The Egmont site was officially called a "Detention Camp".

The accommodation for people was primitive at best, and it was located in a swampy area of the island on the east side. Canvas tents left over from the Civil War were sent to the island to house the people. These tents were subjected to fierce storms from the north at this time of year and proved inadequate for protecting people from the elements[3]. The camp was surrounded by a barbed wire fence as well. The food was deplorable at best, and there were clouds of mosquitoes because of the marshy areas on the island and in the camp.

These conditions made for crowding and tensions between the people forced to endure the camp. There is one documented account about a minister and his wife who were billeted with a prostitute, who was busily plying her trade while quarantined there. The minister wrote an angry three-page letter to the military complaining about the situation and the indifference of the local soldiers to do anything about it. The minister alleged that the soldiers were partaking of the prostitute's services as well.

In addition to handling people, there was an urgent need for decontamination facilities to ensure the yellow fever pathogen was not brought ashore in baggage. All personal contents of troop transport ships had to be removed and fumigated with formaldehyde vapor. What follows was from a report on those facilities:

> "Taking possession of the light-house wharf and buoy shed was a happy idea of Assistant Surgeon Corput, and without the wharf, we would have been unable to land either troops or baggage. Immediately upon taking possession of this wharf, we proceeded to construct thereon five tight chambers, each

---

3 John O'Neill, a private in Theodore Roosevelt's famed 1st US Volunteer Cavalry, the Rough Riders, came to the island with pneumonia and died after enduring one of these winter storms.

having a cubic capacity of 1,000 feet, for use as formaldehyde disinfecting chambers. We also constructed a chamber in our own disinfecting shed, having a cubic capacity of 1,300 feet, giving us a total of six chambers besides the steam chamber. Immediately upon the landing of the first troops, the disinfection was begun, using the air-tight rooms and the steam chamber, all with formalin. The first troops landed were set to work unloading baggage and pitching tents. About dark, we succeeded in landing the last of the troops, got them into camp, and had them all fed and supplied with disinfected blankets by midnight."

The detention camp on Egmont Key was not in service for very long. When the construction of permanent buildings for Fort Dade began, the military insisted that the camp be shut down, and the people relocated to the facilities Mullet Key out of fear of infecting the construction personnel.

Nurse Lucy Graves' Diary

What follows are some relevant diary entries of Nurse Lucy Graves, one of Barton's staff who left Cuba for Egmont Key and quarantine. These diary entries are from the Library of Congress Collection.

Havana, Cuba, August 31, 1898.
Wednesday.

Every day deputations come on board from Havana and the surrounding country and towns, stating the condition of the people and of their urgent need of assistance. These appeals are very pathetic in many instances, as are the floods of written appeals received. One of the most urgent is the official letter from Cienfuegos asking help for that place.

Miss Barton fell several days ago and hurt her right eye somewhat, and today flies have been troubling her a good deal, so that both eyes have become sore; we fear that they have been poisoned by the flies.

Havana, Cuba September 1, 1898
Thursday

It is decided by Miss Barton that the best thing, and in fact, the only thing to be done now is to meet all obligations here, pay the fine of five hundred dollars imposed by the government here, and return to the United States. Accordingly, the necessary arrangements are made in view to leaving in the afternoon, but Captain Wursch is opposed to leaving until morning and neglects to have the fires up, thus delaying us till after nightfall and necessitating the payment of double pilotage—fifty instead of twenty-five dollars. Miss Barton is feeling very sick but asks for an interview with the officers of the *Comal*, and they call accordingly. When told of her decision to leave Havana, Captain Miles said: "How I wish, Miss Barton, that we could just weigh anchor and sail away with you." They are thoroughly tired of the business entrusted to them but must, of course, await instructions from home. (In connection with our departure from Havana, see attached short pages for the press written by Miss Barton's direction).

En route to Tampa, September 2, 1898.
Friday

Miss Barton continues quite ill, her eyes troubling her a great deal, so little office work is done. Miss Graves is day and Miss Fowler is night nurse, and Dr Egan is the attending physician. There is a little sea on (rough seas), so none of the ladies are feeling quite well. We bring the mules with us and will send them through to New Orleans in charge of young Cottrell and the two colored men who came from that place. Mr. C.H.H. Cottrell will also go to New Orleans and rejoin Miss Barton in Washington. Beautiful moonlit evening we are having now.

Egmont Key, September 3, 1898.
Saturday
Showers in afternoon.

Early this morning, we arrived at the quarantine station, the doctors came aboard, and we were ordered to Egmont Key for detention and disinfection. We are glad to hear we will be there only five days, and so do not complain, though we all know how anxious Miss Barton is to get north. We reach Egmont Key in the forenoon, but do not go ashore till late afternoon, the interim being spent in packing our personal and office belongings. The men are hard at work getting off the cargo, and work until long after midnight as it will be hard to get laborers tomorrow, Sunday. The three ladies are assigned to a very nice house, and the men are made as comfortable as possible in tents. Everything is, however, beautifully clean, and the physicians have given their table to us, eating later themselves. Miss Barton is glad to find in the chief surgeon here, Dr. Geddings, the son in law of her old friend, Mrs. Moses of South Carolina. The only drawback to a very pleasant stay here is the mosquitoes—their name is legion, and they are simply ferocious. Our baggage is, of course, left at the office for fumigation, but we are allowed to bring our satchels to the house, and so make the necessary arrangements for the house. For a time at least, Miss Barton is to have her meals brought to her, though her eyes are much better.

Egmont Key, September 4, 1898
Sunday.
Storms in afternoon.

In the morning, the entire party were busy unpacking and sorting clothing in the trunks for fumigation, and after the process, drying and repacking it. Miss Graves made several copies of a paper for Mr. Cottrell—a tribute to Miss Barton from her staff. A dozen copies of an article for the papers were made. Dr. Partello, who is in charge of Red Cross work at Tampa, Fla., has promised to see that it gets to the Associated Press; he will call for it tomorrow morning.

Miss Barton's eyes are much better, but she still does not go to table (to eat).

The *Clinton* leaves the dock and anchors some distance out to take on coal, which has come down from Tampa.

Egmont Key, September 5, 1898
Monday.
Storm in afternoon.

Clinton comes in and Mr. Cottrell and his son come ashore. Miss Barton calls a meeting of the entire party while the two gentlemen are with us and asks that all financial matters be arranged at this time with Mr. Cottrell, as she has nothing whatever to do with money matters and wishes them fixed up before the accountant leaves. The expedition closes at this point, and all salaries must, of course, be discontinued. All the party except Messrs. Cottrell will proceed to Washington from New Orleans after having arranged matters there. Miss Barton expressed her regret that the party must break up, and also that we were returning to our homes without having accomplished the relief of the island of Cuba. She called attention to the fact that the Red Cross relieved Santiago in less than a week and said she was certain that Havana and the surrounding country could have been fully relieved in six three and the entire island in six weeks had we been allowed to work. There will, of course, be medical work for a year or more to overcome the effects of famine and disease, but the work of relieving the actual starvation, of putting food into hungry mouths could, in the hands of experienced and energetic Red Cross people, could have been accomplished inlLess than six weeks

Monday, September 5, continued..

Speaking of the refusal of the Havana authorities to allow the Red Cross to land supplies, Miss Barton said, "There was nothing left for the Red Cross but to accept the decision, draw its anchor, and come away to the land of our birth, which we have done. Each one of the party from that time was free. I had no more occasion for help, you understand, and sorry, sorry enough I was. I would be so glad to know today that I was free to go over to that island and, with your help, finish up the work, and all go home with the work done; but we cannot do it, therefore other persons must finish it. Under the military, the Government will probably take it up. There is Cuban relief work in New York and will probably want to use its funds; they will not, however, use them through me and we want that perfectly understood, in order that each may know what to expect. There must never be one minute of misunderstanding between me and my staff, my officers and my workmen. The following telegrams was written and sent:

September 6, Egmont Key

"Please arrange transportation Port Tampa to Washington for Clara Barton, Lucy M. Graves, Anne M. Fowler, J. G. Hubbell, E. W. Egan, A. Van Schelle, J. A. McDowell, J. K. Elwell, Chas. R. Gill, Geo. J. Hassett, Jos. Langley, and Miguel Cervantes. Party will be out of quarantine ready to leave probably Sunday, possibly before. I go to New Orleans on steamer. Please send me pass New Orleans to Washington, care Western Union Telegraph, New Orleans."

The following article appeared in *Harpers Weekly* on this day:

RED CROSS AND RED TAPE

"There has been a good deal of apparent friction between the Red Cross and the medical authorities in the army, but we are inclined to think that it has been more apparent than real. We know that many of the best surgeons of the army have accepted the Red Cross aid and relief not only willingly but gladly, and we have read testimonials written from the front by regular surgeons to the efficiency of Miss Barton and her aids. A good deal of trouble has been caused by the red tape system prevailing in the army, but this system is not to be charged to the medical department, although it's responsible for much, or to any executive department. It comes from the disposition of Congress in every administrative function of the Government. The result of this interference is that not a dollar can be expended, and not a bit of property of the Government used, without following certain minute directions contained in statutes, except at the personal risk of the man primarily responsible. An instance of this petty character of Congressional interference in administrative functions is furnished by a story, which we have recently heard, of an officer who hired a tug, in an emergency for the purpose of hauling into the stream a ship that was on fire, and which threatened some very valuable Government stores upon the wharf, which were in his charge. This was illegal—that is unstatutory—on the part of the officer, who under the law, should have advertised for bids for hauling out the vessel. The consequences to him were very unfortunate. He paid the captain of the tug out of his own pocket, and a grateful country—meaning Congress—did not appropriate the money to repay him till two years had gone by. The medical department is hampered and tied up, as all other administrative departments are, by Congressional acts such as that which made this officer smart for his diligence. The Red Cross has encountered this kind of entanglement, and we trust its officers and aids know where the responsibility lies. As to the Red Cross itself, and Miss Barton in Particular, most work has been done, great self-sacrifices have been made, and enormous good has been accomplished. Miss Barton is of the heroic figures of the war, and the suggestion that she should be the first woman ever thanked by Congress is one worthy of serious consideration."

Barton, New York.

Post War Endeavors

After returning to Tampa, Clara Barton and her staff spent one night at the Tampa Bay Hotel before boarding a train for New York. Her last fieldwork was assisting the victims of the 1900 Galveston hurricane. She established an orphanage there for the children.

After being criticized for mixing personal and professional resources, she was forced to resign as president of the American Red Cross in 1904. She was 83 years old. She continued to reside in Glen Echo, Maryland, which had been the Headquarters of the ARC since 1897. At this time, she published her autobiography, *The Story of My Childhood*. She died on April 12, 1912, at age 90 from tuberculosis.

Chapter 23

Major Francis Langhorne Dade

C ountless articles and books about Major Francis Dade and his final days in Florida have been written. The late Frank Laumer authored several books on the battle and spent many days in the field, walking the old Fort King Military Road route, which connected Fort Brooke in Tampa with Fort King in Ocala. He even had the remains exhumed of Private Ransom Clarke, who survived the battle and made his way back to Tampa to see if Clarke had been wounded five times, as his account of the battle claimed. Ransom Clarke's telling of the story had been accurate since the remains indicated five injuries.

Francis Dade was born in King George County, Virginia, on February 22, 1792, to parents Townshend and Elizabeth Dade. The Dade family lineage goes back to England.

He attended the Military Academy at West Point, but his first assignment was a field promotion, not from the academy. He started as a 3rd Lieutenant in the 12th Infantry Regiment on March 29, 1813. Two years later, he was transferred to the 4th Infantry Regiment. A year after that, he was promoted to 1st Lieutenant. Dade was again promoted, this time to Captain, on February 14, 1818.

He met and married Amanda Malvina Middleton of Pensacola, Florida, in 1826. His only child, Fannie Langhorne Dade, was born in 1830.

In 1825 and 1826, Dade led troops from Fort Brooke in Tampa to Fort King near present-day Ocala. In 1826, Captain Dade commanded an infantry company, which, along with another company, established the route that

Major Francis Langhorne Dade

would later become the Fort King Military Road. This road was twelve feet wide and cleared of trees, with the stumps being cut short enough to permit the passage of wagon axles. This road ran very near the present-day US Highway 301. These experiences would play a part in his life a decade later when he led the ill-fated 1835 trip. Meanwhile, he was made Brevet[1] Major on February 24, 1828.

Before the start of the Second Seminole War, Brevet Major Dade was stationed at Key West in command of the Army post. This assignment would eventually expand to include the southern part of Florida from Cape Florida to Charlotte Harbor. In December 1835, he was sent along with Company B of the 4th Regiment to Fort Brooke aboard the schooner *Motto*. This company would soon be sent to Fort King.

---

1 Brevet ranks were given to officers for meritorious service but without a corresponding increase in pay to the regular rank. So, a Brevet Major would still be receiving Captain's pay.

Initially, Captain George Washington Gardiner of Fort Brooke was assigned to lead the 108 infantry and artillerymen to reinforce Fort King, which had been threatened by attack from the Seminoles. The garrison there was inadequate for its defense. However, Captain Gardiner's wife had been seriously ill, and Dade offered to lead the expedition to Fort King in his place. He had traveled this road twice before and knew the route better than anyone.

As Captain Gardiner was sitting on his horse, preparing to leave, he accepted Major Dade's offer to lead the column north to Fort King. On December 23, 1835, Dade and his troops set out for Fort King, about a six-day journey away. Meanwhile, Captain Gardiner had family in Key West, and the medical facilities and climate were better there, so he decided to send his wife and children to be cared for by family. They boarded the *Motto,* which was returning to Key West.

Shortly after leaving Fort Brooke, Major Dade was forced to leave his lone six-pounder cannon behind on the trail since the oxen used to pull it were not up to the task. Dade sent word back to Fort Brooke detailing his predicament and requesting a team of horses be brought to him to pull the cannon. Captain Gardiner saw his chance to rejoin the column, so he volunteered for the task. He caught up with the column after bringing a team of horses and using them to pull the cannon and limber. Captain Gardiner's decision to return to the expedition would prove to be fateful in just a few days.

The soldiers knew that a small force of Seminoles had been shadowing the column, at least since they had crossed the Hillsborough River. When they were encamped each night, they could hear the warriors' shouts and war cries. However, they had no idea of the size of the force that was gathering to ambush them when the time was right.

That day came on December 28, 1835, about a day's march away from Fort King. The Seminoles had fired no shots during the night to worry the troops. The terrain was more open, which made it less likely there would be an attack. Major Dade had been most concerned about river crossings since they would have been more vulnerable with part of the column on each side of a river till the crossing was complete. As a precaution, the column had troops that moved along with the column but flanked the main column. In addition, there would be advanced guards and a rear guard to prevent surprise attacks. These precautions slowed the advance of the column, and on December 28, Dade and his officers made a decision that would prove to be disastrous.

To speed the advance towards Fort King, the officers decided to bring in the troops that flanked the main column. This action by the soldiers allowed the Seminoles to get closer to the column when they attacked. Even though they expected more warriors to join them soon, the Seminoles stalking Dade's column decided to attack as they approached the present-day site of Bushnell. The column was getting near Fort King, and the warriors were concerned that troops from the fort might come to the rescue if they waited much longer. The soldiers had been lulled into believing an attack was unlikely since they were so close to the fort and in more open country, and they were looking forward to a belated Christmas celebration when they reached Fort King. The trap was set!

The Seminole force was now at nearly one hundred and eighty warriors and were waiting in ambush on the west side of the road when the column of soldiers arrived. The first volley of rifle fire from the Seminoles killed or wounded half the soldiers, including Major Dade and most of the officers. Captain Gardiner was one of only two officers left after the initial volley, and he assumed command of the remaining troops. The soldiers fired at the elusive Seminoles who were hiding among the palmettos, pines, and live oaks. The cannon was brought into action and fired at the warriors with little effect. The warriors were wary of artillery since they had no effective defense against them.

After the initial fighting, the warriors withdrew a short distance to decide how to finish the battle. Meanwhile, the soldiers put up a small log enclosure with the artillery piece just outside. This tactic by the soldiers greatly simplified the task of ending the battle for the Seminoles. They picked off the soldiers, one by one, including the artillerymen. All the ammunition for the cannon was fired. Captain Gardiner, who had relinquished his command at the start of the expedition to Major Dade and then rejoined the column, was among the last to fall with several gunshot wounds.

The Army Returns to the Dade Battle Site

Only three soldiers and one civilian scout survived when the battle ended and left the battlefield. Privates Ransom Clark, Edward DeCourcey, and Joseph Sprague managed to avoid being killed by the warriors as they walked the battle site looking for survivors..

The Seminoles took anything of military value from the dead but refrained from taking personal items. Private Sprague crawled to a nearby pond, hid in the brush, and was undetected. The other two survivors began making their way back down the road towards Tampa and safety. Privates Clark and DeCourcey were helping each other down the road when a warrior on horseback came up the trail and spotted them. The two soldiers split up, each going off the trail in an attempt to elude the warrior who was searching for survivors. The warrior went after DeCourcey and killed him. He then looked for Private Clark but was unable to find him.

Even after being wounded five times, Ransom Clark eventually returned to Fort Brooke and told the soldiers there what had happened. An enslaved man named Louis Pacheco, who had been forced to scout for the expedition, and Private Joseph Sprague lived to tell their stories of the battle.

It was six weeks later before the Army felt they had gathered enough soldiers to return to the battlefield to bury the dead safely. When they arrived, the trees were filled with hundreds of vultures that had been feasting on the bodies to the point that most were just skeletons. The remains were quickly buried at the location of the log enclosure. Later, the Army returned to the site and relocated the remains to the National Cemetery in St. Augustine, inside vaults underneath coquina pyramids. Private Ransom Clark wrote a memoir about the battle but lived only a few years more; his premature death was probably the result of his injuries that were inflicted at the battle.

Major Dade's wife returned to Pensacola and lived there until 1867, receiving half his annual salary until her death. Dade's daughter, who would have been five years old when he left Tampa for Fort King, lived until 1848.

An Interesting Story

While visiting a local museum, I read a handout that listed facts about Egmont Key's history. One of the "facts" was that Major Dade had once visited Egmont Key to hunt deer. In all my research on Major Dade, I found nothing corroborating this statement. So, the question is, could this have happened?

It's shown in the historical records that Dade had been in Florida in 1825 and 1826, traveling between Fort Brooke and Fort King. He returned to Tampa from Key West in December of 1835 to bring troops that would eventually reinforce Fort King. The two earlier expeditions may have been an opportunity for a hunting trip.

Were there deer on Egmont Key? At that time, the island was more than 580 acres, and that is enough acreage to support a small herd of deer. The only problem with that possibility is the shortage of fresh water on the island. There were marshy areas and some small springs, which made it more likely. It is known from the historical accounts of lighthouse keeper Charles Moore that he hunted deer on nearby Mullet Key, claiming to have killed nearly 200 over the years. Was it possible that Major Dade might have been on Mullet Key instead? The story of Major Dade hunting deer on Egmont Key is possible but will probably never be known for certain.

Dade's Legacy

If he had ever come to the island, Major Dade would not have been the most famous of Egmont Key's many visitors for hundreds of years. Robert E. Lee and Clara Barton are more well-known among the many visitors. Dade, however, has had more places named in his honor around Florida. Dade City and Dade County are the most obvious. He had two forts named after him, one from the Second

Seminole War and the one we know today on Egmont Key. The battle site is now a state historic site with a museum and a short section of the Fort King Military Road preserved where the fateful ambush occurred. There is a replica of the log enclosure that was built in an attempt to protect the soldiers. Every December 28, a memorial ceremony is held at the park to remember the sacrifices made by both sides that day. On the first full weekend in January, there is a reenactment each day near the original battlefield to tell the stories of both sides, Seminole and soldier, and to honor both. There is a monument at the West Point Military Academy in honor of Major Dade.

Chapter 24

The Story of Fort Dade

The origins of present-day Fort Dade and its sister site, Fort DeSoto, go back to 1849, just five years after Florida became a state. At that time, major seaports in the United States were protected from potential enemy attack by the construction of coastal fortifications. In 1849, the Board of Engineers (forerunner of the Corps of Engineers) sent an expedition around the coast of Florida to survey sites for future coastal defenses.

The group stopped at fifteen sites along the way, with Egmont Key and nearby Mullet Key among them. They recommended that these islands be reserved for possible future military use. Lee commented at the time that the entrance to Tampa Bay would be difficult to defend due to the size of the bay. His assessment was based on the range and accuracy of the artillery at the time, which didn't have the improvements that would be developed during the coming Civil War. These technical advances, such as rifled bores, would not be available for another twelve years but would dramatically improve artillery range and accuracy.

The property reservations were form alized in 1870, and the islands were not used for permanent military fortifications for the next twenty-nine years. Egmont Key had a lighthouse, and Mullet Key had a quarantine station operated by the Marine Hospital Service for people arriving from the Caribbean to prevent the spread of yellow fever. The Army had used the island as an internment site for Seminoles awaiting relocation to reservations from 1856 to 1858. the Union Navy used Egmont during the Civil War as a coaling station to prevent blockade runners from getting through. These were temporary uses of the island, and the military abandoned the island after the war.

In 1898, the tensions in Cuba finally erupted into war between the United States and Spain when the armored cruiser *USS Maine* exploded in Havana Harbor. Even though a Spanish mine did not cause the explosion, the United States saw the opportunity to both assist the Cuban rebels who had been fighting Spanish oppression for thirty years, as well as engage in a bit of imperialism. The US government saw an opportunity to get control of the Philippines, Puerto Rico, and Guam, all Spanish possessions. The US government also thought it might be an excellent way to help heal the divisions caused by the Civil War by fighting another war as a reunited country.

Henry B. Plant, the railroad, steamship, and hotel magnate, had many friends in Congress and convinced them that his newly completed Tampa Bay Hotel would be a suitable headquarters for planning and implementing the war. The hotel was not used during the hot summers in Florida, so this would be an opportunity to profit during a slack time. His rail line ended at Port Tampa City, and a spur line went to the Tampa Bay Hotel, where troops could depart for Cuba.

It was decided by the Army to follow Plant's suggestion, and soon, tens of thousands of soldiers and horses converged on the sleepy city of Tampa, overwhelming the inhabitants and straining municipal services. There was concern that Tampa, which only had the small Fort Brooke as a defense, might be attacked by the Spanish Navy, which was thought to be in the Caribbean waters. Such an attack would disrupt military operations and threaten the city. It was decided by the Army to hastily construct two gun batteries behind earthworks on Egmont Key, one at the north end next to the main shipping channel and another to the south, covering that smaller channel. Each battery housed two small cannons, which would have been woefully inadequate for stopping enemy warships. It was soon realized that the Spanish Navy was nowhere in the area, and the artillery was later shipped to Cuba for use in the conflict.

The war lasted only three months, but Henry Plant saw another opportunity for Tampa. Once again, using his friends in Congress, he convinced the Army that Tampa needed to be included in the coast defense network. Tampa was now a growing city and had become well known nationally and internationally due to the wartime activities there. Congress agreed, and since they had previously reserved Egmont Key and Mullet Key for military use, plans were made to build Fort Dade and Fort DeSoto, with Dade being the main fort and DeSoto being secondary but capable of operating independently if needed.

As construction started in 1899, the Army was concerned about the Quarantine Detention Camp that had been hastily built on the island's east side, near the lighthouse and buoy repair shed. The camp was considered temporary due to the large number of troops returning from Cuba, which would have overwhelmed the more permanent station on Mullet Key. The Army was concerned that an outbreak of yellow fever among the construction workers would disrupt the fort's completion. The detention camp was closed, and the construction work continued.

Fort Dade stands out among US coastal forts due to its unique design as a Fourth System (Endicott[1] Era) installation. Unlike its predecessors, Fort Dade was constructed from steel-reinforced concrete, with earthen embankments to the front and sides, strategically placed as additional protection and for camouflage. This innovative design provided protection from modern naval artillery and concealed and protected the gun crews operating each battery. These batteries would appear to the enemy as nothing more than beach dunes. This forward-thinking design only hardened the command, control, communication structures, and firing positions. On April 4, 1900, General Order 43 formally named the Egmont Key installation "Fort Dade" in honor of Major Francis Langhorne Dade.

Third System forts are like Fort Clinch near Amelia Island, Florida, with imposing masonry walls, bastions, and sometimes tiers of artillery. There are other defensive structures like moats, drawbridges, and structures to protect the main gate from direct artillery fire. They were expensive to build and maintain, and improvements in artillery, such as exploding projectiles, rifled cannons, and breech-loading, rendered Third System forts obsolete. However, many Third System forts, such as Fort Pickens at Pensacola, were modified with artillery and batteries as recommended by the Endicott Board.

Work continued at Fort Dade for several years with the construction of five gun batteries of varying calibers and mine casemate buildings on each end of the island to store and operate moored underwater mines that would be placed in the channels if needed. In

---

1 In 1885, President Grover Cleveland appointed a Board of Fortifications headed by Secretary of War William Endicott, comprised of Army, Navy, and civilian members. The board recommended modernizing the Coast Defense forts to counter improvements in enemy warships. The board is commonly referred to as the Endicott Board.

addition, a telephone bunker and other storage bunkers were built. At the peak of activity, Fort Dade had about seventy buildings, including a gymnasium, fire station, bakery, power plant, and hospital. There were numerous barracks, housing for officers, a tennis court, and single-family homes for civilian workers. A narrow-gauge train brought supplies from the Quartermaster Dock to the gun batteries and coal to the power plant. A small airstrip allowed military planes to land on the island. It was a small city with families and their children, civilian workers, infantry and support troops, and even some cavalry troops.

In its early years, the fort had about three hundred soldiers plus families and civilian workers. During World War I, the number of soldiers increased to more than a thousand because Fort Dade became a training site for artillerymen needed in Europe. The fort was shut down in 1922, and a small caretaker group was left behind.

Like many coastal forts, this fort became a victim of improved military technology. Ship artillery received more technical development and grew in caliber, accuracy and range, outclassing forts like Dade. In addition, the development of airplanes as a military weapon made coastal forts vulnerable to detection and bombardment from the air.

Eventually, the cannons were removed to be used elsewhere, made into historical monuments, or scrapped. During World War II, Egmont was used for training, and the lighthouse was used as an observation tower, looking for German U-boats prowling in the Gulf of Mexico. During that war, most metal structures were removed from the site to contribute to the many scrap metal drives civilians held to support the war effort.

Postscript

In 2023, I was asked to give a presentation to the Friends of the Island Library on Anna Maria Island. I gave what I thought to be a pretty complete talk covering the major topics about Fort Dade and the Egmont Key Lighthouse. A few days later, I received an email from someone who had attended the presentation. She asked me why I had not mentioned the barracks that had been moved from Fort Dade to Anna Maria and were now part of the Bungalow Beach Resort properties. I had never heard this story, so I began researching the history of Fort Dade after 1922 when the fort had been taken out of service. I had the pleasure of meeting A. Gale Luper and her family, who operate the resort.

The historical account she told me about was that several buildings that make up the resort were supposed to have been barged over to the island from Fort Dade and renovated to be used as vacation cottages. This story had been handed down from two previous owners of the property. So, I began by consulting history books about Anna Maria and looking online at Newspapers.com. This is where historical research becomes a little bit of detective work!

In the late 1920s and early 1930s, the government began auctioning off items on Fort Dade that were "moveable." This could have been vehicles, machinery, tools, and contents of the buildings there. It could also have included buildings since they could be moved. Records compiled by historian Bruce McCall show that many years ago, barracks[2] were built in 1918 when the fort was expanded to accommodate the surge in occupancy due to World War I. Officers'

---

2 The term "barracks" is not technically correct. Barracks are for housing groups of soldiers, while the buildings at Anna Maria are single-family officers' quarters. However, the term barracks is more understood as military housing and is an acceptable word to use in this instance.

housing had been built before 1918. They were two-story buildings that had been demolished when the fort closed. The 1918 officers' housing was simpler one-story buildings. This is similar to the style of buildings at the Bungalow Beach Resort.

Researching the history of Anna Maria Island, one finds that a building was brought to the island by a barge from Parrish down the Manatee River. This shows that buildings had been repurposed from other places and brought to the island. In her research with the Manatee County Library, Ms. Luper found out that several, but not all, buildings had been built on site, and there were records of who paid for the construction. So, what about the other buildings? It is very likely that the other buildings were indeed at Fort Dade and brought to Anna Maria Island when the fort property was being sold off. If government records could be found that showed the sale at auction, that would be irrefutable proof. These buildings would be the only surviving structures from Fort Dade besides the Guardhouse. (Authors note: tragically, these buildings fell victim to Hurricanes Helene and Milton. They were damaged beyond repair and will be demolished).

Today, the concrete gun batteries and other structures are silent and slowly deteriorating. Two of the batteries on the south end have been lost to erosion as well as the mine casemate on the south end. At this writing, the US Coast Guard owns the north fifty-five acres, and the U.S. Fish and Wildlife owns the south 150 acres, managed as a wildlife refuge and bird sanctuary. The Florida Park Service co-manages the island with USFWS, and a ranger lives on the island year-round. The Tampa Bay Harbor Pilots also operate from the island in a ten-acre private compound.

Chapter 25

The Fort Dade Gun Batteries

Battery Mellon

This battery, the northernmost emplacement on the island, was named after Army Captain Charles Mellon and was the first permanent battery to be constructed on the island. In 1904, General Order 194, issued and published, formally renamed it Battery John Mellon.

General Order 194

Battery Charles Mellon, in honor of Captain Charles Mellon, 2d US Artillery, who was killed in action with Seminole Indians at the head of Lake Monroe. Florida, February 8, 1837.

Charles Mellon was born in Pennsylvania in 1794 (approximately). Nothing is published about his early life, but records show that he entered the military during the War of 1812 and was sent to Michigan to fight against the British. He was made 3rd Lieutenant in 1814 in the Army First Artillery. By 1816, he was a 2nd Lieutenant and sent to Baltimore, Maryland. He was later stationed at Fort Gratiot, Michigan, where he met his future wife, Eliza A. Scott of Detroit.

They married in Michigan and had their first child, Mary Ann, in 1825. Their first son, Charles William, was born in Baltimore in 1827 while Mellon worked in the Ordnance Department. The Mellon family relocated to Pennsylvania in 1831 wheretheir third child, Matilda, was born. In 1833, the fourth child, Henry, was born at Fort Monroe, Virginia.

The Mellon family remained at Fort Monroe until Lieutenant Mellon was sent to Florida to fight in the Second Seminole War in early 1835. He was present at the Battle of the Withlacoochee, which occurred just three days after the massacre of Dade's command at present-day Bushnell, Florida. After the Battle of the Withlacoochee, he was promoted to the rank of Captain due to his bravery and valor under fire. He was placed in command of the 2nd Artillery and held that post till his death.

Captain Mellon returned to his wife and family at Fort Monroe, Virginia on a long furlough (June to December 1836) from his duties in Florida. Eliza became pregnant with their fifth child. He soon returned to Florida and was tasked with locating a site for a camp that would eventually be named Fort Monroe.

Fort Monroe was a newly established supply depot on the shore of the St. Johns River near Lake Monroe. It was a three-sided picket fence, with the fourth side open toward the river to allow supply boats to land.

On that fateful day, several hundred Seminoles led by King Phillip and Coacoochee attacked before sunrise. The date was February 8, 1837. The fierce battle lasted for three hours, and the Seminole warriors were routed with the help of artillery aboard a ship anchored on the lake. A single shot to the chest killed Captain Mellon. He was the only fatality, but there were about fourteen soldiers wounded in the encounter. He was buried nearby with a simple wooden marker.

His commander, General Fanning, issued a proclamation that Fort Monroe be renamed Fort Mellon.

Twenty days later, Major General Macomb wrote to the President of the United States with a list of officers who "highly distinguished themselves in the several affairs in which they were engaged in the course of the war with the Creek and Seminole Indians and for uniformly meritorious services and good conduct during these campaigns. These officers are deemed to be entitled to the special consideration of the President for their gallantry and good conduct and are respectfully recommended as deserving of being brevetted." Captain Mellon was thus promoted to "Major by Brevet" for his actions at the Battle of the Withlacoochee as well as the battle at Lake Monroe. A few months after the death of Captain Mellon, his wife gave birth to their fifth child, Eliza.

A small town founded near the battle site was named Mellonville after Captain Mellon. This town eventually became part of the city of Sanford. Fort Mellon was eventually abandoned, like many forts built during the Seminole conflict. A historical marker now stands at the site of the fort.

After the founding of Fort Dade in Tampa Bay, the first and northernmost battery was informally called Battery Number One. This battery featured 8-inch caliber artillery installed on barbette[1] mounts. After Battery Macintosh was constructed several hundred yards to the south, the 8-inch artillery barrels on Battery Number One were removed and installed on the disappearing carriages[2] there. Battery Number One was renamed "Battery Charles Mellon."

---

1 Barbette Mount is a type of mount where the gun rotates on an axis left and right to aim it, and it is raised on the mount, allowing it to fire over a parapet.

2 Disappearing artillery carriages are articulated mounts that allow the gun to be raised from the loading position to fire over a wall or other protection, with the recoil returning the gun to the loading position.

Battery Mellon was then rebuilt to house three 3-inch rapid-fire, masking parapet guns to cover approaches to the underwater mines that could be placed in the channel in wartime. When Fort Dade was decommissioned in 1922, the artillery pieces were removed and eventually scrapped.

Battery Howard

The middle battery on the island's north end, is named after Guy Howard. He was born on December 16, 1855, at the Kennebec Arsenal, Augusta, Maine. He was the first of seven children of General Oliver Otis Howard[3] and Elizabeth Ann (Waite). Not much is known about his early life, but it was most certainly typical of a military family.

Oliver Otis Howard, a noted officer in the US Army, having led troops in the first Battle of Bull Run and the Battle of Seven Pines. During the latter battle he won the Medal of Honor but lost his arm after being wounded. Howard returned to duty in 1863 and later received criticism when his corps broke during the Battles of Chancellorsville and Gettysburg. Transferred to the Western Theater, Howard rose to command the Army of Tennesee during Sherman's March to the Sea. After the war served as Superintendent at West Point. He founded Howard University and served as commissioner of the Freedman's Bureau.

Guy Howard entered the regular army as a Second Lieutenant on August 31, 1876. He was promoted to First Lieutenant in 1882 and assigned to the 12th Infantry. Guy Howard married Jeannie

---

3 Oliver O. Howard has a Tampa connection as well. In 1851, the first permanent Methodist church was built in downtown Tampa. The pastor was Leroy G. Lesley. In this church, Oliver Howard became a Methodist.

Woolworth in Douglas County, Nebraska, on February 14, 1884. The couple had two children, Helen, born in 1884, and Otis Woolworth, born in 1887.

In 1893, he was promoted to Captain and assigned to the Quartermaster Department. On May 12, 1893, Howard was advanced to Quartermaster and Major of Volunteers. His career progressed

Guy Howard

quickly, and he became Chief Quartermaster as a Lieutenant Colonel.

Guy Howard's first combat actions occurred in the Philippines. This combat was the result of the Spanish-American War of 1898 and the naval battle with the Spanish Navy at Manila. Admiral Dewey and the US Navy quickly and soundly defeated the Spanish Navy. The United States government saw an opportunity to keep the Philippines as a naval base in the Pacific and a colony. The Filipino population disagreed with the colonial ambitions of the United States, and guerilla warfare broke out to get the occupying Army forces to leave the Philippines.

Guy Howard was killed in action on October 11, 1899, near Arayat, Province of Pampanga. He was one of eleven soldiers reported killed that day.

A Death Notice in the *San Francisco Call*, November 1899, reads:

MAJOR GUY HOWARD BORNE TO THE GRAVE

"OMAHA, Nebr. Nov.2 – Major Guy Howard, who was killed in the Philippines last October, was buried here today with military honors in Prospect Hill Cemetery. The funeral was private and was conducted at the residence of J. M. Woolworth, father-in-law of the major, and included only the burial service of the Episcopal Church, read by Bishop Williams, assisted by Dean Fair. Military funeral rites had been observed in Manila on October 25. At the conclusion of the services the body was borne to the cemetery in charge of six commissioned officers from Fort Crook and an escort of 100 men commanded by Captain Purcell of the Tenth Infantry. At the funeral was General Oliver O. Howard and Mrs. Howard, the parents; Miss Howard, a Mister James, Henry and Chauncy, and John Howard, brothers; General Charles Howard, an uncle: the wife. Mrs. Howard, relatives of Mr. Woolworth's family, army officers from headquarters in the city, and a few old and intimate family friends."

Construction of Battery Howard began at Fort Dade in July 1903 and was completed in August 1904. It consisted of two six-inch disappearing guns, an ammunition magazine, a generator room, housing for personnel, and an observation platform. Erosion has significantly damaged this battery in the 1970s, but parts are still open to the public.

Battery McIntosh

James Simmons McIntosh came from a long family heritage of military service. They were known as the "Fighting McIntosh's." His father, John McIntosh, was a Revolutionary War hero; his siblings and children all had military careers. His mother was Sara Swinton.

James McIntosh was born in 1784 in Liberty County, Georgia. Not much is known of his early life. He married Eliza Matthews Shumate.

James S McIntosh

His military service in the US Army began with his participation in the War of 1812. He also fought in a brief border war with Canada (part of the War of 1812) in 1814. He was severely wounded in a battle near Buffalo, New York.

He fought in the Creek War (1813-1814), also called the Creek Civil War, since there were two opposing Creek factions. It took place primarily in Alabama and Georgia. The war ended with the Creeks surrendering 21 million acres in southern Georgia.

James McIntosh received several promotions in the following years: Captain in 1817, Major in 1836, and Lieutenant Colonel in 1839.

His subsequent involvement in combat came in the Mexican War (1846-1848). This war was fought over the annexation of Texas since the Mexican government refused to recognize the Treaties of Velasco, signed by General Santa Ana after the battle at the San Jacinto.

McIntosh was severely wounded by bayonets at the battle at Resaca de la Palma in 1846. He led his troops in the battle at Palo Alto. He was fatally wounded at the storming of El Molino del Rey on September 8, 1847, and died on September 26. His remains were returned from Mexico after the war, paid for by the State of Georgia, to the family vault and interred with military honors.

His sons continued the McIntosh military service traditions. Son James McQueen McIntosh was a General in the Confederate Army and was killed in action in Arkansas. His other son, James Baillie McIntosh, served in the Union Army and lost a leg at Winchester, Virginia.

The 8-inch disappearing gun battery[4] was named Battery McIntosh in General Order 78 on May 25, 1903. It was in service until 1922, when Fort Dade was decommissioned. One gun was taken to an American Legion Post in St. Petersburg for display and remained there until the building was demolished. The other gun went to Plant Park in Tampa, next to the University of Tampa. Both guns were eventually scrapped. Plant Park still has a monument to the Spanish-American War, but the artillery presently there is from a railway mount from Fort Morgan, Alabama.

Battery Burchstead

Henry Burchstead was born in New York around 1791. He entered West Point as a Cadet on February 6, 1809, and graduated on March 1, 1811, as an Ensign in the 2nd Infantry. An announcement of promotions in the *Aurora General Advertiser* of Philadelphia on March 25th reads: "Hyppolite H Willard, John Bliss and Henry A. Burchstead,

---

4

cadets, appointed ensigns in the second regiment of Infantry, to rank as they stand on the list."

His first assignment was in the Northwestern frontier in the same year, and he was quickly promoted to 2nd Lieutenant on March 12, 1811. His first combat was during the Campaign of 1811 in the Indiana Territory at the Battle of Tippecanoe, where he was wounded on November 7, 1811. A document called *U. S., Returns of Killed and Wounded in Battles,* shows this battle "At the Confluence of the Tippecanoe River with the Wabash, near Prophets Town." The report lists four killed and twelve wounded.

His next assignment was on the frontier in the Gulf States region from 1811 to 1812. His regiment fought the British in the War of 1812, which lasted until 1815. During this time, he was promoted to 1st Lieutenant of the 2nd Infantry on May 5, 1813.

His following military actions occurred during the Creek War, a regional war between opposing Creek factions within the Creek Confederation. It's usually considered part of the War of 1812 since it was concurrent with the war between the British and Americans. The battles of the Creek War took place in the states of Georgia, Alabama, and Mississippi and ended in 1814.

Henry Burchstead's final actions happened at the Creek towns of Autossee and Tallassee near present-day Shorter, Alabama. General John Floyd, with about 900 militiamen and 450 allied Creeks, attacked and burned both villages, destroying about 400 houses and killing about 200 Red Stick Creeks. Floyd lost 11 soldiers and was wounded himself. Henry Burchstead was killed the following day, on November 30, possibly in an ambush. He was buried probably near the Alabama River.

Battery Burchstead was built on the southern end of Egmont Key in 1901 and included one three-inch rapid-fire masking parapet gun and two British-made Armstrong rapid-fire guns. Pinellas County rescued these two Armstrong guns in 1980 when the battery was nearly lost to erosion. They were preserved and are now on display at Fort DeSoto Park near the mortar batteries.

Battery Page

John B. Page was born in Maine in the year 1795. Nothing has been written about his early years. He joined the US Army as a Lieutenant in February of 1818.

His first assignments involved actions to remove Native Americans, specifically the Seminole and Creek tribes in the south, and relocate them to reservations. He was sympathetic to the plight of these native peoples, something unusual among the military and civilian population. During the removal of the first group of 630 Creeks en route to Little Rock, Arkansas, he noted in his journal:

> "I have to stop the wagons to take the children out and warm them and put them back again 6 or 7 times a day. I send ahead and have fires built for this purpose. I wrap them in tents and anything I can get hold of to keep them from freezing…there was continued crying from morning to night with the children…I used to encourage them by saying that the weather would moderate in a few days, and it would be warm, but it never happened during the whole trip."

He was transferred to the 4th Infantry, promoted to Captain on April 30, 1830, and assigned to Fort Gibson, Oklahoma. This fort was a center for relocating the Creek and Seminole tribes.

Captain Page's next major assignment was in the Mexican War (1846-1848), leading his troops under "Rough and Ready" General Zachary Taylor. His final battle in that war happened at Palo Alto, where he was supporting an artillery unit under the command of Major Sam Ringgold. He was severely wounded, and an account by Ulysses S. Grant, who was also in the 4th Infantry, commented that a nine-pound cannonball had taken off the head of one soldier and another shot "broke in the roof of" the mouth of Capt. Page and "nocked [sic] the under Jaw entirely away...The under jaw is gone to the wind pipe and the tongue hangs down upon the throat. He will never be able to speak or to eat." A wound of this type would be impossible to treat and to reconstruct his face, and given the state of medical care in the 1840s, this would certainly prove fatal in a short time.

The wounding of Captain Page became a national newspaper story. The *Philadelphia Daily Sun* reported, "As soon as she (Page's wife) heard of the terrible wound received by him in the Battle of Palo Alto, she left the luxuries of home and relatives to hasten to the side of her battle-scathed husband. She reached New Orleans two weeks ago, having traveled more than two thousand miles without pausing for an Hour's rest. At this place she embarked the *Alabama* for Point Isabel."

Her transit was delayed a week due to confusion in uniting Page with his wife, and she feared he might die before she could get to him. Captain John Page died on July 12 from his wounds. The July 23, 1846, edition of the *Pike County Free Press* noted:

DEATH OF JOHN PAGE

"This gallant officer, who distinguished himself in the battle of the Polo [sic] Alto and in which he received a dreadful wound, breathed his last on Sunday morning, at half past 3 o'clock on board of the steamer *Missouri*, when a short distance from Caire [sic]."

Page's remains were buried at the Jefferson Barracks in St. Louis on July 13, 1846. Captain John. Page' service would not be wholly forgotten. Page County, Iowa, was named in his honor.

Battery Page was on the island's southern end and had two three-inch rapid-fire guns on barbette mounts. Its remains were also lost to erosion and are now one hundred yards offshore.

Chapter 26

Congressman Sam M. Gibbons

In researching all the people in this book and their contributions to the island's history, I found that a few stood out as having the greatest and longest-lasting impact. First is Don Francisco Celi, the Spanish explorer who mapped Tampa Bay, first surveyed the island and gave names to the many geographic features in the area. Then, a survey expedition led by British explorer George Gauld gave the island its longest-lasting name, Egmont Key. Next was the Expedition of 1849, which mapped the coastline and harbors of the new State of Florida. Robert E. Lee gets most of the credit, but in fact, it was a group effort. They recommended that Egmont Key and Mullet Key be reserved for future possible military use. Because of this reservation, formalized in 1870, these places have remained undeveloped except for the military structures built at the beginning of the 1900s. The last major contributor was Sam Gibbons, who began the process to permanently protect Egmont Key from possible commercial development, starting in 1985. His efforts preserved this island and others in the area, thus far lasting more than thirty-five years.

I had the good fortune to meet his eldest son, Clifford Gibbons, many years ago and worked with him on Egmont Key and its preservation. He is as passionate as Congressman Gibbons was about preserving the island. I consulted with him on the story of Sam Gibbon's life and the complete story of his preservation efforts. I could not write a better version, so what follows is in Cliff's words, and I think you will find it as fascinating as I did.

Sam. M. Gibbons

Early Life

Sam M. Gibbons was a Tampa legend, admired statesman, and a stalwart supporter of education, the environment, and responsible land use; a political legend for almost five decades, a distinguished military combat veteran who helped many, many people and families in the Tampa Bay community improve their lives. Sam M. Gibbons is widely recognized as the founder of the University of South Florida. Gibbons was a man of profound integrity, dignity, and empathy for people from all walks of life and the challenges of their lives.

Sam Melville Gibbons was born on January 20, 1920, in Tampa, Florida, at an infirmary on what is now the University of Tampa campus. He frequently quoted his grandmother's words during the Great Depression: "Be ever mindful of the needs of others."

Sam was the eldest of a third generation of Gibbons in Tampa. His family lived on Jetton Avenue, and he attended Roosevelt Elementary School, Wilson Middle School, and Henry B. Plant High School. Much of the early years of his life growing up in Tampa were during the post-World War I recovery, the Great Depression, and President

Roosevelt's social and economic programs during the New Deal. Helping your neighbors and others in the community and treating others like you would like to be treated was chiseled into his early character and was a way of life for Sam and the extended Gibbons family through the Depression era in Tampa.

Beginning in the late 19th century, the extended Gibbons family were predominantly lawyers in Tampa. Growing up, there were always robust conversations around the Gibbons family dining room tables about issues of the day, politics, government, history, and local personalities.

From age six through college and the Army, Sam spent most of his summers and leave time with his grandparents at their home on Indian Rocks Beach, a two-story wooden clapboard beach house they had built in the early 1900s with a large front sun porch and large windows throughout, overlooking the pristine waters of the Gulf of Mexico. The house was located between 6th and 8th Streets across from the "yacht basin." During these special times, Sam gained a deeper appreciation of the natural ecology of the coastal areas. He would walk the natural vegetation beaches with his grandmother and aunts and take his rowboat and little plywood pram sailboat out on the island's east side in the mangrove-bordered bay waters. During these youthful, carefree times on the beaches, he honed his deep appreciation of the beauty of the wilderness coastline and bayous. Sam would also see the local watermen bring in hauls of fresh mullet daily. He would talk with the fishermen and hear their stories of the mighty silver tarpons in the Tampa Pass and the elaborate forts with their big guns on Egmont Key and Mullet Key. There was a growing curiosity to discover the adventurous wilderness of those Robinson Crusoe islands, but he had no means to get there.

College and the War Years

Sam joined the Plant High School JROTC program to prepare to be an officer if war broke out. After graduating from Plant High School in 1938, Sam attended the University of Florida. There, he became a member of the ATO (Alpha Tau Omega) Fraternity like his father and moved into the sprawling house next to campus. It was here his world opened up. He continued his ROTC training at the University of Florida. He was commissioned a 2nd Lieutenant when the war broke out following the Japanese bombing of Pearl Harbor and the relentless German aggression in Europe.

By the time he was a senior in college, his grandparents were required by the military to draw down blackout shades at night at their Indian Rocks house to prevent the German U-boats that may be in the Gulf of Mexico from seeing the coastal homes[1]. The apprehension of having to draw down blackout shades at night at the beach due to German submarines in the Gulf waters gave firsthand concerns that another war against Germany was imminent.

Following basic training, Sam qualified for one of the Army's elite Airborne Divisions as a lieutenant. After two years of relentless preparation in camps around the United States and later in England, Sam was one of the early morning Pathfinders[2] of the 101st Airborne to land on top of the well-entrenched, heavily armed German forces the night before the D-Day invasion in Normandy, France. It was in

---

1 German submarines wreaked havoc along the eastern seaboard of the United States in the early years of the war. Some U-boats were sunk in the Gulf of Mexico while prowling for defenseless cargo ships.

2 Pathfinders had the hazardous job of parachuting into the Normandy dropzones before the rest of the troops arrived. They set up Eureka radar transponder beacons that were intended to guide the transport planes to the correct locations. In practice, the beacons were not effective in guiding the aircraft, and paratroops were scattered across the French countryside.

that Normandy cow pasture that night that Sam said a little prayer and said: "Dear God, if you ever get me out of this mess alive, I promise to devote my life to public service to make sure this senseless carnage never happens again."

Following the invasion of Normandy and the ensuing months of intense conflict with Nazi forces, he led parachute infantry forces in major combat actions, including the invasion of Holland (Operation Market Garden), the Battle of Bastogne (Battle of the Bulge), the capture of Berchtesgaden and further operations in central Europe and Austria. Gibbons rose to the rank of Major and was awarded the Bronze Star for valor. He wrote a book about his D-Day experience, *I Was There*. On the 65th anniversary of D-Day, French President Chirac presented Sam Gibbons with France's most prestigious award, the Legion of Honor. Sam's experiences in World War II were the inspiration, as the author Tom Brokaw noted, and is the first profile in his best-selling book *The Greatest Generation*.

Following the War

At the conclusion of the War on May 8, 1945, Sam returned home to Tampa. Soon after, he married Martha Hanley on September 14, 1946, and a new life began. After a brief honeymoon in Daytona Beach with his new bride, Martha Hanley Gibbons, they returned to the University of Florida while he studied for and earned his law degree. Following graduation, Martha and Sam returned home to Tampa, got an apartment, and joined the Gibbons family law firm in the First National Bank Building in downtown Tampa.

After the birth of their first son, Clifford, in 1950, Sam launched his career in public service and won a seat in the Florida House of Representatives in 1952. He firmly believed education was the key to civilizations instead of fighting wars to resolve their differences. He served for ten years in the Florida Legislature, where he was instrumental in establishing the University of South Florida, now the seventh-largest university in the United States. He is widely recognized as the "Father of USF." Former USF President and Florida Education Commissioner Betty Castor told the *Tampa Bay Times*: "His legacy is the University of South Florida. I know he had a great career in Congress, but he was the person who made USF happen."

Gibbons also played a critical role in guiding Federal appropriations through Congress with the backing of Presidents John F. Kennedy and Lyndon B. Johnson, bringing the Veterans Administration Hospital to Tampa and establishing the medical school at USF. That changed the University's destiny forever, giving the Tampa Bay area the world-class medical school that was desperately needed on the west coast of Florida.

"Both the University and the Tampa Bay community owe Sam Gibbons great appreciation for his vision, his support, and his accomplishments," Judy Genshaft, former USF President, said. "He had the vision to fight for these great institutions to build this community. He was the founder and best friend of the University of South Florida and the USF Medical School. And he had a great vision for the powerful role of a university in building a community. He was Tampa Bay's great pioneer."

His driving passion for the future preservation of the fragile ecology of Florida led to his creation of the Southwest Florida Water Management District (SWFWMD) and the Four Rivers Basin Initiative. Gibbons gained President Kennedy's support. President Johnson ensured significant Federal funding for decades following. Other Tampa programs included Sam's signature initiative in his early years in Congress, the Head Start Program, which he pushed through. The first Head Start Program in the United States began in Tampa. Other early environmental programs included the Tampa Bypass Canal to mitigate the annual flooding of downtown Tampa and persistence in driving major Federal appropriations for the Army Corps of Engineers to deepen and preserve the Tampa harbor channel to forty-five feet from its downtown ports and shipbuilding and maintenance operations to well into the Gulf of Mexico beyond Egmont Key. The United States Federal Courthouse in Tampa bears his name.

Preservation of Egmont Key

Egmont Key was always a special place for Sam Gibbons. Throughout his forty-four years of public service, he ensured that Egmont Key remained in Hillsborough County and within the jurisdiction of his Florida House and Senate Legislature districts and Congression District to maintain control over its destiny.

From his childhood years living his summers in Indian Rocks Beach and hearing from anglers all about the forts built there during the Spanish-American War and the abundant fishing in surrounding waters, he finally made his maiden journey to the island while he was in the Florida legislature around 1958. Two developments made his life curiosity come to be.

First, Sam and his younger brother Myron always wanted a boat, so they had one custom-built by a noted local boatbuilder. I would often go with my father to the boatbuilding shop in an old warehouse just north of the Platt Street bridge on the east of the Hillsborough River to the right (north) of Mirabella's Fish Market. The boat was an 18-foot molded plywood craft with two 35-horsepower Johnson outboard engines. We often went to the boatbuilding shop after church to see its progress. When the boat was completed in the fall of 1960 and launched at the Davis Islands yacht basin for its first test run, I was convinced it was the fastest boat in Tampa. Soon after that, Sam, his close friend George Nettles, and his two sons would take their journey of discovery to Egmont Key.

The boat was trailered over to O'Neill's Marina in St. Petersburg, just north of the Sunshine Skyway Bridge. It was a quaint rustic marina with a delightful little restaurant that served the best fresh fried mullet, hush puppies, and grits. The launch from O'Neill's was filled with excitement and anticipation. Going to a deserted island with old forts and likely pirate treasures buried in the beaches made us all eager to go fast in the boat to this fantasy island. I had never been to an island before. The excitement was accentuated by a fast ride out of Tampa ship channel into the Gulf of Mexico in their new boat and all the images conjured up by movies about pirates and the castaway island adventures of the Swiss Family Robinson movie.

With the mighty roar of the two 35 horsepower engines, the boat reached plane, and we were off out the Tampa Channel to Egmont Key. I recall my father driving the boat, saying, "See, there is the island out there." Oh – what excitement! As we approached, I could see the lighthouse at the island's north end nestled in the tall Australian Pine trees (these trees have since been eradicated from the island) that densely covered the island. Sam had studied the island maps he had obtained from the Tampa Bay Pilots who had working houses on the island's southeast side. The biggest of the two forts with two massive guns[3] was located at the island's southern end and our destination. We made our way to the south end of Egmont Key, anchored the boat fifty yards off the beaches, and swam to shore.

---

3 The guns are British-made by the Armstrong Company. They are 6-inch caliber and have reusable brass casings. Pinellas County rescued the guns when the concrete battery was being lost to erosion. They were preserved and on display at Fort Desoto Park.

The fort was bigger than life, with the enormous guns pointed southwesterly towards the Gulf. I recall, "We spent the day having a picnic lunch with Cuban sandwiches and Coca-Colas and crawling all over the forts. It was an out-of-body experience." Surprisingly, there were no other people on the island. After a thrilling day of deserted island discovery, we returned to O'Neill's Marina at full speed and arrived just before dusk. I remember my Egmont Key adventures, which were all I could talk about when he went to school the following Monday. None of my friends could relate to what I was reporting because very few had access to a boat to make the journey out to the island.

The second trip to Egmont Key was an overnight camping trip Sam had planned and arranged through his Florida Senate jurisdiction over Egmont Key for Cliff to complete some Merit Badges for his Boy Scout rank advancement. We departed O'Neill's Marina early on a Saturday morning, I recall, with enough provisions for an army. Cliff took along most of his father's World War II gear for the adventure. Tents were pitched on the beach a few yards from the dense palm tree jungle. The campsite was set up just east of the forts on the south end of the Island. The discovery adventures began with no worry about the time of day. Around dusk, we assembled at the campsite and cooked hamburgers over a charcoal fire on the beach. We were the only people on the island. I later learned that this was a fact-finding journey to his father's legislative district and why they were the only people allowed on the island to camp and have a campfire for cooking.

Mosquitoes swarmed from the dense jungle-like foliage as darkness rolled in around our campsite and the gentle winds subsided. "The mosquitoes ate us alive", I recalled.

But no one wanted to mention this annoyance because we were on a deserted island out in the Gulf of Mexico. We wore large mosquito net headgear that helped a lot during the night.

Sam Gibbons' passion for Egmont Key was ignited. Just about every time he and his boys went fishing, it always included a visit to Egmont Key – usually with tasty Cuban sandwiches and ice-cold Coca-Cola. As a Florida State Senator and later as a member of Congress, he made sure during Florida Legislature redistricting that Egmont Key always remained in his legislative districts for his forty-four years of public service.

Florida's Development Boom Years

With the advancement of air conditioning technology in the 1950s and 60s, the Tampa Bay area, especially Pinellas County, became ground zero for coastal dredging and uncontrolled development. Development was out of control in Florida and the coastal regions. Florida had no zoning or coastal development planning, and the notion of environmental preservation was virtually non-existent. No coastal property in Florida was safe from rapacious out-of-state developers.

Locally, the damage of unfettered dredging of mangrove estuary wetlands to the sprawling wasteland of concrete seawalls a foot or so above hightide hideously transformed Hillsborough and Pinellas counties' pristine coastal areas into uncontrolled and unregulated development with little concern or regard to environment sensitivity or long-range adverse consequences. All the bays east of Pass-a-Grill, St. Petersburg Beach, Madeira Beach Treasure Island, Reddington Beach, Indian Rocks Beach, Belleair Beach, Clearwater Beach, and the barrier islands of Caladisi and Honeymoon Islands were impacted by relentless development and ecological devastation by developers. Local municipalities were all complicitous with the developers. They made no efforts to place any limits on the permanent and widespread dev-astation of coastal wetlands to build more and more houses, motels, and apartments. Paved streets and parking lots replaced tens of thou-sands of acres of mangroves, sabal palms, and Australian pine trees.

With just about every square foot of bay bottom dredged and filled by the middle of the 1960s, land developers turned their atten-tion to the western Gulf Coast barrier islands for their insatiable envi-ronmental carnage. They first obtained permits to dredge and fill new islands and bridges from a causeway connecting Pass-a-Grille Beach with the mainland and the US 19 highway near the Sunshine Skyway Bridge on the east. They called these dredge-and-fill islands encircled by concrete seawalls Tierra Verde (ironically meaning "Green Earth"). Finally, developers were stopped as they approached their prized des-tination to turn Mullet Key, with its 1,200 acres, into a develop-ment. Mullet Key had more than six miles of stunningly beautiful virgin beach frontage, several miles of mangrove tidal waters along Mullet Key Bay, and historic Spanish-American War mortar batteries that strategically complemented the Egmont Key forts to defend the port of Tampa. Senator Gibbons and his Florida Senate colleague, C.W. "Bill" Young, worked hand-in-hand to set the stage for Pinellas County to purchase Mullet Key. Extensive plans were drawn up, and Fort De Soto Park was officially dedicated on May 11, 1963.

The developers were not deterred. They devised another mindless plan to build a bridge from the north end of Anna Maria Island to Egmont Key (it didn't get built). Meanwhile, developers focused their attention on building a bridge from Dunedin across the Intracoastal Waterway from Dunedin to Honeymoon Island.

In the 1960s, another developer purchased Honeymoon Island. Developers planned to make the 200-acre island into 3,000 acres by pumping in fill from the Gulf of Mexico. These undeterred commercial developers planned to build 4,500 residential units along waterfront canals. In total, there would be housing for an astounding 16,000 residents. The dredging did not go well. Much of the ill-fated 1.5 million cubic yards of fill material pumped onto the Island was rock, which remains a reminder on the island's south end. In 1969, the dredging permit expired, and because of the efforts of local environmentalists, the permit was never renewed. However, the developer's lasting impact with the 1963 construction of bridges and causeway over the bay and the building of seven high-rise condominiums and associated facilities that affect the pristine beauty of Honeymoon Island today[4].

Preservation and Protection of Egmont Key – Federal Jurisdiction Affirmed Some Background to this Fortuitous Meeting to Save Egmont Key

Sam Gibbons's eldest son Clifford attended Georgetown University Law School and worked part-time as a Doorman (Officer of the Door Keeper) in the U.S. House of Representatives. When asked what he did as a Doorman, I said the job was like a fireman, "when the House is in session, and there are lots of votes, things get really chaotic; otherwise, it provided a good time to study for law school." The Doorman is a historical position in Congress and stands by the various House of Representatives entrance doors and welcomes members as they enter the Chamber. Frequently, the newly arrived members did not know what a vote was on, and the Doorman provided a short brief of the bill and a short title.

Being a Doorman provided full access throughout the US Capitol building and all the office complexes. I took advantage of these perks and walked everywhere around the Capitol when the House was not in session. One summer afternoon, when there were few people around, I was over on the Senate side of the Capitol, and walking towards me was a familiar face of Rogers C. B. Morton. I had the opportunity to get to know Mr. Morton well when he and his father took a ten-day congressional delegation (CODEL) trip on large river rafts down the entire length of the Grand Canyon to understand the catastrophic carnage that would occur if the entire canyon was to be made into a reservoir by building another massive dam on the Colorado River. There were two dams already that had caused irreparable damage to the Grand Canyon: the Glenn Canyon Dam and the Hoover Dam. The California delegation had the votes to authorize and appropriate funding for a major new dam that would cover the entire Grand Canyon as we know it today. I know this sounds unbelievable, but there were enough votes to get the bill out of Committee, and the new dam was essential to enhance the growing California agriculture business.

This critical CODEL was organized by Congressman Morris K "Mo" Udall (D-AZ), Chairman of the Interior Committee in the House of Representatives. It included about thirty-five House and Senate Members on the trip. Back in those days, if a spouse could not accompany a Member on a CODEL, the Member's oldest son or daughter could join the Member on the fact-finding trips. So, I had the opportunity to spend ten days on a raft on the Colorado River through the Grand Canyon with Rogers Morton. They became good friends, and the Gibbons' visited the Mortons at their home and farm on the Wye River in Easton, Maryland. Congressman Morton and Congressman Gibbons were elected to Congress together in 1962 and served together for almost a decade.

So here we were in the US Capitol together. By this time, Congressman Morton had been appointed US Secretary of the Interior by President Nixon. He was the perfect person to head the Department of Interior because he was at the vanguard of environmental protection of the Chesapeake Bay and was known throughout the country for his leadership in preserving public and private lands. Remember, it was President Nixon, a Republican, who established the Environmental Protection Agency.

The Secretary asked me what I was up to. Thinking quickly on my feet, I could not possibly say I was a Doorman in law school – and immediately said I was working with a coalition to save Sand Key from the onslaught of development by US Steel and the preservation of other Gulf coast barrier islands. Well, this really caught the attention of the Secretary of Interior. We talked in the hallway for about ten minutes about how terrible the developers were in destroying scenic barrier islands on the west coast of Florida. As we were wrapping up our conversation, Secretary Morton said to me – "tell your father to invite me down to Florida because I want to take a look at these barrier islands. I have some ideas to help you."

I reported to my father the meeting I had with Secretary Morton's interest in coming to Florida and seeing the barrier islands we were trying to protect. The next day, he drafted a letter of invitation to Secretary Morton, and I hand-delivered the letter to Secretary Morton's office. A response came back immediately. The Secretary said he would meet Sam at MacDill Air Force Base, have a helicopter waiting, and see these barrier islands that were in jeopardy of being destroyed by developers.

About a month later, all the advance work was in place, and I joined my father and Secretary Morton at MacDill Air Force Base early one morning. We had a large twin-rotor troop carrier helicopter with large open doors on the right and left sides of the aircraft. We briefed the pilots on where we wanted to go, got strapped in with life jackets and radio-controlled hearing protection, and away we went. I had never been in a helicopter of this size nor any aircraft with huge open doors a few feet away. It was scary at first. But my father was well seasoned at this kind of flying from leading his combat para-trooper regiments with his 101st Airborne unit troops in World War II. As we lifted off and gained altitude over MacDill, we flew west out over the Tampa Ship Channel. Within moments, we were over a tiny bird sanctuary island, a group of small tidal sandbar islands in the west Tampa Bay south-south-east of Egmont Key (today called Passage Key Wildlife Refuge).

It is relevant to point out some personal characteristics of Interior Secretary Morton. He was a big man in great shape. He had a full head of white hair and a deep, commanding voice. He looked just like John Wayne and had the same swagger and demeanor. He had a confident and imposing presence. Once on board the helicopter, he stood in the middle and faced the right open door of the aircraft, wearing aviator sunglasses and a flight jacket. He was ready for action and the staff on the helicopter gave him all the space he wanted. This had all the makings for a scene right out of a Hollywood film set.

As the helicopter approached the island and began to bank around the west side of Egmont Key, I pointed to the little island off the north side of Anna Maria Island. Within moments, we were off the west side of Egmont Key. My father was standing to the left of the Secretary, and I stood up (as we were tethered to an overhead cable) next to the right of Secretary Morton and pointed out Egmont Key. Despite the tremendous noise and vibration of the aircraft and the intense wind blowing through the aircraft, the big headsets with small microphones provided clear communication. Secretary Morton communicated to the pilots to circle slowly. I began to point out the Spanish-American Forts (c. the 1900s), Fort Dade (commissioned in 1898). There were two 6-inch bore rifled cannons, weighing seventeen tons each, breach loading, utilizing shell cases that were refillable with thirteen pounds of powder. The projectiles weighed one hundred pounds and had a maximum range of 10,000 yards (5 ½ miles), reaching a targeted vessel in about twenty-five seconds. The Fort Dade remains and brick roads, the historic lighthouse, and the Tampa Bay Harbor Pilots facility are on the south end of Egmont Key.

As the helicopter made the second turn around the island below, Secretary Morton stood in the aircraft's open door, waved his arm and hands from left to right, and declared in a robust and clear voice, "National Wildlife Refuge."

I was stunned. I turned to my father, who had a big smile. All the microphones and headsets were set for communication with everyone, including the pilots. My father said, "Mr. Secretary, let us show you more barrier islands that are in jeopardy." With that, I said, "Let's proceed north."

Within ten seconds, we were west of another barrier island called Mullet Key, where there were more forts guarding the entrance of Tampa Bay in the Spanish-American War. The forts on Mullet Key were earthen forts with twenty or so feet high of sand on the west side of the forts with concrete bunkers and four twelve-inch caliber mortars. These were big, short, rifled guns that fired mortar projectiles at high angles at enemy ships. They were still in good condition compared to the rest of the long-range guns on Egmont Key.

Secretary of Interior Morton repeated his arm and hand wave and said in a loud booming voice – "National Wildlife Refuge. ' I felt chills race down my spine at the proclamation. I turned to my father to see his affirming smile.

My father said, "Rogers — let's continue north — I want to point out some more islands that need Federal protection." Secretary Morton said, "Sure — let's continue north."

The helicopter was flying at about a thousand feet or less, and we had a bird's eye view of Pass-A-Grille, the large pink Don Cesar

Hotel, St. Petersburg Beach, Reddington Beach, Indian Rocks Beach, Belleair Beach, Sand Key, and Clearwater Beach. Then, at the north end of Clearwater Beach and the Carlouel Yacht Club was the pristine Caladesi Island. The helicopter slowed a little, and I pointed out the perimeter of the Island and its proximity to the next Island north — Honeymoon Island, where developers had completed a bridge from the mainland to the barrier islands. I also indicate that there was a pass at the north end of Clearwater Beach about 500 yards north of Carlouel Yacht Club that separated Caladesi Island from Clearwater Beach, but the pass was closed during a hurricane in the 1960s.

Secretary Morton repeated his pronouncement as we passed Caladesi Island — "National Wildlife Refuge!"

I said, "Let's continue north. I want to show you two more barrier islands that developers are targeting."

Within a moment, we were at Hurricane Pass, separating Caladesi Island from Honeymoon Island. I pointed out the Dunedin Causeway, the two bridges and the dredged causeway that developers had pushed to be built to connect Honeymoon Island[4] with the mainland, and the two environmentally destructive bunker-style condominium buildings on the north side of the Dunedin Causeway. "Mr. Secretary," I said, "these structures are what developers aim to do to all these barrier islands."

As Secretary Morton gazed across Honeymoon Island and the causeway — the sweeping arm motion and refrain: "National Wildlife Refuge!"

I said, "One more pristine island I want to show you." The helicopter continues north and across Saint Joseph Sound towards

---

4 The developer went bankrupt after building the high-rises. The State of Florida acquired the land and developed it into Honeymoon Island State Park, one of the most beautiful and visited state parks. It has received national recognition for its beaches, amenities, and recreation.

Anclote Key. We passed over a cluster of sandbar islands off the north of Honeymoon Island that, at the time, was barely noticeable. Today, those little sand spits we passed over in the early 1970s have evolved into a beautiful string of fragile islands where hundreds of boaters anchor and traverse the beach on weekends.

As the helicopter approached Anclote Key, I pointed out the 1887 Anclote Key Lighthouse on the south end of the pristine deserted island. I told Secretary Morton that Anclote Key was the most ecologically unspoiled barrier island in Florida's Gulf Coast and needed federal protection. He agreed, waved his hand, and said as he overlooked the Island, "National Wildlife Refuge." In less than one hour, the United States Secretary of the Interior declared five Gulf Coast barrier islands National Wildlife Refuges. There were no proclamations, no authorizations by Congress, hearings, discussions, or debates—just a pronouncement that these five islands would receive the protection necessary to prevent further development. Indeed, it was a glorious historical day in Florida's coastal environmental protection!

The helicopter turned around at the north end of Anclote Key[5], and we headed southeast over the Pinellas County peninsula back to MacDill Air Force Base.

Once back on the tarmac at MacDill, my father and I profusely thanked Secretary Morton and his staff for this momentous visit to Florida and for protecting the environmentally sensitive five islands' coastal wetlands. We knew that there was a lot to be done to formalize what had just happened verbally.

---

5 Anclote Key is now a State Park, and the lighthouse has been restored. The state swapped land it owned on Sanibel Island, which was then added to the Ding Darling NWR so that the park would have the whole island.

My father flew back to Washington with Secretary Morton on his plane to Andrews Air Force Base. He had two hours to continue discussing with Secretary Morton and his senior staff what he was going to do in Congress to inject a protective network of other Federal agencies into supporting the National Wildlife Refuge designations and protection of these Gulf Coast barrier islands by the Bureau of Land Management (BLM).

As soon as I returned to Washington, he called Secretary Morton's office and scheduled a meeting to draft a trip summary and the decisions made by the Secretary to preserve the five barrier islands that were declared Federal Wildlife Refuges. I returned the draft to my father's office for him to review and clear off the document. He said he wanted to talk with his good friend Congressman Bill Young (R-FL), whose congressional district the five islands were located. Congressman Young reportedly agreed and said anything Secretary Morton wanted to do was OK with him to protect the five barrier islands.

I returned to Secretary Morton's office to tell him that Congressman Gibbons and Congressman Bill Young had signed off on the draft language. Secretary Morton called the Interior Department's General Counsel and asked him to meet with me and to formalize the draft language legally. I learned a lot in those subsequent meetings. The legal basis for the Secretary's action did not require congressional approval or further administrative review. The law used to affirm the transfer of the five barrier islands to Federal jurisdiction was The Antiquities Act of 1906, signed into law by President Theodore Roosevelt. The Act was the first US law to provide general legal protection of cultural and natural resources of historic or scientific interest on federal lands. This law gives the president of the United States the authority to, by presidential proclamation, create national monuments from federal lands to protect significant natural, cultural, or scientific features. The Act has been used more than a hundred times since its enactment. This Federal designation remains in effect for Egmont Key today.

To erect further barriers for developers and future efforts of the Florida Legislature and a pro-development governor to change the status of Egmont Key as a Federally protected property, Congressman Gibbons crafted further Federal legislation and Federal agency administrative declarations as early detection tripwires for preservationists to know whether any developer was to try and make a run at commercializing Egmont Key. He entangled a number of Federal agencies, including the US Department of Interior, the Bureau of Land Management, The US Department of Agriculture Fish and Wildlife Operations, the U.S. Department of Transportation, and the Department of Homeland Security for jurisdiction over the Egmont Key lighthouse property. Moreover, he devised an interlocking patchwork of Federal and state agreements between the US Interior Department, BLM, the State of Florida Department of Environmental Protection, and the Florida Fish and Wildlife Conservation Commission jurisdiction. Congressman Gibbon's knowledge of Federal law and his tenacious persistence to establish a long and thorough legislative and administrative history of protections for Egmont Key is in place to keep Egmont Key a historical and environmentally sensitive barrier island in perpetuity. (End of Cliff Gibbons' narrative.)

The Coast Guard would own the northernmost fifty-five acres, but the Florida Park Service would manage the property as a state park. A ranger would live on the island and look out for the Coast Guard's interests while managing the wildlife and habitat in cooperation with US Fish and Wildlife.

The Cleanup of Egmont Key

The event was to be called Egmont '88 and was planned to take place over three days in May: the 12th, 13th, and the final day of work, with the opening and closing ceremony on the 14th. The planning had started the year before with the formation of a steering committee that would organize and coordinate the many agencies and groups that would be participating. A list of the committee members is in Appendix C. This event would be the largest joint civilian and military cleanup operation in Florida and possibly the nation. Over the three days, the participants would total six-hundred civilians and five-hundred military personnel. The local military organizations (a complete list of the units involved is in Appendix C) were a significant presence, providing landing craft, heavy earth-moving equipment, jeeps, and other logistical support. The local volunteer community provided support with volunteers coming to the island to pick up trash (a list of those groups is in Appendix C). The ferry service was provided by the *Miss Cortez*, who brought volunteers to and from the island over the three days. An executive committee (the list of people is in Appendix B) organized the activities and planned the ceremonies for the event's last day.

The Tampa Shipyard Company provided a barge capable of transporting the many dumpsters required for the cleanup to the island. The City of Tampa Solid Waste Department disposed of unrecyclable materials, and Reynolds Aluminum Recycling disposed of the hundreds of aluminum cans removed from the island.

On Wednesday, May 11, 1988, environmental organizations marked the sensitive areas used by birds for nesting habitats and areas with sea oats, which are protected plants. Thursday was for military units with heavy equipment to clear roadways that were covered with sand over the decades. Friday, the Marines assisted in the operations. Saturday, May 14, was led by Boy Scouts, 4-H Clubs from the local area, and other youth organizations. The Tampa Bay Pilots, the *Miss Cortez* out of Bradenton, along with military boats, provided transportation for volunteers from Fort DeSoto to the island on the first day. US Fish and Wildlife closed the island to visitors during this time.

Governor Bob Martinez, Congressman Sam Gibbons, water management officials, and reporters were on the island Saturday. Over seventy tons of trash and debris were removed, including bottles and cans, old refrigerators, air conditioning ducts, and an old portable toilet. This effort has been followed up with the many volunteers and Park Service staff to keep the island trash-free and safe for visitors and wildlife.

The event went well, but one incident received local press coverage. The May 18 issue of the *Tampa Tribune* reported that about seventy-five airmen from MacDill Airforce Base came in contact with poison ivy and experienced rashes. The vine is found all over the island and is very dense on the southern end, so it is no surprise that people were affected. Fortunately, there were no severe cases, and they quickly recovered.

This cleanup effort, including its planning and implementation, also had national significance. Egmont '88 became one of the entries in a national program called "Take Pride in America." A group of leaders from the Egmont '88 project were invited to the White House for the event, where President George W. Bush presented awards to the many groups nationwide that had similar projects. A song also titled "Take Pride in America" was written for the occasion and recorded by the Oak Ridge Boys.

150th Anniversary of the Lighthouse

When I had been a member of the Egmont Key Alliance for less than a year, plans were being made for the 150th anniversary of the lighthouse on the island, which was first put in service (the current one) in 1858. The event happened on November 8-9 during Discover the Island, and the ceremonies were held on the 8th. Festivities involved Park Service officials and several speakers, including Rodney Kite-Powell of the Tampa Bay History Center, Congresswoman Kathy Castor, and Sam Gibbons as special guests.

Sam Gibbons at the 150th anniversary of the Egmont Lighthouse. He's wearing the Hero of Egmont Key medallion. Author's photo.

Rodney Kite-Powell talked about the island's long history and the lighthouse; Congresswoman Castor and the park managers commented. Then Sam Gibbons took to the podium and spoke about what he had to do to put all the agreements together and about the island's cleanup event. He was quite at home talking to a group of people about his work to preserve the island, and it was an opportunity for many to find out what he had done more than twenty years before, making this possible.

After he finished speaking, Richard Johnson, the President of the Egmont Key Alliance, and the Past President, Jim Spangler, presented him with our "Hero of Egmont Key" medal. The Egmont Key Alliance occasionally gives this medal to people who have gone above and beyond to protect and preserve the island and its natural and cultural resources. In Sam Gibbons' case, he had done more than any one person in modern times to protect the island.

Sam Gibbons passed away on October 10, 2012, at the age of ninety-two. He had lived a remarkable life as a soldier during World War II, had a successful career in politics, and left a legacy on Egmont Key that is still being felt today.

Chapter 27

The Egmont Key Alliance

"A wonderful and wonderous place"
Quote about Egmont Key by Past President Jim Spangler

No discussion of island history would be complete without telling the story of one of its volunteer organizations, The Egmont Key Alliance. In 1989, the US Coast Guard removed its personnel from the island, and rangers from the Florida State Park Service began managing the fifty-five acres on the north end as a State Park. The park manager began living in the concrete barracks building that had housed the Coast Guard personnel.

The beginnings of the Egmont Key Alliance came after the end of the cleanup event called "Egmont '88", detailed in the previous chapter about Sam Gibbons.

Becoming a Park Service Citizen Support Organization (CSO) takes several steps. First, a group must apply to the State of Florida to form a corporation. This requires the corporation to have a board and officers. The list of people who were charter members of the board is listed in Appendix D. It comprised seventeen members and two ex-officio members, representing a cross-section of the local and state environmental protection community. Several Egmont '88 Steering and Executive Committee members served on this first board.

An important decision had to be made about what to call this new organization. There were three main interest groups regarding the island. Some were interested in the lighthouse and its history; others were more military history buffs, and a third group of people were interested in shorebirds, sea turtles, and other wildlife. The members of these three groups felt they would be more effective as one larger entity than three smaller ones, so they became an "alliance." After much debate and discussion, the Egmont Key Alliance was born! The date of filing for the corporation was June 24, 1991.

The next step is for the organization to apply to the Internal Revenue Service for a Nonprofit designation. The Nonprofit designation was awarded on June 3, 1993. Lastly, an agreement (CSO Agreement) between the Park Service and the group is signed, and the work could begin. This was completed in 1993. This agreement spells out the responsibilities of both the volunteers and the Park Service. A CSO is dedicated to one park only, in this case, Egmont Key State Park.

Another essential part of the Alliance's story was creating the new organization's logo. A lot of discussion by the board members went into achieving the final design. Every design element of the logo represents some significant part of the island. The lighthouse is prominent, but there is also the water, a sabal palm, the sunset, and even a seashell. At the bottom of the logo are the words "Restore, Preserve, and Protect," which state the primary purpose of the new organization. The mission statement of the new organization was, in essence, "to preserve the island's natural and historic resources for future generations to enjoy."

The Alliance's first president, Susan Kessel, played a pivotal role in shaping the organization. Her extensive knowledge about Egmont '88 and the cleanup effort has been instrumental in the Alliance's journey. Her new board included Hillsborough County Commissioners, a Hillsborough County Sheriff's Office representative, and others in the local environmental preservation community.

The Early Days

In the park's early years, the volunteers traveled to and from the island in the Park Service utility boat or sometimes rode on a harbor pilot boat. There was no regular ferry service, and island visitors could only visit by private boat. This volunteer transportation situation was alleviated when a forty-nine-passenger boat from Hubbard's Marina began regular daily service to Egmont Key in 2004 and Shell Key in 2009 from the Fort DeSoto Bay Pier.

Activities included beach cleanups, trail clearing, and maintenance projects for the park's buildings. Volunteers have also helped with bird stewarding during the nesting season and have acted as docents in the Guardhouse visitor center.

Over the years, the Alliance grew to about two hundred members. A non-profit software package called Wild Apricot, which included a website, e-mail, and a membership database, was implemented. This full-featured and integrated software suite greatly aided the organization's management and events. It also provided visitors to the website with information about the island's history and wildlife. The organization started a Facebook page and posted about activities. Hubbard's Marina became a generous supporter of the Alliance and Egmont Key by providing ferry services for our volunteers on workdays and events.

Charles Canerday, a past Vice President, led a project to create an informational brochure to be handed out to visitors, both on the island and on the ferry while being brought to the island. On one side was historical information, and on the other was a detailed map so visitors would know where they were permitted to go and see where the various building ruins were located. Later, the Alliance published a plastic laminated nature guide that visitors could purchase. It had the most common plants and wildlife on and around the island and was a great educational tool.

The Alliance also provided funding for island needs that were not always in the park service's budget. The money was raised through donations, dues, gift shop sales, and fund-raising events like Discover the Island.

Past Presidents

Over the more than thirty years of the Alliance's existence, many presidents have served. Some served for a year or two, and others much longer. Richard Johnson served a combined total of twelve years, and Richard Sanchez served fifteen consecutive years. Most of the presidents served for a year or two.

Below is a list of the past presidents:

Susan Kessel

Sandy Colbert

Gregory Wilson

Richard Johnson – first term

Sandy Mallett

Jim Spangler

Richard Johnson – second term

Richard A. Sanchez

Award Recipients

Several individual awards were given to Alliance members and others over the years. Below is the list of the "Hero of Egmont Key" award, which was a medallion worn around the neck. This award was given to individuals who had contributed significant accomplishments to the island. There were no specific criteria; there was just a consensus among the board members that the award was appropriate.

- Charles Canerday – Donated time and resources from his architectural firm for the Guardhouse Project

- Jim Spangler – For his work getting sand placements on the island.

- Richard Johnson-For being project manager on the Guardhouse Restoration Project

- Sam Gibbons – For his work in getting the agreements in place from all the government agencies for the preservation of the island.

- Tom Watson – For his tireless efforts during a major fire on the island that damaged eighty acres.

Finally, there was the "Environmental Protection Award" given to the recipients below:

- Jan Platt

- Lee Fox

- Peter Clark – for his work improving the water quality of Tampa Bay

- Jerry Shrewsberry Charlatan

- Dave Mason

- Jim Igler (posthumously) for his many years of local environmental work.

- Richard (Rich) Paul – For his work in protecting the nesting shorebirds

- Jim Spangler

Discover the Island

The park's signature fundraising event was "Discover the Island," allowing the Alliance to showcase the island to visitors. The event included walking tours, exhibitors from various non-profits, food, and presentations by knowledgeable volunteers in the Guardhouse. Initially, there was no regular scheduled ferry service, so the Alliance hired local captains with suitable-capacity boats to bring visitors to the event. Later, Hubbard's Marina provided ample ferry capacity to support the event[1].

---

1 Wilson Hubbard began running trips to Shell Key, Mullet Key, and Egmont Key as individual charters from 1958 to 1976. From 1990 to 1994, trips to Egmont and Mullet Keys departed from John's Pass. Currently, Shell Key trips depart from the Fort DeSoto Boatramp, and Egmont Key trips depart the Bay Pier.

Richard Johnson, one of our past presidents, would portray a lighthouse keeper, complete with a replica uniform and hat. He would stand in the lighthouse, open to the public during the event, give short talks, and answer visitor's questions. His portrayal of a lighthouse keeper was very popular with the visitors, and hundreds of people took his picture. This was the only time of year that the tower was open. Climbing wasn't allowed, but you could go to the first level and get a look up at the spiral staircase.

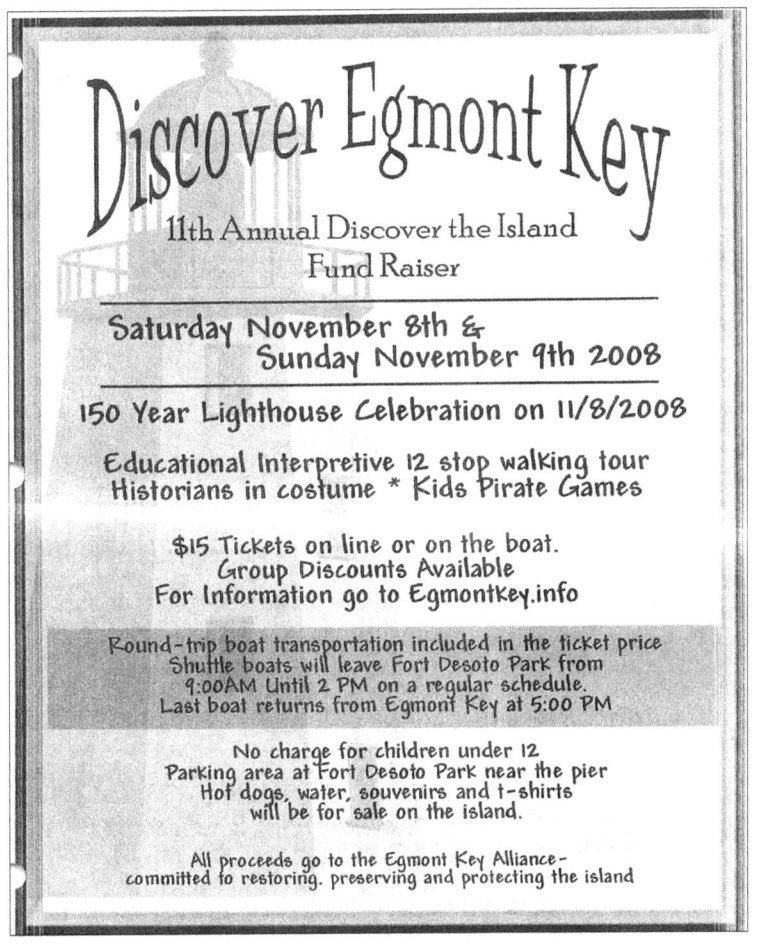

Event Flyer for the year 2008

Over the years, the Discover the Island event grew from just a few volunteers and activities to a much larger event involving Civil War reenactors, the Tampa Rough Riders, and many local non-profits representing the environmental community.

The Guardhouse was open, and visitors could attend presentations by various experts on wildlife or military history. The guided walking tours became very popular, and the topics covered native plants, wildlife on the island, and military history. Scuba divers from the Bay Area Reef Runners had an exhibit at Battery Mellon about the *USS Narcissus* that was sunk offshore. The event was intended to attract people to the island and educate them on all it has to offer.

In the beginning years, the event was held in the springtime. One year, due to some well-placed publicity in the *Tampa Bay Times*, some two thousand visitors showed up at Fort DeSoto on the first day, intending to go to Egmont for the event. There were traffic jams, long wait times for the ferry and parking was a nightmare. Due to these problems, management at Fort DeSoto insisted the event be moved to another, less busy time of the year. The event was shifted to October and then to early November to take advantage of milder weather. The event was a major fundraiser, and the public enjoyed it. COVID-19 restrictions paused the event for two years, and declining attendance ended the event. It was held twenty-two times and was a popular local nature and history event.

Supporting Organizations

The Alliance benefited from several organizations in its mission to "Restore, Preserve, and Protect" the island. Being in a major metropolitan area and Egmont Key being a part of Hillsborough County (yes, that's correct!), we had the support of several organizations. What follows is an overview of the generosity of these organizations.

Hubbard's Marina

Hubbard's Marina has been mentioned elsewhere in this chapter, but the importance of their support cannot be underestimated. With Egmont Key being accessible only by boat, having reliable transportation with adequate capacity was indispensable to the Alliance. We were able to transport our volunteers to the island any time we needed and could transport large items when a work project required it. They supported our Discover the Island event for setup on Friday, the event itself, and the breakdown of the event afterward. Hubbard's shared the cost of printing our information brochure, allowing us to get a better rate and also by handing them out to guests on the trip to the island. Their captains and crew educated visitors on the way over to the island about what not to do regarding the wildlife and where the closed areas were. Many of the projects and workday activities would have been difficult, if not impossible, without the support of the Hubbard family and their staff. They continue to work on the island with TakeMAR under the leadership of Tara Hubbard and her staff, who are now handling the volunteer activities on the island.

The **Friends of Tampa Bay Refuges** is a support group for US Fish and Wildlife in the refuges, which extends from Crystal River in the north to Passage Key in the south, a distance of ninety-five miles, and comprises many small islands. Established first in Crystal River, Barbara and Dave Howard formed this second group in 2005, operating at the refuge's southern end. Many volunteers on Egmont Key were members of both the Alliance and the Friends, and information and work projects were shared. Each group had representatives at the others board meetings. During Discover the Island, the Friends operated the Guardhouse and had activities for kids, such as a fossil pit, where they could "dig" for fossils. Volunteers from both groups would provide docents in the Guardhouse during the year so it could be open to visitors. The Friends managed the bird steward program, where volunteers monitored the nesting shorebirds and educated the public about bird nesting.

The Florida Parks Foundation (formerly The Friends of Florida State Parks) is an organization whose members are made up of the various volunteer groups at state parks. The Foundation provided several benefits, such as project grants, access to administrative services, and, at one time, liability and board of directors insurance. The Foundation granted the Alliance $2,600 to replace a flagpole in the former cemetery near the ranger house. The Alliance also used the insurance services when they were available.

The **Tierra Verde Business Partnership** (TVBP) was formed to promote businesses on Tierra Verde through advertising and sponsorship of fundraising events in the community. On two occasions, the TVBP awarded the Alliance donations to fund whatever the Alliance needed. One year, when Discover the Island was weathered out and was not a financial success, the grant from the TVBP kept the Alliance solvent for another year. The Alliance also had an outreach table at the Tierra Verde Oktoberfest and the annual car show, which allowed the Alliance to promote the park and our events.

The Hillsborough County Board of County County Commissioners awarded the Alliance a grant of $25,000 to fund the cost of the sea turtle monitoring interns hired from the Eckerd College Marine Biology program. I initially contacted Commissioner Stacy White about my request. I met him in his office and explained what I wanted. He thought $25,000 was a good amount to ask for. The cost per year was $5000, so the county grant would have funded the turtle monitoring program for five years. Due to COVID-19, the interns were not hired for several years, and so one year's grant money was repurposed to fund an electric cart for the turtle monitoring program. This was a generous grant, and the county commissioners were eager to help with this funding request. Being awarded this grant necessitated me as President to go before the entire commission, make a presentation, and answer any questions they may have. It was broadcast on live county television. The Commissioners asked several questions about the island and were very interested in its condition and preservation.

Florida Lighthouse Association Many Alliance members were also members of the association. Past President Richard Johnson was a charter member of the association when it was founded. Over the years, the Florida Lighthouse Association provided three grants for various lighthouse-related projects. One grant was for restoring and preserving the lens pedestal, another for refurbishing the DCB-36 beacon display, and the last for rehabbing the Radio Room, Compressor Room, and Oil House. These projects are detailed in the following sections under Significant Accomplishments.

Tampa Bay Regional Planning Council is an organization that works with local governments on economic development, emergency preparedness, planning/design visualization, and geographic information systems (from the TBRPC website). Attendees at these meetings comprise local county commissioners, mayors, city managers, and concerned citizens. The meetings are public and open to anyone.

During these meetings, programs and projects were discussed that could affect the communities with shorelines on Tampa Bay and the Gulf of Mexico. The purpose of the Council was to take a regional approach to these projects rather than each being local in scope. Attendance by Jim Spangler and later Richard Sanchez helped keep the Alliance informed about projects in the Tampa Bay Area.

The TBRPC generously allowed the Alliance to use its facilities for our general meetings, which were usually held quarterly. It was a great meeting space with audiovisual equipment for presentations by anyone who required it.

Visit Florida is a statewide organization that works to promote tourism in Florida. Its members represent venues and tourist destinations of all types. The Alliance joined, and as President, I attended several state conferences held by Visit Florida. The Alliance was granted $2,400 towards an advertising campaign to boost attendance at Discover the Island. It was a matching grant, so the Alliance had to put up an equal amount. We worked with the *Tampa Bay Times* on print and digital marketing in the surrounding counties. We got a boost of about eighty visitors who probably would not have known about the event.

The Murielle Winery worked with the Alliance to produce what they refer to as private-label wines. Located in Largo, Florida, Michael and Janine Biglin own the winery. They make both the wines and create the custom-designed labeling using a photo provided by the Alliance. The winery hosts tastings every week, and on several occasions, the Alliance had an outreach table in the winery. The Alliance would promote the event to members via our website.

Finally, **Tampa Bay Watch**, a local nonprofit dedicated to restoring water quality, protecting shorelines, and educating the public about issues that affect Tampa Bay, provided meeting space for our annual banquets and visits by the Florida Lighthouse Association. They have excellent facilities, and the sunsets off the back porch of the building are spectacular. Having meetings there helped to boost attendance at these meetings, and the TBW staff was accommodating and great to work with. In addition, founder Peter Clarke was an Alliance board member in the early years.

Significant Accomplishments

Several significant accomplishments contributed to the park's success during the years the Alliance CSO was in operation. The first significant accomplishment was the restoration of the Guardhouse. The second was the agreement to bring sand placements from dredge operations to the island. Next, the original lens pedestal that was in the lighthouse was refurbished. After that was the 3D laser scanning of the various buildings and gun batteries, and last was the restoration of a U.S. Coast Guard beacon display.

The Guardhouse Restoration

One of the great success stories on Egmont Key is the restoration of the Guardhouse, which housed the military police and a small jail. After Fort Dade was abandoned in 1922, the building, constructed of solid reinforced concrete, was left to the elements. The US Coast Guard used the building to store oversized metal pallets. At one point, a group of vandals set fire to the building, which destroyed the wood roof framing, causing the collapse of the roof. Eventually, nothing was left but the concrete walls, floor, and debris left by the fire.

Since it was the only building left standing on the island from Fort Dade, members of the Egmont Key Alliance proposed restoring the building and using it as a visitor education center. At that time, the friend's group for US Fish and Wildlife, The Friends of Tampa Bay Refuges, had not been founded, and so the Alliance, the Park Manager, Bob Baker, and the refuge manager agreed to let the project proceed. The project started in 1999, with the Alliance raising nearly half a million dollars ($915,000 today) to fund the work.

Actual work began with volunteers cleaning out the debris inside the structure. The Tampa Rough Riders, a local, well-known historical organization, arranged for a crane to be barged to the island. The crane was used to remove the steel pallets put inside the building by the Coast Guard, which were too heavy to lift by hand. After the cleanup work was completed, the project was turned over to the contractors.

Experts were brought in to assess the condition and make needed structural repairs to the concrete walls. The project moved ahead with the construction of new roof trusses, windows, air conditioning, and other modern amenities. However, the money ran out before the roof tiles were installed, so US Fish and Wildlife generously funded that part of the project.

Since the building needed to be as historically correct as possible, an unbroken sample of the roof barrel tiles was found, and research led to the original manufacturer, who was still in business in Georgia and still made the same pattern tile. The roof was tiled with historically accurate tiles, which completed the reconstruction of the building. This contributed toward meeting the Secretary of Interior's historic restoration standards. Several years later, US Fish and Wildlife funded the cost of interpretive displays for the interior. Over time, lighthouse artifacts and other historical items have been added to tell the story of Egmont Key and Fort Dade. The building is open to the public when there are docents available to staff the building.

Sand Placements

One of the significant accomplishments that has done the most to preserve Egmont Key was what past president James Spangler was able to get done. It involves the maintenance dredge projects that are done periodically by the Army Corps of Engineers to keep the shipping channel at the proper depth and width.

Typically, the easiest and least expensive way to dispose of the dredge materials was to put it on a barge, take it twenty miles into the

Gulf of Mexico, and dump it. James Spangler arranged through the Corps of Engineers to place the sand on Egmont Key. This was done as the "best use" of the sand.

The process is much more involved in this type of sand placement. A large-diameter pipe system has to be put in place from the location on the shoreline where the sand will go back to a flexible pipe that extends into a connection point out in the water off the island's north end. This pipe system could be hundreds of yards long and would need heavy equipment to install. The dredge will remove the sand and then bring it to the connection point, pumping it through the pipe as a slurry of sand and water. Bulldozers and other earth-moving equipment brought ashore spread the sand where it was most needed.

The shipping channel maintenance dredge projects will occur about every five to seven years unless conditions require it to be done sooner. Without these dredge projects and the sand placement on the island, Egmont Key would be significantly smaller than it is today, at about two hundred acres. Like the ones on the island's south end, the gun batteries on the northeastern shore might have been lost. All three batteries have been threatened by erosion over the decades, with Battery Howard suffering significant damage.

Lens Pedestal Refurbishment

In 2015, Neil Hurley, a retired U.S. Coast Guard Commander, proposed a project to refurbish the 1858 lens pedestal discovered in the old Fort Dade mine casemate building where the State Park Service had stored it. The pedestal was original to the 1858 tower and had been cast in France by the Augustin Henri-Lepaute Company. It was removed when the lighthouse's watch room and lantern room were dismantled in 1944 as a part of the Coast Guard's automation of lighthouses.

After getting permission from both the Coast Guard and Florida State Park Service, Neil Hurley traveled to Fort Desoto Park from his home in Virginia and then made his way to the island. The pedestal parts were removed from the museum building where they had been stored since being moved from the mine casemate bunker. It was transported to the Park Service utility boat and secured. The total weight of these iron pieces was about seven hundred pounds! Neil and a group of volunteers loaded the parts onto his truck, and he transported them to Tallahassee, where the Florida Division of Historical Resources Conservation Lab is located, for the next steps.

Lab scientists submerged the pedestal into a chemical solution with electrical charges that, over the course of six months, removed salts from the iron's pores to stabilize the metal. Without this procedure, the paint would not adhere properly to the metal. After this process was complete, the parts were painted in a historically correct green color[2].

In the meantime, Neil had a steel bracket custom-designed and welded to serve as an interior support for the pedestal. All this came together in the Guardhouse on a workday. Putting these parts together on the support bracket was quite a task, but with many hands, it was finally done.

To finish the pedestal and prepare it for public viewing, a wooden frame was built around the base to cover the support legs, and a railing was installed. Some interpretive signage was added, and later, a

---

2 The historically accurate shade of green, as it turned out, was Rustoleum "Hunter Green." The lighthouse restorers conducted extensive research, even discovering a spot on a lens pedestal that the sun had not affected. The closest match they found was the standard, off-the-shelf green from the Rustoleum Corporation, a fascinating detail that adds a historical context to the project.

full-scale photographic image of a third-order lens was placed atop the pedestal so that visitors could appreciate its size.

The Florida Lighthouse Association provided a grant of $1,200, and the Alliance provided some additional funding. Thanks to the co-operation and efforts of volunteers, the Florida Lighthouse Association, the U.S. Coast Guard, Egmont Key State Park, Florida State Parks, the Florida Division of Historical Resources, and the Egmont Key Alliance, a valuable island artifact was saved and preserved.

Replica of the Watch Room

In 2012, I received a call from Neil Hurley, who proposed a project to build a full-size replica of the watchroom and lens pedestal, which were removed from the lighthouse in 1944. As he described what he wanted to do, I admit that I was a little skeptical, owing to the project's complexity. However, with the park manager's approval, he moved ahead with the work. I agreed to have some volunteers available when it was time to transport and assemble the parts.

Neil lives in Virginia, so whatever he built had to be transported via a trailer. He built the watchroom in pieces that would be fastened together in the museum. These were complex pieces since the watchroom was round. He eventually brought the parts to the Fort DeSoto boat ramp, and the park manager met him there with the park utility boat. Once the parts were on the island, Neil guided the assembly of the pieces. Several volunteers were on hand to help get the parts assembled. To my surprise, all the parts fit very well, and the finished product was an accurate replica of the watchroom. It has been used countless times to show visitors to the island what the watchroom was like and how the lens was mounted on the pedestal. There was even a replica of the Argand lamp that illuminated the lighthouse beacon.

Refurbishing the Coast Guard Buildings

The lighthouse has several support buildings that are occasionally open to the public as exhibits. There is the Radio Room, where the transmitters were housed, a generator room adjacent to that, and the Compressor Room, where the air compressor and air tank for the foghorn were housed. Finally, there is the oil house, built around 1890 to store the fuel for the lighthouse lantern.

The last time these buildings were painted was in 2008, before the lighthouse's 150th anniversary. The doors to the buildings were rotted, the door frames were in bad shape, the lighting was inadequate, and the switches and receptacles had corroded from decades of being in a salt environment.

A plan was put together to address these issues, and funding was acquired from the Florida Lighthouse Association for the majority of the funding. Work began with fabricating new doors that had to conform to the Secretary of the Interior's historic standards. The doors were not standard sizes, and each was different. Once the doors were built and transported to the island, the door frames and hinges were replaced next. Before the door on the Radio Room could be installed, repairs to the concrete wall had to be made. The doors were installed and painted, and new latches were installed so the doors could be padlocked.

The electrical work was another set of problems. The wiring was not updated from the original electrical code, and the lights were halogen, generating significant heat. Modern wiring, switches, receptacles, and conduit were installed where needed. The halogen lights were replaced with energy-efficient LED lights that better illuminated the displays in the room.

The project's final phase involved painting the concrete walls of the buildings. Because there was a lot of peeling paint, the first step was to manually scrape the loose paint so that the new paint would adhere properly. The work was done in the summer, so the outside temperature was oppressively hot, which made the work difficult. Due to restrictions on the number of volunteers we were allowed to have on each ferry trip, the painting and all this work spanned several months. Through the efforts of a few dedicated volunteers, the work was completed, and it dramatically transformed the look of the buildings.

USF 3D Laser Scanning Projects

In 2018, I was contacted by Dr. Laura Harrison, head of the University of South Florida Access 3D Lab, and her colleague, Dr. Brooke Hansen, wanted to do laser scanning of the various buildings on the island. They had been referred to me by Dr. Paul Backhouse of the Seminole Tribal Historic Office down at Big Cypress. They were looking for historic buildings to scan and to take on a challenging structure like a lighthouse.

They used two different technologies to complete the projects. One was the Faro System, which uses lasers to create a "point cloud" of data points. Using specialized software, the data can be converted into images and videos. The Faro System is accurate down to a millimeter and can generate paper documents in case a structure needs to be rebuilt.

The second system, Matterport, uses digital photogrammetry to accomplish similar tasks. It has specialized imaging equipment and even an iPhone app.

The work was done as part of coursework for students wanting to learn these systems and methods. They scanned the lighthouse, Battery Mellon, and Battery McIntosh using Faro and the Guardhouse and Coast Guard buildings using Matterport. The Access 3D Lab created stunning images that enable people to take virtual tours of these sites without traveling to them. These videos are a great teaching tool for historic preservation and education.

Beacon Refurbishment Project

When the lighthouse was automated in 1944, the original lantern room and watch room were removed, and a double DCB-36 beacon was installed and powered by an electric motor mounted inside the lighthouse. After many years of service, that beacon was "retired" and replaced with a single aerobeacon. This model of light had an electric motor in a housing directly below the beacon, and the entire unit was installed on top of the tower. The old DCB-36 beacon was placed on a concrete pad near the US Coast Guard flagpole as a static display. It sat there for decades with no maintenance and was showing its age. It leaked water when it rained, and the baseplate had severely corroded to the point it was unsafe. Trying to maintain it in place was inadequate, and more extensive work needed to be done.

In May of 2022, David Barker, then vice president of the Egmont Key Alliance and former Coast Guardsman, proposed refurbishing this display beacon on Egmont Key. The light station at Egmont was David's first duty station as a new service member, so the beacon project meant a lot to him. He had learned how to maintain the light and the low-frequency navigation radio at the site. Since joining the Alliance, he became concerned about the deterioration of the beacon and wanted to see what could be done.

He began by contacting the US Coast Guard staff at St. Petersburg and proposed the idea to them. At the same time, Richard Sanchez, then President of the Alliance, began looking for a facility to handle the work. Mr. Frank Kearny, Manager of the Manatee Ship Repair Company in Tampa, agreed to do the work and quoted a price.

Richard was on the board of the Florida Lighthouse Association and began working on a grant proposal to see if the FLA could fund the grant. With a vendor willing to do the work, the USCG was agreeable to assist with the project.

A grant was applied for through the Florida Lighthouse Association, which funds projects like these, and $10,000 was awarded for the refurbishment. This included all the hardware, cleaning and sealing the glass lenses, new seals around the access doors, and cleaning and painting the exterior of the housings. The USCG Aids to Navigation Team took on transportation to and from the island and dismantled the beacon.

Since this was not a high-priority project for the Coast Guard, we had to wait until there was time in their busy schedule to dismantle and remove the beacon. This required four of the staff from the Aids to Navigation Team to travel to the island by boat with the tools necessary to do the work. Without the base, the beacon was large and more than six hundred pounds. All involved did a lot of work, including Sanchez and Barker, as well as park staff, and the team used a tractor with a front loader to handle the weight. It was dismantled into six major pieces, placed on the boat, and returned to the St. Petersburg Coast Guard Station.

Again, as time permitted, the USCG transported the pieces to Manatee Ship Repair's facility in East Tampa. The beacon was fully disassembled, and an assessment of the work to be done was made. Any parts that had to be purchased or manufactured were also determined. Since the original mounting base was unusable due to corrosion, a new one had to be designed and fabricated. This part alone weighed more than one hundred pounds.

During the refurbishment process, Manatee Ship Repair had to move from its shop in East Tampa to a new shop nearer to the Port of Tampa Bay. They made the move on short notice, and not a single part of the beacon was lost or damaged in transit!

Before the beacon could be returned, the new base needed to be taken to the island and mounted on the original concrete base. David Will, owner of Caveman Concrete in Pinellas County, had the equipment, materials, and experience to do this work. Mounting the base required drilling six holes in the base and installing 7/8 inch threaded rods with epoxy adhesive to keep it in place. The epoxy would have plenty of time to cure before the beacon was brought back to the island, and the Coast Guard was ready to bring everything back and reinstall the beacon on the new mounting base.

After many months of waiting, the project was nearing completion! The beacon parts had to be taken from the station at St. Petersburg to the Coast Guard Air Station at St. Pete/Clearwater Airport. It would require two trips from there to Egmont to get everything on site. Four Coast Guardsmen came to the island by boat with tools, ready to begin the work. There was a delay in getting the first part of the beacon to the island, so things didn't start till after 1 PM. With the help of the front loader tractor, they were able to lift the two beacons and put them in place after assembling the parts. It was a long day's work for everyone involved, but the beacon was finally in place and ready to continue educating the public about lighthouse history for many years.

A few months later, a bronze plaque designed by David Barker and funded by the Tampa Rough Riders was placed on a post near the beacon, acknowledging the hard work of all involved. It took a full year from start to finish! Many people were involved with this project, from the Alliance to the US Coast Guard ANT Team, the US Coast Guard Air Wing, and the shops of Manatee Ship Repair. Also, it would not have been possible without the generosity of the Florida Lighthouse Association and the Tampa Rough Riders.

The beacon and mounting system were put to the ultimate test with the arrival of Hurricanes Helene and Milton in 2024. The beacon and mount survived without damage and will represent the US Coast Guard for decades to come.

The End of the Alliance CSO

In December 2023, I notified the board of directors that I was no longer willing to serve as president of the Alliance. I had been a member for seventeen years and president for fifteen, the longest serving in total years. Nobody was willing to take on the president's tasks, and several board members intended to resign anyway. Thus began the process of closing down the organization, which took several months.

Tara Hubbard of Hubbard's Marina had recently founded a nonprofit called TakeMAR. Within her organization, she created a subcommittee called the Egmont Key Alliance Committee that handles the park's volunteering activities.

During my time as president, I was fortunate to have some of the best volunteers and board members. The organization made significant contributions to preserving its natural and historic resources. The Alliance's motto was "Restore, Preserve, and Protect" Egmont Key, and for more than thirty years, the organization was faithful to these goals.

Chapter 28

Epilogue

There are probably very few places like Egmont Key in the United States, but certainly none like it in Florida. It has a unique geological and human history. It has had many names and has been visited by countless famous and ordinary people. Each has brought something to the island regarding what they did when they came. Each has taken something with them as well, whether something significant or just memories.

The island has witnessed storms, wildfires, disease, hardship, births and deaths, war and peace, human bondage and freedom, and has been a place of safe haven. It will continue to do these things in the coming years. Throughout it all, the island has been a refuge for wildlife regardless of the activities of its human visitors.

The island has steadily decreased in size over the years, from nearly six hundred acres when it was first surveyed to the present two hundred acres, as the forces of development, climate change, and sea level rise continue to affect it. Passage Key has also suffered, going from one hundred acres to completely submerged a few years ago after a storm to reappearing in a slightly different spot and growing to four acres.

Ownership has changed between the Spanish and British, and finally, to the United States. The island has played a part in many United States conflicts, from the Seminole War to the Civil War, the Spanish-American War, and both World Wars. Fort Dade and nearby Fort Desoto stood guard over Tampa Bay for more than twenty years, and a shot was never fired in anger from their guns.

The island remains a very significant site for wildlife as well. Loggerhead sea turtles return to the island every summer from their travels around the world's oceans to nest at the place where they hatched decades before. Egmont Key is an important nesting site for many species of shorebirds, and at the height of the nesting season, more than 100,000 birds will inhabit the island after hatching and fledging their young. The island is also part of an eastern United States seaboard flyway for migratory birds. Egmont Key is recognized internationally as an essential site for both shorebirds and migratory birds. The island is home to the threatened gopher tortoise, found all over the state in the past. The island has a stable, healthy, and thriving population of this important keystone species.

Egmont Key is currently managed as a US Fish and Wildlife Refuge and Bird Sanctuary on the southern three-quarters of the island, as well as a Florida State Park, which overlays the US Coast Guard property on the northern fifty-five acres. The Tampa Bay Harbor Pilots occupy about ten acres on the southeastern side of the island and help to safely guide the many cargo ships in and out of Tampa Bay. They have been providing this vital service for more than one hundred years. The Coast Guard, which has been on the island since 1939, and before that, the US Lighthouse Service, keeps the lighthouse in good working order.

Epilogue

Egmont Key has been a destination for tourism and recreation since the 1850s when guests at Henry Plant's Tampa Bay Hotel came to the island on steamships to picnic and explore. The visitor numbers have varied over the years, but more than 200,000 people currently come to the island on the numerous ferries that operate locally or by private boats.

But things are changing with management as well. The Coast Guard started relinquishing its property in 2001. It is not certain when this relinquishment will be completed or what will happen afterward. Hopefully, the island that has been so much a part of Florida, U.S., and world history and an important natural resource will continue to be protected for future generations to enjoy and learn about its rich history.

Appendix A

Note: The Recorder to the Board was Captain Robert E. Lee, who had written the final report to his superiors. It was a handwritten document that sometimes presented problems in transcription. The layout of the document below is intended to resemble the original one. All spelling and grammar mistakes are left in as they appeared. When you see an asterisk (*), it is because the original, handwritten document was illegible. These records are from the National Archives. RAS

Florida Lands in General
14 March 1849

Report of the Board of Engineers
Upon their examination of
The West and East Coast of Florida
From Pensacola Harbor to
Amelia Island

Rec. Mar. 19

Savannah, Mar 14, 1849

Board of Engineers

Coast of Florida

Their Report Recommending certain
Reservations of land
On the coast of Florida

2 enclosures
Report
List of lands so
Recommended

14 March 1849

Report of the Board of Engineers,
upon their examination of the West & East
Coast of Florida, from
Pensacola Harbor to Amelia Island

(B4562)

Fwd. To: G. Totten Chief Engr.
Washington City D. C.

Savannah
14 March 1849

Sir,

*** to your instructions of the *** 1849 relieving Col. Thayer
from the duty of examining the Florida Coast, *** that particular
Service upon the other members of the board of engineers

Lt. Col R. E. Delrusy(DeRussy)
Major R.[Richard] Delafield

Appendix A

Bvt. Col J.[Joseph] K. F. Mansfield
Bvt. Col. R. E Lee

Proceeded to Mobile to embark on the U. S. Schooner *Phenix* [*sic*] provided for the purpose by the Department, in execution of the order of 8th Sept. 1848.

Col. S. Thayer, Pres: Bd. of Engrs. *(Note: Sylvanus Thayer)*

Engineer Department

Washington 8 Sept. 1848

Sir,

The Board of Engineers will make an examination during the coming winter of the coast of East and West Florida from Amelia Island around Pensacola Bay, not including the latter, which has been comprised in previous examinations.

It is hoped that the engagements of the Officers of the Board permit the duty to be taken up in time for the proceedings results to reach the Department before the close of the next Session of Congress. When informed of the time & place appointed by the board for the commencement of the examination, the Dept. will ask the Sec. of War to solicit the Sec. of the Treas. the aid (hitherto granted with great promptness) of a Revenue Cutter, to transfer the Board along parts of the Coast otherwise inaccessible to them.

The main object of the Board, in the contemplated exploration of the Coast of Florida, will be the selection & designation of the Bays, Harbors and Inlets, that should enter into the New System of Coast defence [*sic*]. To this end it is expected that they will examine all such, so as to satisfy themselves of the true points of defence [*sic*] in each, & also to be enabled to append to their report, memoranda comprising instructions for the necessary surveys & levellings. In a general description of the localities of interest as connected with defence [*sic*], the Board will discriminate to the relative value & importance of each; will mark out the order of time in which they *** should receive the attention of Government in surveys, in the erection of defenses [*sic*].

In the account of harbors *, should be comprised a description, with a sketch (at least) of all existing works (except Fort Marion, St. Augustine, & Fort at Matanzas inlet now in this office) and the opinion of the Board on the propriety of maintaining the same in the system.

A special board having already reported on the Florida Reef, including Key West & the Tortugas, the Board of Engineers will use their discretion as to further examination of the same or any points thereof, in reference to the Commission [*sic*] of this reef with the general defensive System of the Gulf.

The Board is aware that every other part of the Coast from Eastport to the Sahire [*sic*] has been heretofore examined by the Board of Engineers – whose valuable reports thereon are in file in this office: the design now is to supply the a***pay[*sic*] knowledge for the deficient portion of the Coast indicated in the beginning of this letter. The above general instructions are all that can be a***pay [*sic*] to the accomplishment of this object, in a perfect manner.

I have however particularly to instruct the Board, that in anticipation of the necessity for occupying certain points, islands on the Coast of Florida as defensive sites, reservations have been made of the public lands to an extent that interfers [*sic*] *** in some places, with the with the progress of improvements & settlement of the Coast and therefore the Board will as soon as practicable, in a special report, point out all the localities that should be reserves – giving limits to each reservation to sufficiently guide the Land Offices.

Applications have been more than once made from high quarters for all land to be liberated that is now under reservation along that shore and I have had action therein postponed only under a promise that at the earliest day practicable, the Board of Engineers would make a selection of the sites actually *** for our purposes.

It may be advantageous for one member of the Board, before going south, to visit this city for the purpose of selecting such maps, Reports useful in the duty before the Board, as can be procured here.

I have the honor to be
(Signed) Jos. G. Totten
Chief Engineer

The Board assembled at Mobile on the 26th and the Schooner *Phenix* being reported ready for sea on the 30th, sailed that day for the Coast of Florida.

The various bays, harbors, inlets around the Coast will now be considered under their respective heads, with a view to their being embraced in the general system of defence [*sic*].

I.   Pensacola Bay.   This Bay having been examined by previous Boards of Engineers, was by the orders of the 8th Sept. excluded from the Coast of Florida directive to be examined by the present Board.

II.   Bay of Santa Rosa.   This Bay being connected with the Pensacola Bay & forming one of its entrances, the examination of which has been stated, was to be omitted by the Board, was not visited.

III.   St. Andrews Sound.   There were formerly three entrances to this Sound. The <u>western</u>, near the termination of the western point of the main land, called Coe Point, has now about 5 feet of water at common low tide. The <u>middle</u> entrance near the west end of St. Andrews island, has about 15 feet at low water. The <u>eastern</u> entrance, between St. Andrews island & the eastern point of the mainland, called Crooked island, is now closed. Within the Sound, formed by the points & island mentioned, there are 24 feet of water & a smooth(?) Anchorage. The islands & necks of land, separating it from the ocean, are *** with breaches through their barriers of trees and settlements. The upper end of the St. Andrews Sound called St. Andrews bay is a good harbor for Coasters *(ships suitable for coastal use)* & the banks are covered with pine timber.

At present therefore, but a few vessels? would enter this sound except as a port of refuge, of which there are others that that might be within their reach. No work of defence [*sic*] is therefore recommended, but in consideration of future events of commerce & development of the resources of the County, reservations of lands or the points commanding the several entrances have been recommended. Owing to the changeable character of the bars & channels, & the absence of Surveys necessary to locate the exact positions, the Board considers it advisable to have the designation of the points to be occupied until the time appropriate when it may be necessary, & after the Surveys have been made.

IV. Bay of St. Joseph.   St Josephs bay, situated southeast of St. Andrews Sound, is formed by a low neck of land, stretching on a Southerly direction to Cape San Blas. Its entrance is between the southeast extremity of the shoal, making it from St. Andrews Sound & the northern extremity of the neck which is called St Joseph point. The channel passes close to the latter point is clear & easy & about 15 feet of water can be carried over the bar at low tide. The bay is about 2 ¾ miles wide at its mouth and & about 14 miles long. It increases in width after passing the entrance & furnishes excellent anchorage. Near the neck of land separating it from the ocean, there are from 4 to 5 fathoms water & a secure harbor in all winds. The neck of land is covered with a thick growth of pine for about 1 ¼ miles from its north extremity but is destitute of trees in some parts of its extent and varies in width.

About 8 miles from the mouth of the Bay, on the main land is the site of the town of st. Joseph, formerly the terminus of the railroad from the Apalachicola river & was the seat of some commerce. It is now abandoned & the Lt House that was then established at Point St. Joseph has been removed to Cape San Blas.

As a harbor of refuge, though somewhat removed from the course of trade, Bay of St. Joseph is one of the best on that part of the Coast, but at present has no other value. Its defence may therefore be designed like that of St. Andrews Sound with the circumstances there referred to, shall point out its necessity. To meet this contingency & to preserve the harbor the reservation of the whole Peninsula has been recommended. The preservation of the harbor depends on the preservation of the trees that protect the sand beach & it is for that reason that the reservation of the whole peninsula, which is necessary for agricultural purposes, has been urged. A work on St. Josephs when acquired will it is believed sufficiently command the entrance.

V.   St. Georges Sound.   The <u>west</u> entrance of this sound is between the N. W. extremity of St Georges island & the southern extremity of St. Vincent's. After crossing the bar, the channel passes near a small sand island, called Flag island about 2 miles south east of the entrance. There are about 12 feet of water on the bar at low water, with an average rise of tide of 2 feet. Directly at the entrance, which is about ¾ of a mile wide, there are 7 fathoms of water. St Georges island which forms the sound & separates it from the sea is low and flat and thinly covered with trees about 30 miles long and varies in width from ¼ to 1 ½ miles. It receives the water of the Apalachicola river. The Apalachicola formed by the junction of the Chattahoochee & Flint rivers takes its use several hundred miles from the Coast. Its waters at its mouth or junction with St Georges Sound spread over extensive flats & oyster reefs & form Apalachicola bay. The shores of the bay are low and marshy. On the west point of the main land is situated the town of Apalachicola. It contains a population of about 1300 inhabitants. The amounts of its imports for the year ending 30 Sept. 1847 was $2,661,000 & of its exports for the same period $5,435,789. The principle article of export is cotton which is estimated will amount this year (1849) to 160,000 bales. The business period of the year is limited to the winter season or about 6 months. There the Apalachicola is navigable for small steamers & the climate is healthy. The channel from the town to the Apalachicola bay is narrow and winding & at low water is not over 5-6 feet deep. Ships consequently cannot approach nearer than Apalachicola bay & receive the greater part of their cargo in St Georges Sound. Those that draw over 14 feet are obliged to enter the sound through the middle entrance, which is between the east end of St. Georges island & the west end of Dog island. Sixteen feet can be carried over the bar at this entrance at high tide, but ships cannot approach by it nearer than 14 miles to the town of Apalachicola, inconsequence of a sand bar called the "Bulk head", that stretches from Cat point, the east point of Apalachicola bay to St. Georges island. This bar has only 6 ft. of water on it at high tide & is probably formed by the meeting of the tides through the two entrances. It interrupts the passage of ships drawing over 6 feet through the sound and effectually prevents their approach from the middle & eastern entrances to the town or bay of Apalachicola.

The east or third entrance is east of Dog island. But 14 feet of water can be carried over the bar of this entrance at high water & the channel passes within a quarter of a mile of the east end of the island.

In consideration of the present & growing commerce of the town of Apalachicola, the amount of its exports and interior trade, the number of *** engaged in its commerce and the position of St. Georges Sound as a port of refuge for *** Coasters, the board consider the latter of sufficient importance to require that preparations with a view to its defence in case of need be commenced. The precise system & plan of defence cannot be given until after the necessary surveys for that object be made, but the Board will state generally from their personal examination that the occupation of the west end of St. Georges island by a suitable work will give not only some protection to the general commerce of that section of the Country but also confidence to the trade & partial security to the inhabitants of Apalachicola. It would prevent an enemy's ships entering the bay of Apalachicola from which by his boats, he would have ready access to the town & give shelter under its guns to such of our ships as might be in the Sound.

To close the Sound eventually against an enemy & complete the defence of Apalachicola, may require other works at this entrance, as well as at the points commanding the other entrances.

VI.   St. Marks river.   The next harbour [*sic*] to St. Georges Sound worth considering is St. Marks river. Ochlocknee bay, at the west end of Apalachicola bay (a shallow & unprotected sheet of water) has only 7 feet of water at its entrance at high water. St. Marks river empties into Appalachie bay near its center. The approach to the river is plain & direct. The bar is about 5 miles from its mouth, over which not more than 12 feet of water can be carried at ordinary high water. The channel across the bar, though straight & well defined, is not more than 100 yards wide. Within the bar it expands to about 300 yards in width & deepens to 14 feet. The basin thus forms called "Spanish hole" extending to the mouth of the river is the usual anchorage for vessels trading to St. marks river & the only shelter against southerly winds in Appalachie (Apalache) bay.

The distance from the mouth of the St. Marks to its junction with the Wakulla river, the site of the old Spanish fort of St. Marks is about 8 miles. The channel is narrow and winding passing through the oyster reefs; is not more than 6 feet deep at low water & varies in width from 50 to 100 yards. There are two tides in the river in 24 hours & the ordinary rise of tide is 4 feet. The banks of the river below Fort St. marks is liable to be overflown [*sic*] during southerly gales & Port Leon situated one mile below has been destroyed by a recent gale. There appears therefore to be no site for a town below that point. The Fort is situated on the point of confluence of the two rivers & is in a dilapidated state. It is well situated to defend the passage up the river & to prevent the approach to the town of Newport 5 miles above. A rail road from Fort St. Marks to Tallahassee is the chief means of communication with the interior. The cotton is principally carried by freighters from Fort St. Marks down the river to the shipping anchored at its mouth. The quantity of cotton that will probably be shipped from St. Marks this season is estimated will amount to 30,000 bales.

For the purpose of defence of this river, should circumstances hereafter require it, the Board would recommend that the old Spanish Fort of St. Marks & the ground attached to it be reserved for military uses.

VII. Cedar Cays Passing Deadmans [*sic*] & Horseshoe bays, two more indentations in the Coast, the next harbor is that of Cedar Cays. The group of islands forming this harbor is situated 3 or 4 miles from the main land & about 13 miles S. E. of the Suwannee river. The mouth of Wakassa[Wacas-

asse] river is about the same distance east of these islands &
the Awisura[?] or Withlokkoochee[Withlacoochee] pours
its waters into the Gulf at an equal distance S. E of them.
They are therefore nearly equidistant from the mouths of
these three rivers, towards which they all converge & their
harbour is of nearly equal value to each. The principle islands in the group are named North Cay, Seahorse Cay,
Snake Cay, Depot Cay *(present-day Atsena Otie Key)* and Big
Way Cay *(now present-day Cedar Key)*. The best approach
from the Sea now known is between Seahorse & Snake
Cays, which are in the outer line of islands. The channel
passes near the South point of Seahorse Cay & there is
an anchorage of 2 fathoms water, close to under it. From
Seahorse to Depot Cay, *** of the inner islands, the channel
is contracted [?] at common low water does not exceed 8
feet in depth. There is an inner anchorage of 2 fathoms water between Depot and Way Cays. Depot Cay is the site of
the storehouses & wharf, erected by the U. S. in the Florida
War of 1836 which has formed the basis of a small town. It
is situated N. E. of Seahorse Cay & about 4 miles distant.
There are three other channels from sea, besides the ones
described, to Depot Cay. One east of Snake Cay, another
between Sea Horse & North Cay & the third west of North
Cay. Neither of them at low tide has more than 5 feet of water. The islands are above the reach of inundation & covered
with a growth of trees.. The mouth of the Suwannee river
being closed by shoals & oyster reefs & having but 3 feet
or 4 feet of water over them , the cotton and other produce
descending the river is brought to Cedar Cays in lighters

(*flat bottomed barges*) for shipment. The Suwannee takes its use from Georgia from many sources & is now navigable by a light draft steamer as high as Columbus about 200 miles from its mouth where it is joined by the Withlacoochee & Alapaha. The shipments at present from the port of Cedar Cays, are derived principally from the Suwannee. The average amount of cotton shipped per year for four years, including the estimated quantity for this year is 2234 bales. That of hides & skins, about 200. In addition there are yearly shipments of cedar & pine lumber.

The country East and South of Cedar Cays is as yet now & uncultivated. It is represented to be rich and adaptable to the growth of sugar & cotton, as far as the Chasowiska (*Chassahowitzka*) river. The immediate defence of this point, although well situated in reference to the Suwannee and Wakasasa (*Waccasassa*) and Awisura (*possibly Withlacoochee*) rivers , & now the depot of commerce, may in the opinion of the Board, be advantageously defended. The present trade is not sufficient to require it to be fortified, & the development of the resources of the country may cause the construction of railroads that would direct commerce to other points. After the surveys of the Coast, now in progress, have reached this point the true and best approach from sea will be discovered & the particular surveys of the harbor will indicate the points of the erection of defences. A reservation of certain islands have been recommended for this purpose.

VIII.   Tampa Bay.   The Coast South of Cedar Cays as far as Anclote Cay, or Anchor island is so low & shoal that the land is not visible to the naked eye until you get into less than 2 fathoms of water. From that point it becomes more prominent & bolder. Anclote Cay, about 4 or 5 miles from the mainland, has an anchorage for Coasters *(coastal boats)* under its Southern point. Like Clearwater Harbor *(present-day Clearwater),* still farther South, this anchorage is open to the north & can only be entered from the South. It is accessible only to small vessels. South of Anclote island the shore is bolder and covered by a range of low islands *(barrier islands)* The principle of those which extend across the mouth of Tampa Bay , are called Mullet, Egmont, Barnaby & Long islands *(present-day Mullet Key, Egmont Key, Passage Key and Anna Maria Island. The names have changed many times over the years, and even a coastal survey done in 1855 has different names for Passage Key and Anna Maria).*

The lower part of this Bay was called <u>Espiritu Santo</u> *(Holy Spirit).* The upper part is divided into two branches. The western branch is called Tampa and the Eastern, Hillsborough. The whole bay is generally known under the name of Tampa. It is about 30 miles long & 5 miles wide, as far up as Gadsden's Point, where it separates into East and West branches.

There are now two principle entrances from sea. One on either side of Egmont island. The channel north of Egmont, called the <u>West entrance</u>, runs nearly east & west between the shoals extending from Egmont & Mullet islands sea-wards, which bound it on either side. Both shoals stretch several miles to the sea & even at high water are well defined & mark the channel way. The bar is at their outer termination, where they spread into one & g=has 21 feet of water on it at common low tide. Hn pgea Within the bar the channel is from 7 to 10 fathoms deep & about a mile wide to within the bay. The distance from the north point of Egmont island to the South point of Mullet island is about 2 miles.

The entrance south of Egmont island, called <u>East entrance</u>, lies between Egmont & Barnaby islands. This entrance is also broad & open. The bar has 15 feet of water on it at low water & is not so distant to sea as the bar of the west entrance.

Besides these two main channels there are other minor ones north & south of them, between islands covering the mouth of the bay, which vary in depth from 4 to 7 feet.

All of these channels except the <u>west entrance</u>, change in their positions and depths after every severe storm. The storm of October 1848 *(possibly the one that damaged the first lighthouse)*, washed away a portion of Barnaby island & diminished the depth of the channel between that island & Long island. In this latter channel there had been previously 116 feet of water. The channel of the <u>west entrance</u> differs from all the rest in not being subject to the alterations produced by storms. It remains always the same.

The islands covering the mouth of Tampa are low & sandy & bear a stunted growth of Spanish bayonet, palmetto. The shores of the bay as high as Gadsden's point, are also low & subject to be overflowed by storm tides. Above Gadsden's point the banks are higher. Those on the western branch are above the reach of inundation & 3 fathoms of water can be carried up to the head of the branch. The banks at the head of the Eastern branch, the site of Fort Brooke, are barely above the reach of severe storms. Four fathoms water can be carried from the mouth of the bay to Mangrove point. There the water begins to shoal & the channel becomes winding. Only 8 feet of water can be carried up to the mouth of the Hillsborough river at the head of the Eastern branch and the Hillsborough is not navigable more than 12 miles from its mouth. The Manitee *[Manatee]* river enters the bay at near its mouth & the little Manitee about half way up. There are a few settlements on these rivers, but as yet that around Fort Brooke is the principle.

In a military point of view, this large and spacious bay of greater capacity than any on the Coast of Florida of easy access & having as much water over the bar of its principle entrance as Pensacola is diminished in value in consequence of the many & width of its entrances which renders it difficult to defend. In itself it has but little trade & commerce & it would be difficult to state the period when it would be likely to be of sufficient importance to authorize the expenditure necessary for its complete defence. Yet its position intermediate between Cay west *[Key West]* and Pensacola, the only points on the Gulf where vessels of a certain draft could look for safety, added to its advantages as a harbor, may hereafter render it advisable, if not to close against our enemy's fleet; at least each a work on the on the north end of Egmont island, which in addition to interrupting the passage of the main entrance , would give some protection under its guns to our own vessels, with the aid of war steamers stationed in the Gulf, secure the advantages of the harbor to vessels & wrest them from an *** . The Survey of this part of the coast will honestly establish the relative position of the islands & channels now imperfectly known & show how the defence of the harbor can be best effected. With this view & preparatory to the completion of the Survey the Board have recommended certain islands at the mouth of the harbor be reserved for military purposes.

IX. Charlotte Harbor.   The Coast between Tampa & Charlotte harbour is bordered with low flat islands, about 4 miles distant from the main land, allowing an interior boat passage between them & the shore. Outside this range of islands the shore is bolder than north of Tampa. The principle islands that cover the mouth of Charlotte harbour are called Ulena [*possibly present day Cayo Costa*], Gasparilla, Boca Grande & Captiva.

Like Tampa, Charlotte harbor has several entrances. The main entrance called Boca grande, lies between Gasparilla & Boca grande islands. The distance between them is about a mile. From each island flat shoals extend 5 miles to sea & confine the channel on either side. The bar is near the extremity of these shoals & about 4 miles distant from the line of islands. At common low water there are 15 ft.

of water on the bar. After crossing the bar there are from 4 to 7 fathoms water in the channel. The channel is plain and direct & the shoals on either side well defined. North of Gasparilla & between it and Clena island is another entrance called Boca Gasparilla. At low water there are not 7 feet water in this entrance & the passage thence to the interior of the bay, between the mangrove islands is shoal & intricate. South of Boca grande island & between it & Captiva island is a third entrance called Boca Captiva. This entrance at low water is not over 7 feet deep. Besides these three entrances, there are others north of Clena & south of Captiva islands admitting the passage of boats between the islands that border the shore & the mainland. They are however shoal & at low water not more than 2 or 3 feet deep. They are all too, as well as those just named, liable to be changed by storms, except Boca grande which remains unaltered. The islands that protect the mouth of the harbour from the sea, are low & narrow & sparsely covered by trees of stunted growth. There are besides many others of similar character in the interior of the bay. Several streams empty into this bay, which take their rise in the Indian Country & are fed from overflow of the swamps & lakes.

This harbour bordering on the Indian Country has no trade beyond that relating to the Indians & a few fishermen. It would therefore scarcely ever be sought, except by Coasters as a port of refuge. Its proximity to Tampa, although affording perfect shelter & good anchorage, even lessens its importance in this respect. Measures for its defence may be therefore with propriety deferred until time shall indicate its necessity & after the surveys of that coast have been completed. With this view the reservations of certain islands appropriate for the purpose, have been recommended by the board.

X.   Carlos Bay   Sanybel *[Sanibel]* island South of Captiva island is the most southern of the group that covers the mouth of Charlotte harbour. The indentation in the coast South of this island is called San Carlos bay. Sanybel Shoal stretching to the S. E. for 4 or 5 miles, protects the head of San Carlos bay towards the west. Between this shoal & Semon *[possibly present day Estero Island]* island in the east is good anchorage in 9 fathoms water. After passing the north end of Semon island, which is separated from the mainland by a narrow bayou, the water shoals to 1 ½ fathoms. Beyond the shoal it again deepens to 2 fathoms. Near the S. E. point of Sanybel island, there are from 2 to 3 fathoms water, extending ½ mile north of the point. The waters of Charlotte harbor communicate with the waters of San Carlos bay, by the passage between Sanybel and & the main, which is narrow & winding channel of not more than 5 feet deep.

The Caloosahatchie *[Caloosahatchee]* river which takes its rise in the swamps around Lake Okee Chobee [Okeechobee] discharges its waters into the head of San Carlos bay. It is navigable for 10 miles from its mouth in boats drawing 4 or 5 feet of water.

Punta Rasa *[Punta Rassa]*, the south point of the Caloosahatchie is low and sandy & apparently subject to be inundated during severe storms. A flat shoal juts out from this point & only 7 feet of water can be carried up to it.

From the above description it will be apparent that though Coasting vessels might in times of necessity find anchorage in San Carlos bay, it is not of a character to enter into the system of Coast defence.

XI.   Gallivan's Bay *[present day Gullivan Bay]* A group of small low islands imbedded for many miles within the line of coast, lie south of San Carlos bay. The creeks or bayous which separate these islands communicate with the sea. Their mouths are shoal & interrupted by storms & they are only accessible to small boats. Many of these creeks have local names & the sheet of water formed by them among the islands is called Otsego bay.

The Coast south of Otsego bay is low & flat as far as Cape Romano & is sparsely covered by a small growth of trees. The shore is clear & free of shoals, with 4 fathoms water at 1 ½ miles from land. Before reaching Cape Romano, it is again broken into islands of similar character to those already described.

Cape Romano is a low flat point, putting out a shoal 8 or 9 miles in extent, to the south east. The Coast at this point receding abruptly to the east forms a deep indentation or bay called <u>Gallivans *[Gullivan]* bay</u> which furnishes a harbour against northerly winds. The depth of water after doubling Romano shoal, is 4 fathoms which diminishes to 2 fathoms as you approach the shore towards the north The shore to the north as well as to the east, exhibits a chain of mangrove islands, low and unapproachable except in a small boat.

An open & exposed bay of the character above described can of course form no part in the System of Coast defences.

XII.   Cape Sable   Chatham bay commencing a few miles below Gallivans bay is a mere indentation in the Coast which extends to within 10 miles of Cape Sable. It is shoal and furnishes no harbours.

Cape Sable the south east extremity of Florida, is low & flat, bearing a scattered growth of Palm, Spanish bayonet, mangrove, etc. About 2 miles north of the Cape, on the west shore, there is an anchorage ground of 2 fathoms water, with a narrow channel leading to it. It is protective against northerly & easterly gales, but open to the west and South.

A flat shoal puts out South from the Cape & no channel yet has been discovered of a greater depth than 3 or 4 feet, around the South Coast to <u>Cape Florida</u>, the S. W. Cape of the Peninsula.

There is nothing to recommend this point for military purposes.

XIII.   Biscayne Bay.   There is no direct passage from Cape Sable to Biscayne bay or Cape Florida, except for small boats. The transit from the West to the East Coast of Florida, even coasting vessels, must be through the Florida reef. The usual passage, unless the reef is turned, by passing west of the Tortugas bank, is through the channel at <u>Cay West</u>. There is another passage at Honda bay, east of Cay West &

others still farther east, but they are less known & seldom used. Vessels not drawing more than 15 feet can be brought over the bar or reef at this point. The channel way is direct & open & about 2 miles wide. After crossing the reef the water is smooth & vessels can find shelter from the wind under Soldier cay & other islands within the reefs. The anchorage under Cay Biscayne is sheltered from northerly but exposed to southerly winds. It is nearly 3 fathoms deep though only 8 or 9 feet can be carried up to it. The direct channel, called East Pass lies between two shoals called the Boarers. The east boarer extends from about 6 miles from the South end of Cay Biscayne. The West boarer is parallel to it and lies within the bay. The West Pass is west of the west boarer & unites with the East pass about a mile above the South end of Cay Biscayne, which is called Cape Florida. The channel continues thence to the to the mouth of the Miami river , about 8 miles distant. A third channel of about equal depth to those mentioned, leads from the bay, west of Soldier Cay, to the Miami river. Cay Biscayne is low flat & sandy & covered principally with a growth of mangrove. There is a Light house on its south end. Many of the islands within the reef are large and well timbered.

The importance of Biscayne bay, in a commercial as well as a military point of view, arises from its position. Besides the Harbor it affords our coasting vessels, it is the northern outlet of the passage within the Florida reef & has an important bearing upon this interior navigation. Vessels from the north drawing over 12 ft. water, after passing Cumberland Sound can find no harbor along our Coast until they reach this point. By entering here within the reef, they avoid an opposing current & tempestuous sea & might also escape an enemy cruising in the Gulf. When the Surveys of this part of the Coast are completed & the channels & harbors are well ascertained & defined; the erection of defensive works at this point may become important to complete the system of commenced at Cay West & the Tortugas. It will then be seen, whether this bay can be defended & whether it will be advantageous. Reservations of certain islands have been recommended by the board to meet this contingency.

Before leaving the subject of the Florida reef, the board would remark, that though they did not include in their examination of the Florida Coast in consequence of having been informed by the Dept. that it has been by a Special Board it may be proper to refer in a general way to the important bearing, which is the fortifications now being erected at Cay West & Tortugas, not only have on upon the defence of the reef but also upon the defence of the Florida Coast. Besides the specific harbors they secure to our naval & commercial marine, the salient positions they occupy along the high way of our commerce in the Gulf, upon the Coast to their seas. This influence has been constantly kept in view of the board, while considering the general defence of the Coast, as well as the particular defence of the several harbors. It is this consideration that has chiefly induced the to look rather to the prospective than the immediate defence of some of the points & to wait the result of the Survey of the Coast, as well of the harbors.

XIV.   St Augustine.   There is no harbor on the Eastern Coast of Florida, from Biscayne bay to the mouth of the St. Johns river, that can be entered at low water, by a vessel drawing over 6 feet. New river & Hillsborough inlets furnish even less. Jupiter inlet is closed. Mosquito inlet, the entrance to Smyrna is said to have about 6 feet over the bar. Matanzas inlet only allows the passage of boats. None of these could be entered by the U. S. Schooner Phenix & in consequence of stormy weather were not visited.

The Coast between Cay Biscayne & St. Augustine with the exception of Cape Canaveral is clear & bold. A long flat shoal projects about 20 miles into the sea from this Cape & interrupts the navigation along the shore that would be unobstructed.

At ordinary low water there is only six feet of water in the bay of St Augustine & 11 feet at ordinary high water. Although the wind was from shore, an almost unbroken line of breakers stretched across the mouth of the entrance. After crossing the bar the channel is deep and winding, not exceeding 400 yards in width but well defined by the breakers on either side.

Fort Marion (present-day Castillo de San Marcos) is well situated to defend the approach to the town & in conjunction with the battery at Matanzas inlet is deemed sufficient by the board for the wants of the place. They would recommend that the existing works at St. Augustine be maintained in the System of defence.

XV.   St Johns river   The coast continues clear & bold from St. Augustine to the mouth of the St. Johns & there are 5 fathoms water within a mile of the shore. The channel over the bar is not constant in its position, but works to the north for a certain period.& then breaks in a new place to the South. At ordinary low water there are but 7 feet on the bar & 12 feet at high water. After an easterly blow 14 feet can be carried over it. The bar is flat & about ½ a mile wide. During Easterly & Southerly winds which generally prevail on this part of the Coast for 8 months in the year, the sea breaks entirely across the mouth of the river. The Channel after crossing the bar is 5 fathoms deep; affords good anchorage & 12 feet of water can be carried up the river 100 miles from its mouth. Jacksonville, the principal town on its banks, is situated 95 miles above its mouth. The river is wide & winding with extensive mud flats near its mouth, that are submerged during storm tide. The inland passage from St Mary's enters the river 4 miles above its mouth & the island opposite this entrance, as well as the shores on either side, are of the same character with the flats. There are points in this inland passage between the Nasau [sic] *(Nassau)* & St. Johns rivers that are dry at water. It is therefore not practicable for boats.

The commerce of the St. Johns is now of importance & may increase so as to require protection. The best position for a work cannot be stated until after the necessary Survey but the board are of the opinion work on Baton *(present-day Batten Island)* island would probably prevent an attack from within the passage, on Jacksonville, or vessels lying within the river by boats or small steamers. For this purpose Baton island & certain land west of it has been recommended to be reserved from sale. The proximity of the St. Johns to Cumberland Sound, which is designed to be protected, will in the event of war, will give much security to its commerce & vessels that frequent it.

XVI.   Nasau inlet   is 6 miles north of the mouth of the St. Johns river & separates Talbot from Amelia island. At its entrance it is about 5 miles wide & extends into the interior about 7 miles where it receives Nasau river. It has two channels from sea. One close to the north end of Talbot island & the other close to the south end of Amelia. Neither channel is more than ½ a mile from shore& about 6 feet at low & 11 feet at high water can be carried over the bars of each. These two channels are separated by a middle ground or bank, about 2 miles long & bare at its upper extremity. Like the channel into St. Johns river, they are not stationary but altered by storms & when the wind is from sea, the breakers extend across the mouth of the inlet. The inland passage between St. Johns & St Marys rivers intersects Nasau inlet about 4 miles from its mouth. The inlet at this point is about 2 ½ miles wide & the two channels from sea unite about a mile above. The banks on either side of the intersection of the inland communication with the inlet are low and marsh & liable to be submerged by storms. The Board do not consider any defences necessary for this point.

XVII. Cumberland Sound.   The entrance into Cumberland Sound is between Amelia & Cumberland islands. There are three channels leading into it from sea. The <u>Southern</u> channel has 8 feet of water over its bar at common low water & diminishing in depth. The <u>Northern</u> channel has 12 feet over its bar at common low water & its depth in increasing. These two channels unite before reaching the N. E. point of Amelia island form the main passage & continue along the north shore of said island till opposite the south end of Cumberland, where the third channel, called the <u>Cumberland</u> Channel, joins them. On the bar of this latter channel there are only 8 feet of water at common low tide & said channel previous to its junction with the main channel passes within 400 yards of the south end of Cumberland island.

Between the Cumberland & Main channels, there is a flat shoal, called Pelican bank extending several miles to sea & which opposite the north end of Amelia island, is bare at low water. At the western termination of this shoal, which is about in a line with the South end of Cumberland & the N. W. end of Amelia, there are not more than 3 or 4 feet of water at common low tide.

Cumberland Sound is a safe & extensive anchorage having from 4 to 6 fathoms of water. It s 7 miles long & 2 wide &secure from all winds.

Besides the principle entrance, between Cumberland & Amelia islands, there is another communication with the sea farther north through the St. Simms (*Simons*) Sound, through which 10 feet of water can be carried.

Cumberland Sound forms one link in the chain of inland communications between the St John's & Savannah rivers & St Marys river empties into it, nearly opposite its outlet between Cumberland & Amelia islands.

The examination of this Sound, terminated the examination of the Sea Coast of Florida by the Board, under the orders of 8 Sept. 1848. They have confined themselves merely to a description of its entrance & capacity without considering its properties In a military point of view. It being understood that these last have been discussed by a former board & that plans for its defence are matured.

The board only think it necessary in addition to what has been said to recommend that the Survey of the Florida Coast now is progress, as well as the particular Surveys of the harbors, be completed at the earliest convenience of the Government & will conclude by appending the following table.

Tabular statement of the relative value & importance of the points on the Sea Coast of Florida, marking the order of time in which they generally should receive the attention of Government in surveys & in erection of defences.

Name of Place	Class	Remarks
St Georges Island	1	To receive first Attention of Govt.
Tampa Bay	1	To receive first Attention of Govt.
Biscayne Bay	1	To receive first Attention of Govt.
Cedar Cays	2	Ditto Second ditto
St Johns river	2	Ditto Second ditto
St Andrews Sound	3	Ditto third ditto

Name of Place	Class	Remarks
St Josephs Bay	3	Ditto third ditto
Suwannee river River	3	Ditto third ditto
Charlotte Harbor	3	Ditto third ditto

All of which is respectfully Submitted by the Board of Engineers

Lt. Col R. E. Delrusy
Board of Engrs.
Pres. Pro Tem

R. E Lee, Capt & Bt Col. Engrs.
Recorder to the Board

Office of the Board of Engineers for Fortifications
Army Building, New York, Dec. 20, 1877

Brig. Gen A. A. Humphreys (Andrew Atkinson Humphries)
Chief of Engineers, USA
Washington, D. C.

General,

The Board of Engineers for Fortifications, having carefully considered the subject of certain reservations of land for military purposes on the coasts of Louisiana, Mississippi, Alabama, and Florida, described in your letter of the 11th, inst, and its enclosures, has the honor to report thereon as follows:

Mobile Bay

In order to have sites for defensive works to cover the passes from Mississippi Sound to Mobile Bay, the reservation made of Heron Tower and Grants Island should be retained, while those covering the other small between Dauphine Island and Cedar Point, as well as that on Cedar Point, may be relinquished, as they are of no importance for military purposes.

Mississippi Sound

Cat, Horn, and Petit Bois Blanc islands not being required for military purposes the reservations covering them may be relinquished, except so far as they may be required for Light House purposes. There is now a lighthouse on the western end of Cat Island, and another on the eastern end of Horn Island.

Dog and Hurricane islands mentioned in the list furnished by the Commissioner of the General Land Office as having been reserved. Are not to be found on the charts of the U. S. East Coast Survey and probably have been washed away.

Amelia Island

All the land now held by the United States on the northern end of this island is deemed to be necessary in connection with Fort Clinch and the reservation should therefore be retained.

Tampa Bay

The two and only important entrances into this bay are the main ship channel between Mullet and Egmont Keys and another deep channel between Egmont and Passage keys. The latter key which is supposed to be the one called Barnaby in the list of reservations, is described by the Coast Survey as "a round sand bank, bare at low water". To cover these entrances, Mullet and Egmont Keys will be needed as sites for batteries and the reservation over them should be retained. That over the other Keys at this locality can be relinquished.

St. Johns River

A Battery for the defense of this river would probably be established in time of war, and the reservation of Batton (present-day Batten Island) island should be therefore be retained as a site for the same.

Charlotte Harbor

This is one of the best harbors on the western coast of Florida, and sites for works of defense of the entrance should be retained. For this purpose a reservation of the southern end of Gasparilla island and the northern end of Boca Grande or La Costa island *(Cayo Costa)*, for a distance of two miles on each, should be continued. The remainder of the reservations at this location may be relinquished.

Cedar Keys

The reservation of Sea Horse Key should be retained; and as the point is the terminus of a railroad crossing the peninsula of Florida it would be well to retain North and Snake Keys also as sites for additional batteries – for the present at any rate.

St Andrews Bay

The reservation on the western end of Crooked Island should be retained as sites for defensive works and lighthouses. The others at this locality may be relinquished.

St George's Sound

The reservations covering Flag and Dog islands and a part of St George's island should be retained as sites for defensive works and lighthouses.

St Joseph's Bay

This bay affords one of the best and most accessible harbors of refuge on the gulf coast of Florida, and as the land is believed to be valueless for other than government purposes it is thought best to retain this reservation for sites which may possibly be needed in the future for defensive works and lighthouses.

Entrance to Santa Rosa Sound

As no survey has been made of this Sound or its entrance, so far as this board is informed, the subject stands as it did at the time the reservation was made. It is therefore seems proper to hold on to the reservation till more definite information is acquired.

Reservations on the Coast of Louisiana

He reservations mentioned n the list presented by the Commissioner of the General Land Office are at the west mouth of Bayou La Fourche; on Bay Plat, at East mouth of Bayou La Fourche, near the western entrance to Camanida Bay, near the Pass at the east end of Grand Terre island, near the mouth of Quatre Bayou Pass, near Bastieu Bay (three reservations) and at Bastieu Bay. None of these reservations are important for military purposes and may, in the opinion of this board, be relinquished.

So far as is known to the Board there are no improvements on any of the reservations the relinquishment of which is recommended.

The copy of the list (marked A) from the General Land Office, furnished with your letter of the 11th inst. Is returned herewith the opinion of the Board noted thereon in each case.

Respectfully Submitted

***

Col of Eng. & Bvt. Maj. En.

L. B Tower

Co. of Eng. Bvt. Major Genl.

V. G ***

***

Lt. Col. Of Eng. Bvt. Maj. Genl.

Department of the Interior

General Land Office
Washington, D. C.

Sept 11ᵗʰ , 1882

Hon. H. M Teller
Secretary of the Interior
(Henry Moore Teller was
Secretary of the Interior
from 1882 to 1885)

Sir:

I have the honor to acknowledge the receipt by reference from the Department for report, of his letter from the Secretary of War, both dated the 28ᵗʰ of August, 1882, one requesting to be informed as to the status of Dog Island government reservations in Florida, which the Special Deputy Collector of Customs at Apalachicola, desired to be sent as a stock range, the other letter enclosing copy of letter from the Chief of Engineers, and in accordance therewith, requesting to be furnished with plats of such of the following named reservations in Florida as have been surveyed, and also to be informed whether these reservations as now valid complete, viz:

1. At St. Georges Sound. – The whole of Flagg Island. The west end of St. Georges Island, for two miles from its northwest extremity. The whole of Dog Island

2. At Cedar Cays. – The whole of Sea Horse, North and Snake Cays.

3. At Tampa Bay – Mullett [*sic*] and Egmont Islands.

4. At Charlotte Harbor – Gasparilla and Boca Grande Islands

In reply I have the honor to enclose here with photolithographic copies of the township plats embracing the following named reservations:

Township 15 S. Range 12 East, containing the part of North Key.

Township 16 S. Range 12 East containing the west of North Key and all of Sea Horse Key, which latter Key in addition to being reserved for military purpose by order of the Secretary of War dated March 12, 1849, was declared a reservation for light house purposes by President's order dated Sept. 2, 1851.

Township 16 S. Range 13 East, containing Snake Key

Township 33 S. Range 16 East containing Mullett Key

Township 33 S. Range 15 East, containing Egmont Key, 15 acres of which at the north end was reserved for light house purposes by President's order dated August 12, 1847.

Township 43 S. Range 20 East, containing the south end of Gasparilla Island for a length of two miles, shown by green color on plat.

Township 43 S. Range 20 East and Township 44 S. ranges 20 and 21 East containing the north end of Boca Grande and Cayo Costa Island for a length of two miles, the line of reservation which was adopted being shown by green color on the plats, and the remainder of Gasparilla and Boca Grande Islands having been restored to market in pursuance of the letter from the Secretary of War dated May 18, 1878, enclosing a list of reservations with notations thereon made in office of Chief Engineers, showing what portions were no longer needed for military purposes.

As to the reservations made at St. Georges Sound, I have to state that the records of this office show what the whole of St. Georges Island and Dog Island form part of a private land grant confirmed by decree of the U. S. Supreme Court at the January Term of 1841 and patent was issued therefore by this office on June 9, 1842, to Colin

Mitchell, Robert Mitchell, et. al. Flagg Island at St. Georges Sound does not appear to have been dispose of by the Government, but it remains unsurveyed. Its approximate position in indicated on the enclosed map of Florida.

In reply to the inquiry as to whether the military reservations, plats of which are enclosed, are now valid and complete. I have to state that said reservations exist by virtue of the order of the Secretary of War, dated March 23rd, 1849, requiring the reservations to be made until completion of the surveys necessary for the Coast defences, and also by virtue of said letter from the War Department dated May 18, 1878, with enclosures indicating what military reservations should be retained. The U. S. local land officers have been instructed not to allow any disposal of the lands embraced in said reservations, but in order that the same may be requisitioned suggest that it might be well to obtain a formal order of the President reserving the lands desired. The letters from the Secretary of War are herewith returned. Copies of the plats in the accompanying roll.

Very Respectfully,

N. C. McFarland

Commissioner

Appendix B

Excerpt from George O. Shield's book, *By Mountain and Stream*, published in 1888, describing his visit to Egmont Key.

At one o'clock A.M. we reached Egmont Light, which stands upon a small island called Egmont Key. Here the steamer tied up until day, when the captain sent the steward to call us and say that he would give us an hour to take a walk upon the beach.

We gladly availed ourselves of the opportunity, and after partaking of a cup of hot coffee served in our stateroom, hurried out and beheld a most lovely picture. Egmont Key is a picturesque little isle half a mile wide and one and a half miles long. The government lighthouse and light-keeper's residence are handsome and substantial structures. We found Mr. Moore, the light-keeper, an intelligent, kind-hearted and hospitable gentleman. He gave us some interesting information concerning this island and others in the vicinity. He says there is a heron rokery [*sic*] on the island only half a mile from his house where the birds annually build their nests and rear their young. Last year there were five hundred nests there. He estimates that each nest produced on an average five birds, making the total crop two thousand five hundred. He considers them his pets and will not allow them to be shot or disturbed in any way.

Mullett [*sic*] Key, two miles northeast, is the home of a large herd of deer, and Mr. Moore goes over there and kills one at any time when he wishes some fresh venison. Mr. Moore is an enthusiastic sportsman, by the way, and I am informed that he has killed one hundred and ninety-three deer in the past two years.

During our walk around the island we found many wonders of the deep in the way of shells, fishes, etc. A cold norther had prevailed for two days previously, and many of the more delicate fish having approached too near the beach in quest of food, were paralyzed by the cold air and swept ashore by the surf. Among the curious specimens we picked up, I note the cow-fish, sea-horse, rock-fish, dog-fish, lamprey eel. three varieties of the toad-fish, etc. We also collected many specimens, shells, coral, sea-moss and sponges.

The time for our departure having now arrived, we reluctantly returned to the steamer. On our departure, Mr. Moore gave us a pressing invitation to visit him on our return and spend several days on the island as his guests. We sincerely hope to be able to accept, for it is a most fascinating place, and we feel confident that we could spend a few days here both pleasantly and profitably.

Appendix C

What follows are the lists of the various committees formed during Egmont '88 and the charter members of the Egmont Key Alliance, Inc. Also listed are the different groups that contributed to the effort.

The Egmont '88 Steering Committee was formed to plan, coordinate, and implement the event's activities.

1. Chairperson, Susan Kessel, Manager, Community Relations, SWFWMD
2. Mr. Martin Anderson, Tampa Port Authority
3. Mr. Jim Allgood, Hillsborough County EMS
4. Mr. Robert Baker, Florida Park Service
5. Ms. Cheryl Buckingham, US Fish and Wildlife Service
6. SMSgt. David Clayton, 56th Combat Support Group, MacDill AFB
7. Mr. Hal Cusick, Greater Tampa Chamber of Commerce
8. Mr. Bob Cutler, Jos. E. Seagram & Sons, Inc.
9. Ms. Pamela K. Day, Deputy Director, City of Tampa Solid Waste Department
10. BM1 James A. Flannagan, Chief Petty Officer, US Coast Guard

11. Major Ken Forrester, Public Affairs Officer, Florida National Guard
12. GYSGT W. J. Gober, US Marine Corps
13. SFC Jonnie D. Green, 231st Transportation Company
14. Mr. Patrick Hagan, Refuge Manager, Chassahowitzka National Wildlife Refuge
15. Ms. Debbie Jeannette, Aide, S Representative Sam Gibbons
16. Major Bob Lewis, Florida National Guard
17. Captain Pete Lumianski, US Navy Reserve
18. SFC Mike McDonald, Florida National Guard
19. Mr. Jim Metcalf, President, Metcalf Associates
20. Mr. Richard T. Paul, Manager, Tampa Bay Sanctuaries, National Audubon Society
21. Mr. Anthony Pizzo, Tampa Historical Society
22. Mr. Dan Samborn, American Red Cross
23. Major Steve Saunders, Hillsborough County Sheriff's Office
24. Major Ronald Scott, US Army Reserve
25. Lt. Eric Stillwell, US Navy Reserve
26. Captain John C. Timmel, Tampa Bay Pilots Association

The volunteer organizations participated in the Egmont '88 event over the three days.

1. American Red Cross
2. Brandon High School Junior R.O.T.C.
3. City of Tampa
4. Department of Natural Resources
5. Easy Divers
6. Florida Conservation Association
7. Gulf Coast Maritime Institute

8.   Gulf Ridge Council, Boy Scouts of America

9.   Hillsborough County Emergency Medical Services

10. Law Enforcement Explorers

11. Littoral Society

12. Manatee Audubon Society

13. Manatee Community College

14. Manatee County 4-H Club

15. Manatee County Historical Commission

16. National Audubon Society, Tampa Bay Sanctuaries

17. Order of the Arrow

18. Robinson High School Marine Biology Department

19. Sea Explorers

20. Sierra Club, Tampa Bay Group

21. Southwest Florida Water Management District

22. St. Petersburg Audubon Society

23. St. Petersburg Young Republicans

24. Suncoast Conchologists

25. Suncoast Girl Scout Council

26. Tampa Audubon Society

27. Tampa Historical Society

28. Tampa Port Authority

29. US Fish and Wildlife Service

30. Walter C. Heinrich, Sheriff, Hillsborough County

31. Young Democrats of Hillsborough County

Egmont '88 Participating Military Units

1.   Florida Army National Guard – Temple Terrace

2.   Florida Army National Guard – Lake Wales

3.   Florida Army National Guard - Camp Blanding

4.   Naval Reserve Center – Tampa

5.   United States Marine Corps – Tampa

6.   United States Coast Guard – Egmont Key

7.   United States Army Reserve – St. Petersburg

8.   United States Air Force – MacDill Airforce Base

Egmont '88 Corporate Sponsor that donated funds or "in kind" services to the event.

1.   A. R. Savage and Son, Inc

2.   Bay Transportation

3.   Blount Construction Corp. – Tampa

4.   First Florida Bank

5.   Florida Land Design and Engineering

6.   Fortune Hotels

7.   G. E. Smith Independent Ice Company

8.   Hendry Corporation

9.   Jos. E. Seagram and Sons, Inc.

10.   Lykes Brothers, Inc.

11.   Lykes Pasco, Inc.

12.   Manatee Chamber of Commerce

13.   Merita Bakeries – Tampa

14.   Metcalf Associates

15.   Miss Cortez Fleet

16.   Patrick Media Group

17.   Port-A-Pit Bar-B-Que

18.   Reynolds Aluminum Recycling

19.   Robbins Lumber Company

20.   Sheldon/Cusick & Associates

21.   Southport Stevedores

22. Tampa Bay Buccaneers

23. Tampa Bay Pilots Association

24. Tampa Electric Company

25. Tampa Shipyard, Inc.

26. The Greater Tampa Chamber of Commerce

27. The Q-Morning Zoo (FM radio station)

28. Waste Aid Systems

29. Waste Management, Inc.

Egmont '88 Donor Services

1. Bay Transportation
    Tugboats to move barge
    19 ½ hours @ $125.00 each $2,406.00

2. South Port Stevedores
    Crane 600.00
    Lashing and Welding 200.00
    Labor 800.00

3. Tampa Shipyard
    Garbage barge
    Five days @$400.00 each 2000.00

4   International Longshoremen's Union
    Local 1402
    Loading and unloading barge 2,016.00

5. Waste Aid Systems
    11 roll on/off dumpsters 1,350

6. Reynolds Aluminum
    600 Garbage bags
    Trailer
    T-shirts and hats 1,050

7. TECO – Asplundh
   Wood chipper to clear underbrush   1000.00
8. Waste Management
   Port-o-lets   438.00
9. City of Tampa
   Disposal of trash   6000.00
10. Tampa Bay Pilots Association
    Boat transportation
    T-shirts and hats
    Printing
    Facilities   5000.00
11. Patrick Media
    Four signs   800.00
12. Robbins Lumber Company
    Lumber Company   100.00
13. Port-a-Pit Bar-B-Que
    Food   200.00
    Tent   300.00
14. Fortune Hotels
    Rooms   350.00
15. First Florida Bank
    T-shirts   400.00
16. Q-Zoo (radio station)
    T-shirts   400.00
17. Tampa Bay Buccaneers
    Sun visors   150.00
18. Lykes Pasco and Lykes Brothers
    Food   1000.00
19. G. E. Smith Independent Ice Company
    Ice   100.00

20.	Greater Tampa Chamber of Commerce	
	Food	500.00
21.	Merita Bakeries	
	Food	150.00
22.	*Miss Cortez* Fleet	
	Transportation	500.00
23.	Metcalf Associates	
	T-shirts	250.00
24.	Florida Land Design	
	Ice	50.00
		$28,110.00

Appendix D

Charter Members of the Egmont Key
Alliance Board of Directors

1. Mr. Robert (Bob) H. Baker (FPS)
2. Dr. Judith Breuggeman
3. J. Fred Campbell
4. Ms. Sandra Colbert (Sandy)
5. Mr. Jay Davis
6. Mr. Scott Hampton
7. Ms. Susan Kessel (President)
8. Mr. Dennis McDonald
9. Mr. Michael S. Perry
10. Commissioner Jan Platt
11. Mr. Stephen I. Saunders III
12. Mr. Charles G. Stephens
13. Captain John Timmel (Tampa Harbor Pilots)
14. Mr. Bruce A. Rogers, P. G.
15. The Honorable Barbra Sheen Todd
16. Mr. Gregory Wilson
17. Ms. Susannah L. Thayer

Ex Officio Members

1. State of Florida Department of Natural Resources Representative Mr. Robert J. Seifer

2. US Fish and Wildlife Representative Cameron Shaw, Refuge Manager

References

1. Bethell, John A., 1914, "Pinellas: A Brief History of the Lower Point."

2. Taylor, Thomas W, 2001, "Florida Lighthouse Trail."

3. Romans, Bernard, 1775, "A Concise Natural History of East and West Florida."

4. Hurley, Neil E., "Florida's Lighthouses During the Civil War."

5. Hine, Albert C., 2013, "Geologic History of Florida."

6. Davis, Richard A., 2016, "Barrier Islands of the Florida Coast Peninsula."

7. Silverman, David J.,2016, "Thundersticks"

8. Hanna, Alfred J, 1938, "Flight to Oblivion"

9. Buker, George E., 2004, "Blockaders, Refugees and Contrabands."

10. Wynne, Nick & Crankshaw, Joe, 2011, "Florida Civil War Blockades."

11. Matthews, Janet Snyder, 1983 "Edge of Wilderness"

12. Haddleton, Frank B. 2022, "The Walkers at Tampa Bay"

13. Caignet, Carrie, 2012, "Dedication to Service" (Tampa Harbor Pilots History)

14. Barton, Clara, 1899, "The Red Cross in Peace and War"

15. US National Archives (1849 Florida Survey)
16. Library of Congress (Lucy Graves Journal)
17. Ware, John D., 1972, "Tampa Bay in 1757:Francisco Maria Celi's Journal and Logbook"
18. McDuffee, L. B, "Lures of Manatee" (Tresca Biography)
19. Wheeler, H. J, 1923, "Citrus Culture in Florida" (Tresca Grapefruit)
20. Sheilds, George O., 1883 "Hunting in the Great West"

Newspaper Articles

1. New York Herald, August 24, 1861 – Egmont Key Occupied by A Federal Force
2. St. Petersburg Times, July 1, 1910, Charles Moore article
3. The State Newspaper (South Carolina), November 22, 1910, Charles Moore Obituary
4. Tampa Times, January 4, 1967, Charles M. Moore Obituary
5. Stinemetz, Morgan, Sarasota Herald TribuneJanuary 6, 1999, Union Sympathizers on Egmont Key

Other Resources

1. Florida Master Site File Survey 17510, 2016 survey of Scottish Chief and Kate Dale
2. Find a Grave – Bernard Romans
3. Spessard Stone, 2004, "Billy Bowlegs Seminole Chief"
4. Rollins College Library (Charles M. Moore as a student)
5. Manatee County Library (Moore family)
6. Tampa Bay Pilots History by C. W. Bahrt
7. Tresca vs. Maddox, 1854 trial transcript

References

8. Tresca Notes, Mamatee Pioneer Village, 2020

9. George Gauld Map of Tampa Bay, 2020, U.K. Hydrologic Office Archives

10. Rickards, George V. 1860-4, Poems from a personal journal, courtesy of the Tampa Bay History Center.

11. USACE, New Orleans District, 2000, Contract No. DACW 29-97-D-0017 (Report on steamship *Grey Cloud/ Colonel Kinsman*).

12. Haddleton, Frank B., 2022, The Walkers at Tampa Bay, personal article.

13. Stone, Spessard, 2004, Billy Bowlegs: Seminole Chief, https://freepages.rootsweb.com/~crackerbarrel/genealogy/Bowlegs3.html

Index

Index